D1086417

Zero Dark Thirty

Samuel Brantley

Hellgate Press
Central Point, Oregon

Zero Dark Thirty

Hellgate Press
An Imprint of PSI Research
P.O. Box 3727
Central Point, Oregon 97502

info@psi-research.com

Book designed & edited by Harley B. Patrick
Cover design by Mark Hannah

Library of Congress Cataloging-in-Publication Data

Brantley, Samuel, 1943-
   Zero dark thirty / Samuel Brantley.
      p.cm.
   ISBN 1-55571-624-5 (paper)
      1. Vietnamese Conflict, 1961-1975--Personal narratives, American. 2 Vietnamese Conflict, 1961-1975--Aerial operations, American. 3. Brantley, Samuel, 1943- I. Title: Zero dark 30. II. Title.

DS559.5 .B735 2002
959.704'3'092--dc21   2001051683

Printed and bound in the United States of America
First Edition 10 9 8 7 6 5 4 3 2 1

Dedicated to veterans of actual combat and others
who have stepped beyond normal viewing,
both living and passed.

With a bit of a mind flip
You're into the time slip
And nothing will ever be the same

Rocky Horror Picture Show

Contents

Foreword

War stories, first-hand accounts of people in the thick of fighting, constitute a special literary genre. How to express the inexpressible? How to give voice to an experience that is patently beyond the realm of words? The task is daunting. For those of us with no knowledge of what it's like to be shot at, reading about it can be both disturbing and puzzling. Disturbing in its savagery and horror, puzzling in its utter negation of human value. Combat is the ultimate existential moment, winnowed to its bleakest, starkest, most furious pitch. What else can be said of an activity that takes as its animating factor the extinction of the very people who are trying to extinguish you? "War means fighting," someone once said, "and fighting means killing." It all comes down to that, and for those who engage in it, and survive, making sense of the ordeal in the aftermath must seem like an impossible burden.

As a teenager in the 1950s, Samuel Brantley liked to watch airplanes take off and land at a field near Alexandria, Virginia. The men who flew the aircraft displayed a certain cachet that caught his fancy. When he came of age he knew he wanted to fly—not dinky piper cubs or clunky commercial jets, but sleek, shiny, explosive jet fighters. On the verge of graduating from college, he enlisted in the Marines, hoping to qualify for the Navy aviator training program. He did, and after boot camp was sent first to preflight school in Pensacola and then to various bases around the country where he learned how to fly the latest high-tech fighter planes. He was good at it, a natural, as he describes in the opening chapters of his memoir, *Zero Dark Thirty*; man and machine seemed to fuse into a propulsive thrust that defied the presence of gravity.

But young Sam was soon brought back to earth by the escalation of the Vietnam War in the mid-1960s. There, at the controls of an A4E Skyhawk, he flew sortie after sortie, strafing, bombing, firing rockets, dropping napalm on enemy targets. Combat accentuated and refined the skills he had developed in training. His proficiency intensified as his experience increased. "The most appropriate mechanism for me," he says, "was to become the centrum of the machine I flew; an ultra-complex human system within, attuned to, and managing a complex machine system. That had the advantage of overlaying excellence and professionalism on the destruction I was dealing with. The more professional, the more effective. The more effective, the more excellent."

But what makes this memoir so compelling is what happens next. Inexplicably, in one of those bureaucratic shuffles, Sam finds himself on the ground with an infantry unit (First Battalion, Seventh marines) as a Forward Air Controller (FAC), telling the very same aircraft he had been flying over the hills and jungles where to drop their bombs and release their rockets. The killing he had done at a distance suddenly exploded in his face, and he found himself in the throes of a dirty, savage, ground war that required all his soldierly skills to survive.

Most combat narratives are content to relate what happens to the soldier when he closes with the enemy; what distinguishes *Zero Dark Thirty* is that every step of the way Sam Brantley meticulously details not only his feelings but the deeper, darker thoughts that torment his consciousness as the fighting becomes more intense and gruesome. To understand the ground war in Vietnam we have to understand the conditions under which it was fought. For the average grunt it was under the canopy of a damp, leafy jungle where visibility was limited and ambush routine, and the foliage bristled with booby traps. One moment the jungle trilled and squawked with familiar sounds, the next it convulsed into a fury of explosions and screams, all of which Brantley describes with chilling precision. As a fighter pilot, he was accustomed to cranking the throttle and roaring out of harm's way; on the ground he has to adopt a different tactic. "It's bad if you're slow, sir," a gyrene tells him when he first arrives with the unit. "There's no count like in training. It's always for real. You need to come out of the gate at max. You go as fucking hard as you can on one."

The tempo of the book accelerates with these graphic descriptions. As much as any writer in this difficult genre, Brantley conveys the bitter adjustments that each soldier is compelled to make. The gradual numbing of the senses, the shutting down of the emotions, the conversion of the sentient self into a ruthless and efficient killing machine leaves scars that are virtually impossible to eradicate.

He also conveys the exceptional camaraderie that seizes men at these harrowing moments and enables them to function as an effective unit. "Peculiar amid unbelievable sounds of a firefight was the amount of brief but well understood two-way communication accomplished with nearly mindless grunts, screams, barks, etc. It was as though we were all hooked into the same thread, using vocalizations as indicators of timing for events we all knew were necessary. A high-functioning, exceptional state of togetherness I have missed since. It seems the threat of immediate death is one of the few things that can get a group to that level."

The delineation of human consciousness under extreme duress is one of the masterful touches of this astonishing memoir. Brantley comes as close as anyone to conveying the totality of a (thankfully) limited experience in all its shattering particulars and effects. The book belongs in the company of the great Marine combat narratives—*Goodbye Darkness* by William Manchester and *With the Old Breed* by E.B. Sledge—that have distinguished the genre down through the years. In this struggle to reclaim his humanity in the aftermath of this ordeal, Brantley adds a poignant chapter of anguish and acceptance that brings the war uncomfortably home to those of us who rode out the sounds of its distant alarums in a clamor of dissent and soothing clouds of marijuana smoke. *Zero Dark Thirty* is a riveting account of a war that, in our chronic ignorance and grief, we will continue to mourn and mull over for a long, long time.

Conger Beasley, Jr.
January 2002

Conger Beasley, Jr., is an award-winning writer who has published two novels and three collections of short fiction. *We Are a People of This World: The Lakota Sioux and the Massacre at Wounded Knee*, written in 1995, was given the Western Writers of America Spur Award for best contemporary nonfiction book. He divides his time between Kansas City, Missouri, and Colorado Springs, Colorado.

Preface

Beacon Field, a charming little airfield leftover from the 1930's located on the west side of Route 1 about five miles south of Alexandria, Virginia, was rapidly being overtaken by suburban development that began in the late 1950's. Runways previously approached over occasional clusters of trees and endless grass fields were now cautiously approached over knotted clusters of houses and a shopping center.

The field was a private aviation facility where flight operations were conducted, flying lessons offered, and complete maintenance services provided. The hangars leased by aircraft owners housed various aircraft types and fuel.

The airfield's owners, instructors, maintenance people—all those associated with the place—were easy going and friendly, allowing almost anyone to wander about areas not directly involved with flight or maintenance operations. On summer weekends, and often weekday evenings, people gathered in small groups, young and old. Families and couples sat in clusters of folding chairs, occasionally ambling to and fro observing this and that, releasing the heavier issues of the day into the spacious surroundings. Among these visitors, always tactically positioned for a direct view of aircraft operations, was a group of wide-eyed teenage boys who meticulously scanned anything having to do with flight.

One particularly crystalline Saturday in September 1957, Beacon was busy with private pilots and students wanting to fly as much as possible during the short period between summer's heat and humidity, and fall's rain and wind. A friend and I sat on the low fence that separated the flight line and fuel pit areas from the offices, attempting to imagine what life would be like without school. Technically it was still summer and neither of us was mentally ready for anything so structured as school just yet. So we sat pleasantly stupefied, watching.

A man with light auburn hair, wearing the most beautiful blue leather flight jacket I'd ever seen, emerged from the field office. He walked over to a row of five or so BT-13s, low-wing monoplanes powered by radial engines that were former military trainers now flown at Beacon by aerobatics students. Aerobatics students usually had money, a certain enviable look, and used a language form of which my mother would heartily approve. They were imbued with infinite cool and taught by a high order of aviator—aerobatics instructors. (In our hierarchy of aviation, the test pilots at Edwards were the absolute highest, followed closely by jet fighter pilots—extremely rare creatures as far as we were concerned. While not quite at the top, aerobatics instructors were about as close as one could get to either of those groups and so their students were held in very high esteem.)

This particular aerobatics student, in his oh-so-blue flight jacket and aviator shades with smoke gray lenses, the epitome of Mr. Bluejacket Hollywood Ultracool was about to do some thrilling things all by himself, solo. Just the sky, the aircraft, and the man. Nothing and no one else. My friend and I looked at each other, then him. We were boys, pre-pubescent aviator wannabes in jeans and t-shirts, transfixed by a genuine aviator man in all his coolness.

Presently, the BT-13's radial engine coughed, barked, rattled into life as he taxied by on his way to the runway, propeller wash kicking up thin clouds of swirling dust from the oil-soaked unpaved taxiway. The aircraft paused at the end of the dirt strip, turned onto the hard surface of the active runway, held in position while accomplishing a propeller pitch check. The engine noise rose to totally unreasonable and down the runway into the sky he went.

"I'm going to fly for the airlines," my friend said with just enough volume to be heard over the takeoff clatter. It seemed a correct thing to say as the departing propeller snap-roar and harsh radial engine growl diminished.

"Which one?" I asked.

"Don't know," he said quietly, still focusing on the receding BT-13.

"Makes sense to me." I paused while an Aeronca 7AC taxied past, not drawing much undue attention from us. Everybody, that is any-old body, flew the sixty-five horsepower things. Their horizontally opposed engines were considerably quieter than the BT-13's radial, but were loud enough to interrupt conversation. "You already know how to fly," I continued once the noise abated.

"Oh yeah," he said with a smirk. "I can get around Beacon's pattern when the weather is good, but that's nothing. I want to fly across oceans, see other countries." Then turning to me with a come-on-tell-the-truth-have-you? look on his face he said, "Besides, I've never been up solo."

"Are you kidding? How?" I shot back, knowing that neither of us was of legal age to do anything yet. "You know I have a big deal fifteen or twenty minutes of real stick time, and that's only because the instructors were in such good moods." The 7AC pulled into the fuel pit area, the engine stopped, the field returned to quiet. "Still, we're pretty lucky."

"Yeah," he said, flipping into the air the sheet metal fastener key he always carried. He caught it and looked at me. "What about you?"

I took a huge breath, exhaled loudly, and readied to say an unsayable thing. It was something never said around anyone who wasn't really close. And never around adults, most of whom would just laugh and expound on how one couldn't do that, or start in with the "real-job-real-life" noise and then, when your face dropped in distaste at their response, would switch to routine #11-beta, the nondescript "you'll-see-when-you-grow-up" bit.

But I could say it to him. "Fly single-seat jets."

The words hit the afternoon like a hard afterburner light. He didn't laugh, minimize me, or even say anything for a while. After looking across the field, scanning the length of the runway, he turned back to me.

"Yeah. We all want to do that."

"I know," I said exhaling.

"But I'm going to."

"How?"

"I don't know. I just have to."

Chapter 1
Position

Another day. I sat up, watched a couple of mini-iguanas and a small assortment of strange little bugs scurrying about checking out this and that, then gazed outward to the horizons. The spectacular green flash of the sun's corona breaking had come and gone. I sat in a wondrous panorama of high desert with only the road, its accoutrements, and memory providing any indication of man. An industrious, excitable wind tested my face and hair, busily escorting chunks of atmosphere first one way, then another, whispering all the while, "Just to let you know, I intend a little moderate unruliness later today."

A pinprick, tiny focus of noise from far away to the north —ascendant machine sounds—said something was coming down the road. I checked my gear, ensured the rifle was cold, and dumped my boots before pulling them on. Any of various creatures may have elected to settle in the boots while I slept, some of which could become singularly unhappy when disturbed and were capable of a bite or sting that could twist one's system functioning, perhaps forever. The little collection of sounds to the north rose to normal vehicle noises.

A tractor-trailer rig moved south along Highway 14 curving through the canyon below. Machine sounds attenuated, whisper-rumble peculiarities added at each end of the sound spectrum then passed along by the desert. "This little truck," the desert articulated, "can bang along okay this time because I feel that way right now. But understand this surface is mine, always has been, always will be. I can have the truck and anything else here, anytime."

A car followed not far behind the truck, the sounds of which waned as it slowed approaching the canyon. I moved closer to the edge of the precipice chosen as a safe area for the night, to observe the sources of the clatter. Two dissimilar vehicles in close proximity approached a bona fide freeway rush at that location. The truck sounds diminished as the tractor-trailer continued southward while the car, a 240Z, turned into the considerately constructed pull off below, halted, stopped its engine. The desert passed the sounds around for a minute or so, returning to harmonious quiet as two women disembarked. The ladies moved softly, unpredictably from point to point, with fluid movements, grace, and style only women can display. Long hair wafted gracefully about heads in contrapuntal concert with body motion as they turned this way, then that. Elegant feminine presence in the beautiful high desert canyon, a visual feast. The ladies didn't perceive me; that was fine.

Shortly, also from the north, a pickup truck came loudly and rapidly down the highway, dissonant against the canticle of soft desert sounds and echoes. The truck lurched into the pull off, stopping in a cloud of dust near the 240Z. Two men exited, tossed aside beer cans. The subsequent conversation didn't seem to be what the ladies had in mind. They moved quickly toward their car, but were intercepted by the men, dragged toward the truck. One woman was forced into the bed of the truck. Her assailant immediately began tearing off her jacket, leaving me with no doubt as to his intentions. The other woman was thrown into the dirt at the front of the truck. She valiantly fought her captor until bashed in the face hard enough to snap her head back, knocking her flat.

I didn't know any details, had no idea of what those women may have done to provoke the two men, or if they'd done anything, but there are no reasons to resort to rape. Rape is only a disgusting physical demonstration of internal weakness, lack, inability to accommodate; I was not going to lie around and watch while two women were violated.

What could I do to preserve those women and prevent those two idiots from disgracing themselves and men in general, with extremely low, particularly vile conduct? I was something a little over three hundred meters away, couldn't cover the distance quickly enough to accomplish much. My position above and perpendicular to the truck's longitudinal axis, however, certainly supported safe and accurate placement of a round or two from the rifle, which would get there in small parts of a second.

PLAM-ah-ah! PLAM-ah-ah!

High desert morning tranquility shattered as I placed two rounds under the driver area of the truck; rude weapon sound crashed through the canyon, out into the desert. Before echoes returned, the man in front of the truck jumped under it. The one in the back scrambled into the cab and produced a shotgun that he frantically began to load. The woman in the bed of the truck ran to her friend in the dirt. As she started to drag her, the down woman came to life and they sprinted to their car.

M. Machismo Shotgun sat in the cab of the truck waving his newly found metal and wood courage at everything, while dash two, the one under the truck, slowly climbed into the cab from the passenger side. I could see the women holding each other in the 240Z. Suddenly the shotgun blasted twice at loose rocks away from my position. Mr. Shotgun got out of the truck, walked toward the car shouting, brandishing his weapon, as people unfamiliar with weapons do. The car's engine started, he fired a shot into the air.

Well shit. Mr. Shotgun's little old brain just didn't assimilate data well, did it? Had I not just rather pointedly demonstrated my presence, and that the women were covered?

I positioned a round about a meter in front of him, another in the dirt under the front bumper of the truck as he scurried into the cab, and three more under the tailgate of the truck as he slammed the door. The engine roared, the truck turned abruptly as it shot backward, departing rapidly northward in the southbound lanes of the highway. About a quarter of a mile up the road the pickup bounced across the desert median into the correct lanes for its northward journey. Next town in that direction was Ridgecrest, many clicks away.

Sharp reverberation of the weapon sounds blurred to fuzzy, diminishing with each iteration as the harmonious sounds and presence of the high desert passed them around, reducing them and the departing truck's sounds to nothing. The car sat still, engine idling, burbling softly to itself as the women within held each other.

Was the one seriously hurt? I was about to move down when they started waving at the whole face; they hadn't located me. I scrunched back, lying there trying to decide if I should show myself, stay hidden, make my hat, jump straight up, or just disintegrate. I could not amble down there and talk to them, don't know why. In a few minutes the car moved onto Highway 14, raced down the road, blended with the highway miles farther south, and disappeared into the high desert horizon sheen.

What if I had not been present? Would somebody have eventually discovered the bodies of two violated women? The desert and I just sat there.

Didn't kill him. The thought smashed into me, through me. I actually had not even considered it. The opportunity of doing that of which I was most afraid presented itself, then passed unnoticed. I hadn't blocked anything, the event didn't occur, thoughts of it didn't occur. An intense sense of relief and internal emptiness coalesced as I moved off the rocks into the desert.

One day around noon, about halfway between the northern ridgeline of the Angeles National Forest and the ninety-degree turn in Route 138 where it changes course to the south toward Pinion Hills, I heard a familiar banging in the sky. To the northwest, a UH1 festooned in the colors of the Los Angeles Police Department whupped along a couple of hundred feet off the desert, headed south. Surprise, surprise. The machine passed due west, turned in my direction, approached, and circled overhead while I stood still. The Mini 14 was in my right hand, one of the cowboy style canteens I used sat on my left hip. I wore a sleeveless olive drab T-shirt and my jungle hat, jeans and cowboy boots of course, and gloves with the fingers cut off at the first joints. My essential Kabar hung on my right side, like it always had in combat. Not entirely sure I looked just like some peaceable folk out enjoying the desert, I was completely convinced the police were going to drill me with 38-caliber holes any second. My body felt all the rounds and shrapnel that had near it, and into it. The helicopter hovered more or less overhead as an external speaker crackled, "Put down the rifle. Place your hands in the air and stand still."

Well, I *was* standing still, and was not in the least interested in pitching a clean rifle into sand. So I removed the magazine, locked the bolt to the rear, and held the rifle overhead by the flash suppressor and butt plate, with the empty chamber easy to see. The chopper landed. I stood motionless, spitting sand, holding the weapon overhead, convinced rounds would immediately pound through my body if I did anything, perhaps even if I did nothing.

Killed by the police? For nothing? No, no, couldn't be right, too malicious a twist. There was no one around but the two police officers and me, and there isn't right or wrong in this respect anyway; only what occurs. If that was their scheme, I wished they would just fucking do it. About a month later, rotor blades slowed enough to allow sand to remain on the desert. The police officer in the port seat alighted, walked toward me.

"I'll stand nice and still like this until I can hand you this weapon. It's clean, I don't want to lay it in the sand," I said.

I wanted the police officer to understand I was not interested in any rude behavior just then, but didn't want to fill a clean rifle with sand. The officer remaining in the helicopter had his pistol on me, his buddy well covered. We maintained that little freeze-frame a few moments. I soon realized I would have to do something rather stupid to entice bullets in my direction. Though I may not have displayed much, internal relief was great.

"I can understand that," the officer said as he moved to within a few feet of me. "Toss it to me."

Now, passing a perfectly good personal weapon to a stranger is not an easy thing to manage. His face acknowledged my reticence as he caught the rifle like I would have, gave his partner a signal. The officer in the helicopter relaxed a little, pistol remained ready.

"What are you doing?" He holstered his pistol, checked out my rifle like any old combat Marine would. It helped to know that he was Marine Corps. I wondered about his combat experience.

"I was going to shoot that in at three hundred meters," I pointed toward a break in the ridgeline ahead, "near that break."

Below the break was a flat, open, quiet, cool area surrounded by trees with a little creek trickling along one edge, a normally deserted safe place one could let up for awhile. He looked toward the break, turned back to me, asked about my car parked about five clicks away.

"Was that your SCJ we flew over?"

"If it had a poncho liner behind the windshield."

If they ran the car's plates they had my identity, which may have worked in my favor. I had no police record. He nodded, made no mention of having run plates.

"What kind of ammo have you got?" he asked taking in the shrapnel scars and bullet hit on my forearms.

"Nothing exotic. Plain old ball." I tossed the magazine to him.

"That's a thirty rounder," he clacked the magazine into the rifle.

I almost said no shit.

"Did you use those in country?"

Aha, a little combat vet pop quiz. I guess he had suspicions; it didn't seem at all cool to hide from him.

"No, man. Issue M-16 magazines held twenty rounds, I loaded the things with eighteen most of the time."

His face acknowledged receipt of an anticipated answer. "How many do you have in there?"

"Twenty-six. The return springs aren't all that resilient."

He nodded, handing the rifle to me as his eyes found the bullet scar on my upper left arm. "Who were you with?"

The little quiz, his facial expressions, his bearing, the way he handled the weapon, just the way he stood there: that police officer had been there. I don't know why he gave the rifle back so easily, why I could just stand there talking with the gent like I knew him all my life, or why there was nothing but smooth space between us. More comfortable with him than with any person in a long time, I casually accepted the rifle, removed the magazine, slung the weapon muzzle down under my right arm.

"VMA121 out of Chu Lai, then First Battalion, Seventh Marines, outside Da Nang. You?"

He smiled, "Fifth Marines at Hue."

The fifth Marines retook Hue after the Tet Offensive of 1968 at great cost, likely that won't be found in press coverage of the event, but I'm talking about the actual version. You probably won't find press items regarding the 10,000 or so civilian bodies Marines found left by the NVA in shallow mass gravesites near the city either.

"It's good you're back and okay. I was on Hill 10 during Tet," I said.

"You went from the air wing to the grunts?"

"Yeah. Flew A4s out of Chu Lai, then went FAC with One-Seven on Hill 10."

He nodded about three times. "No shit? I had a friend with kilo in the seventh Marines."

Another pop quiz? Kilo Company was on Hill 55 with the rest of the third battalion. I had just told him I was with the first battalion.

"They worked off of fifty-five, I didn't get down there often."

I smiled, thinking how small and busy my world had been with One Seven. He smiled too, probably at the same sorts of things; there wasn't any need to discuss them. His hand extended, I shook it; a lot passed through the handshake.

"I was an oh-three-eleven the first two weeks," he said naming the MOS of a Marine rifleman, "wound up a machine gunner. Our FAC didn't make it."

A rifleman who suddenly moved to machine gunner likely did that during a firefight in which his machine gunner and probably a-gunner were killed. Somebody had to get the gun back up immediately; he was the gent. Marines working with a machine gunner in whom they can believe really aren't at all interested in making changes just for fun. I guess his people appreciated his work, locked him into the position. I had known good machine gunners, spent a few instants thinking about one who had a lot to do with my continued existence.

"Gotta go." He looked around. "We've been fucking around up here too long. You know what you reminded me of, humping along like you were? I wanted to know." He turned to go, turned back to me.

"Look, Sir. Stay out of trouble, Come on back in. Christ, you were a fucking officer. You have to."

We stood there looking over the desert for a few moments. I hadn't felt that synched with anyone for a long time, it might have been the same for him.

"I know," I whispered, took a deep breath, exhaled, "just don't know how yet. How did you?"

"Man," he exhaled, followed with a long pause as he looked out across the desert, "I'm not sure I have. The police job helps, but there are fucking times."

He looked back as he walked to the helicopter. "It's not easy. Civilization is a turncoat, many-faced bitch of a place. Good luck to you, Sir."

"Thank you." I wanted to say something in reflection of the value of the moment, but was having a hard time talking at all. "The best to you."

He could have confiscated my weapon, incarcerated me while determining whether I was dangerous. I was legal enough, though I guess I may have looked just the most tiny bit suspicious to the untrained eye. But mutual recognition of shape allowed our brief life interface to be clean. That gent probably saw more horror, had been through more plain old combat than most. He seemed okay.

What the hell was the deal here anyway? Me, in the middle of nowhere con nada, ninguna, nunca. Secluded, segregated, sequestered, insulated, isolated. Why? To get along better? To rationalize, internalize, externalize, nuclearize, parabolize, roll snake-eyes, simonize, fantasize? What? I sat down, cradled the rifle, settled into the sand, closed my eyes, and remained a long time, wondering, pondering, remembering.

Chapter 2

Winter Wonder

One cold January morning, as Alexandria was being covered with billions of silver-white crystalline structures, I shuffled through knots of traffic, groups of cheery people, and snowplows pushing snow around to disguise curbs, to a Marine Corps Recruitment office. Recruiters on the grounds had mentioned a Naval aviator training program allowing entrance to flight school prior to graduation from college. Presuming accurate information had been presented, the remaining semesters of school would have to wait while I worked on realizing a boyhood dream. A nascent schema in the shimmering sea of future, a vague way began to form. It seemed I had about a flash in time to make my move.

"YOU want to be a MAH-RINE?" a heavy staff sergeant in an impeccable recruiter's uniform growled.

I removed gloves, thumped off snow, opened my coat, loosened my scarf. His eyebrows arched as he leaned forward at his desk, challenging me to take the only seat in the vicinity. Well, being a Marine was certainly a part, but flying jets was most important to me.

"Yes. A Marine aviator, Sergeant."

Yes, a Marine aviator. Simple answer. I had no idea of the complexity of the task and already had made a mistake. Designating a Marine Corps staff sergeant as sergeant is not a good thing; they're a full stripe and pay grade beyond that, they have entered the ranks of staff NCOs and should be addressed as staff sergeant. I, the brat of an Army officer, had not one clue regarding Marine Corps conduct and courtesies.

"More than that, a Marine fighter pilot," I continued. Unaware of my *faux pas* and state of youthful ignorance, I casually positioned my bones in the seat he dared me to use while he recovered from having been called sergeant.

His heavy face flashed absolute incredulity, but he just bit off a breath, returning instantly to stoic. He was a practiced recruiter, much too professional to vocalize personal thought. "Have you finished college?"

"No, but the grounds recruiters talked about a flight cadet program."

The staff sergeant looked like he just saw me. "How old are you? You have to be twenty-one before you can be commissioned. You have to be a commissioned officer to be an aviator in the Marine Corps."

"I'll be twenty-one before program completion."

He thought a moment, obviously running through his recruiter's mental index. With the desired item located, his attention returned to me. "There is a cadet program, Marine Aviation Cadet, MARCAD for short. The tests are rough, and there are no guarantees. You enlist, apply for the program at Parris Island, take the tests, then hope you're selected. If you aren't selected or if for some reason you don't complete the program, you revert to the enlisted Fleet Marine Force for the duration of your contracted term."

Not exactly what I had been told; didn't matter. It was a shot.

"It's a tough program. You could sign up for platoon leader's course and get to flight school when you finish college," he paused, "if you pass the tests. You'd go through Quantico first."

Quantico, the place designated to accomplish transformation of normal human beings to Marine Corps officers, was a few miles south, not far from Fredericksburg, green and attractive amid Virginia hills. I'd driven by a million times, been on the premises a couple of times, which did not provide even a glint of what went on there. But completing school would mean delay; I wanted to get moving.

"I don't want to finish school right now, I want to fly. When would I leave for boot camp?"

"In about a month," he said looking directly at me. "There's a considerable amount of shit to be done first. You should think about it."

I squirmed, suddenly nervous and sweaty. "Don't need to, but I must have guarantee of a fair shot at the MARCAD program. It's the reason I'm here."

He smiled, laid out a form. "I'll put it in writing. This okay with your parents?"

"Want to call them?"

His head moved from side to side twice, to my relief. I hadn't yet mentioned this to parents, really didn't know what my father, a previous Army infantry officer, would have to say about the Marine Corps, nor had I the slightest idea of what my mother would think of any of it.

"Not now. I want us to fill out a preliminary form and you to think about this a couple of days. You'll obligate yourself for either four years of enlisted service or four years of commissioned service beginning at date of commission. If you are accepted in the program, and you complete flight school, you'll be gone more than six years. Talk it over with your parents, then call me."

Early one morning, so early that part of the world hadn't yet decided if it was going to do anything that day, four tense people boarded a bus full of other apprehensive new Marine recruits in Alexandria, sat silently in various states of paralysis while the bus drove to an induction station in Baltimore. After being inducted, which meant standing around all day, enduring a nearly abusive physical examination, continuously being made aware of our general state of stupidity and total inadequacy, then pledging ourselves to the service of the United States, we boarded a train for South Carolina. A night of traveling in rigid, uncomfortable seats that prevented any kind of rest resulted in arrival in Yamasee not long after sunup. As we disembarked, a cluster of uniformed vocal mechanisms began yowling, moving us into various military positions and formations, quickly slamming us into buses. These mechanisms, eventually identified as Marine recruit handlers, continued to howl all the way to Parris Island, where even more joined them. I didn't know what to do or what it meant, so just stood at attention, attempting to see everything.

Perhaps you've heard about Parris Island, upon which resides Marine Corps Recruit Depot Parris Island, one of two Marine Corps boot camps that dispense linear series of completely unprecedented experiences to calculatedly confused young men. Like thousands before, I was entirely too befuddled to think about anything for a while, just hauled around doing exactly as told, like a good robot. MARCAD tests were given a few weeks into training and as the staff sergeant had indicated, they were definitely something special.

After inordinate running, close order drill, scrambling, sweating, extravagance of discipline, more screaming than I thought possible, the platoon proceeded to the rifle range. Rifles and target shooting weren't new, thanks to my father, and the range routine settled me. Shortly after the platoon returned from the rifle range, the Senior Drill Instructor called me to his office. I halted at his hatch and requested to speak as loudly as I could while pounding on the hatch frame until my hand hurt. Drill Instructors didn't seem to hear until perceiving pain in the screamer's hand, no matter how loudly one wailed.

"ENTER MY HOUSE!"

Where do you suppose I went?

"Listen to me," the SDI growled, his face about one inch from mine while I stood in the most perfect position of attention ever.

"YOU are going over to the second battalion area to talk to a captain in the United States MAH-RINE Corps about this MARCAD detail. YOU WILL present yourself as an exemplary maggot, which has FULLY ASSEMBLED shit. Do you understand me?"

"Aye-aye, Sir!"

"I mean it! Your conduct will be PERFECT, and you WILL NOT talk to those second battalion privates, do you undergahdamstand me?"

"Yes, Sir!" Absofuckinglutely.

"YOU will show the captain we are all Smedley Butlers and Iron Mikes over here," a most brief pause, "and you know what will happen to you if you DON'T."

I did not immediately respond, not exactly a most cool thing in the face of a DI.

"DON'T YOU?"

He closed up to about half an inch. I couldn't manage a response.

"I will have the gahdam platoon kick your ASS, private," the one eye I could see widened, "all over the gahdam ISLAND, private," a one millisecond pause, "then direct them to STOMP what's left, private," less than a millisecond pause, "have you fucking GOT that, private?"

"Ayefirmative, Sir!"

"Well get over there! If you keep a CAPTAIN in the United States Marine Corps WAITING he will have you SHREDDED. We will never find all the PIECES. Your momma will get a box containing incomfuckingplete REMAINS!" He paused again, then asked, "Why are you still here? WHY? Go NOW! Fucking GO-OH!!!"

"Aye-aye, Sir!" I left that instant.

"And get yer ass RIGHT BACK HERE when he releases yoo-oooh," followed me through the squad bay.

The interviewing captain was calm, quiet spoken, gracious, polished, qualities nearly forgotten to me. He was patient with my fixation on his gold wings while observing my conduct and reaction to his questions. We shook hands as gentlemen when we parted, something else nearly forgotten. A relaxed but thorough interview, and manners and dignity amid the Parris Island bop.

Toward the end of boot camp, as the platoon was hard at work arranging for an inspection, a shadow appeared over me.

"Follow me."

My SDI turned away; I followed without conscious thought, halting at his hatch to bruise my hand and scream.

"Just get in here!"

Well?

"At ease." He leaned back in his chair as I halted in front of his desk, then put up his feet. "Your squad okay for final field?" he asked quietly.

All my internal alarms fired. A normal voice? Oh shit, what had I done?

"They will be, Sir," I shouted back, anticipating at least an axe in the skull from behind. This normal conversational level talk stuff was brand new, must herald something truly terrible.

"Good," he said.

Oh God, I thought.

"Time for you to be a Marine. You're about through with this recruit depot routine. There are reasons for all this and one day you'll know them." He glanced at the paperwork on his desk. "Listen. You'll graduate with the platoon, then detach and transfer to casual company. You'll be on the island an additional few weeks."

"Sir?" A DI speaking to me like I was human was unnerving. I had no idea what it, or "an additional few weeks on PI," meant.

"Shit private," the SDI turned eyes upward, "you're selected. You'll wait here for orders."

"For MARCAD, Sir?" I almost jumped through the overhead. I stood for an eternity with my heart halted, sweating, waiting for an answer that would shatter my tenuously constructed new universe.

"Yes Private, for MARCAD," he laughed. "One of these days I'll see you and have to salute you. What do you think about that?"

I didn't know what to think or what to say, just stood riveted to the deck, instantaneously frozen in place. But a good DI can handle any situation.

"But not yet," he said, "so get the fuck out of my house."

Blood roared, sight and sound returned, the SDI's pronouncement slid another block of life schema into place. I executed a rather hurried exit of his cubicle, was not called back.

The next few days led to the dreaded final field inspection, pretty much the last big-deal thing at boot camp before graduation. Though preparatory activity was intense, it blurred for me, I was headed for flight school. The squad aced final field, not of anything I did, but because everyone just wanted to do well, genuine esprit de corps, the elusive stuff wanted by everyone. After graduation ceremonies, we strutted around in tropical uniforms for the first time, feeling incredibly good about having accomplished something, wondering if we were ever as pale and frightened looking as recruits in the newly formed platoons. The platoon boarded Greyhound buses and departed for Camp Geiger. I moved to casual company, most assuredly an appropriately named organization.

Orders came in three weeks. After a run through ITR, I was to report to United States Naval School, Preflight, in Pensacola, where I would officially be a MARCAD. The rank insignia was gold wings vertically bisected by a silver two bladed propeller.

Propeller? Nah.

◉

"Well look here," the platoon troop handler at ITR said as he waved my papers, "we got a PFC that's gonna be a gahdam general. What about that?"

Groans, catcalls, and whistles from most of the platoon; no boos, all friendly noises. One of the things about the Marine Corps was acceptance. Though new at a duty station with no idea of what was to be done, other Marines held that issue open until showed something one way or another, one was a fellow Marine, held rights associated with that without question, and was definitely part of the show, whatever it was—even fresh out of MARCAD. All one had to do was reasonably, that is Marine Corps reasonably, accomplish what was asked and maintain propriety in all things. If those two domains could consistently be managed well, relationships with everyone would remain in good shape.

Of an afternoon in heavy rain, just after a field-prepared gourmet lunch of, um, er, something, the platoon assembled for the renowned barbed-wire crawl under live fire. A field mess is, as a rule, a mess in a field rather open to the elements, and steady rain accomplishes interesting changes to previously pulverized, factitious potatoes and some variety of squingy meat-like substance. After eating whatever that was, we were all still hungry, wet, cold, and some highly trained Fleet Marines were readying to shoot at us with machineguns. The idea of fast moving, acutely real bullets casually zipping along just past our brain housing groups didn't exactly contribute to feelings of well-being. We stood completely still in platoon formation, nervously waiting for the thing to get underway, wondering who wouldn't be there when the exercise finished. I was concentrating on rain smacking against my poncho when a troop handler suddenly appeared right next door and pulled me aside.

"Listen! YOU are going first and YOU WILL set a good example. Settle down. Be cool. I made that crawl."

Sure, he did it; I could do it, yes indeed.

"One of these days you'll be an officer. Marines will watch you. You have to show good so they can be good. Now get your ass out there. Lead."

Using my poncho as a set of makeshift reins, he escorted me to the front of the platoon. "This Marine volunteered to go first." As I moved forward at his urging, he spoke softly, "I expect a class number from you."

Indeed. Care to define class number while shivering in boot nervousness and real-bullet twitches? Well, he hadn't run that little routine just for fun; he was exercising a personal methodology to teach something. The rain fell, I understood, apprehension did not diminish.

So into thick mud slime and under the wire, working on getting my heart from out of my throat, back down where it belonged. Belly-slopping along with each nerve feeling every damned thing, most particularly the sharp pop of bullets above, I realized rounds were passing a reasonable distance overhead. One wouldn't seriously want to consider standing or anything, but down in the slime, the barbed wire and the slime were the problems. Bullets cracking overhead educed new mental pictures, more than normal intensity of emotion, and certainly a little anxiety, but otherwise weren't all that horrible. Perhaps Big Daddy C and the Boys really didn't want all of us killed.

However clumsy, that was my introduction to bullets-in-my direction-with-people-depending-on-me-at-the-same-time; another flash preview as occasionally offered by life.

Chapter 3
High Places

United States Naval School of Preflight sat on the grounds of the Pensacola Naval Station, right on the Gulf of Mexico. The well-kept station was nicely arranged, interesting. Its quarters and buildings were massy yet comfortable. While the school wasn't the Midshipman Academy at Annapolis or even close, it had a little of the same feel.

Down the road from the main gate there existed all manner of locally run businesses anxious to provide their solutions to the stressful problem of what to do with one's pay. Automobile dealers offered any kind of wheels one could wish with any kind of financing one might require. They seemed to understand that a cadet's pressing need for wheels involved a machine of relatively high performance with looks that could attract company for the weekend, as well as a requirement for mere transportation.

Aviation cadets couldn't marry, ostensibly because the demands of the flight training command displaced everything else in life, which did seem to be true; it also may have been the Naval services way of protecting its investment. The institution let us know we were entirely too stupid to accomplish reasonable mate selection at the time and closed the issue by forbidding marriage. The organization didn't actually prevent one from marrying of course, one could marry anytime; however, marriage and flight training were held in exclusive disjunction for aviation cadets: one or the other, not both, end of the issue. We presumed our fearless leaders were covering our best interests and butts well and fairly. But the darlings of Pensacola were nonetheless scintillating, fabulous company who wonderfully amplified weekend pleasantries. Anyone having experienced even one of those incredibly beautiful faces with that look and smile aimed right at you, like you and she were all that existed in the universe, will know what I mean.

At the School of Preflight, instructors taught a wealth of military and academic points and procedures, all essential to one's chosen future. Their specialty, however, was humility, taught by loudly pointing out each individual's complete personal inadequacy at every possible opportunity. People outside the school said things such as "Y'all boys are so cool," while the instructors were saying, "How in phuque can y'all boys be so stupid?" This resulted in a certain state of confusion known as ACJ (aviation cadet jitters), where under various circumstances a cadet would flat lock up, hung upon the horns of a dilemma, unable to resolve the issue, often because resolution favored the group in opposition to that presenting the issue.

Preflight was disciplined, concise, a completely military college. Military aviation required much more extensive knowledge than I would have thought, and the school provided the solid beginnings of a Naval aviator's knowledge base. This was a mostly invisible process from the recipient's viewpoint. The all-the-time preflight environment obscured disconnection from the rest of the world. We spent considerable time in academic brain fry, ran up and down the station's sea wall until silly, swam until unable to shave over the filamentous structure of new gills. Yet In spite of all that, the warmth, solidarity, and order of the place remained intact.

Graduation day at last: structured ceremonies, ladies in formal attire, gents in dress whites, ambassadorial level of conduct. Most cadets included their weekend company of course; the ladies were categorically captivating. Parents were treated especially well by everyone and they displayed obvious delight. Mine, however, were not present for reasons of business. It was a comfortable, superb occasion in sharp contrast with everything else I had experienced in the Marine Corps.

End of ceremonies brought a little pensiveness for possibly one to seven seconds, followed immediately by a state of maximum amplification regarding primary flight training. Next stop was NAAS Saufley Field, where we would encounter the Beechcraft T34 "Mentor" primary flight trainer, and flight.

❂

Reporting to the OOD (Officer of the Deck) at Saufley, I used the set of straight-line, stiff motions declared by the military to be "walk," into the compartment, determined to be the picture of correct military bearing, expecting at least token harassment. A Navy lieutenant inestimably privileged with OOD duties that moment, told me to relax, spoke as if to one of his peers, urged staying up on the books during ground school.

"And don't get all tightened up about flying," he said. "Have some grace, allow it to come on naturally."

He wished me luck after I signed in. I wasn't prepared for his genuine interest, nor could I have been given more appropriate advice. Perhaps he was exercising a Naval aviator form of noblesse oblige.

Ground school, operating procedures for this and that, check lists, T-34 systems, course rules, emergency procedures, more theory of flight, more aerodynamics, hydraulics, academics. I had no idea getting to or from an air station required such complex course rules.

"Get your flight gear," my instructor unexpectedly directed one morning. Actual flight training began, the world once again converted to exciting and new. Flying, my *raison d'être*, went smoothly. I can't begin to relate the consuming nervousness of the first hop, or the all-encompassing elation experienced during first solo. One afternoon while executing touch and go landings at an outlying field named Wolfe, my instructor called for a full stop. When we stopped on the runway he exited the aircraft and said, "Go fly."

Um, er, ah -. All I could do was vigorously nod my head and pant, rather like an enthusiastic puppy. Though a primary flight staff would be hard-pressed to admit this to a cadet, the machine flew well without an instructor. Exhilaration. I was as free as ever I have been in somebody else's machine during that few minutes cranking around the sky alone.

That evening as was the custom, amid liberal dousing with whatever was in dousing glasses or cups, and considerable enthusiastic whooping, my field scarf was cut about halfway down from the knot. Now I had enjoyed the happiness of friends when assisting in the cleaving of their field scarves, but really hadn't understood how that felt until it happened to me. It felt wonderful yet, at the same time, there was a small, immediately perceivable separation. Treatment by friends who had soloed versus those who had not was different. So too was the treatment by the instructor staff.

◉

Not everyone made it. A good friend of mine suddenly found himself under close scrutiny by the primary flight training staff. He could go no place or do anything without somebody of official capacity inquiring as to his whereabouts. It was an unnerving deal for all of us, no doubt horrible for him. The closer they looked, the more unsettled he became.

"What?" I asked one day.

"Nothing special," he replied.

"Anything I can do?"

"Leave me alone."

Huh? Leave me alone? Perhaps my idea of friendship was funny; that response came as a real surprise. I went to see the flight commander.

"Sir, what's the deal?"

"There are reasons," the commander seemed more concerned with me than the issue I wanted addressed. "I'm not at liberty to discuss them. Focus attention on what you are doing and let this go past you, youngster. Some good people aren't able to manage this type of flight well."

It sounded like my friend's flight training was history. I recalled how excited we had been when arriving at Saufley, wondered what happened.

"Can I do something?"

"Not for him," pause, "and don't let this throw you. Take care of yourself, continue to do well. You're going to see more people eliminated as you go through the training command, more still when you get to the fleet."

Eliminated. Such a bitten word when associated with a friend. It wasn't long before his easy demeanor moved to brusque, then to hostile, which I understand now, but didn't then. He elected to DOR rather than hang around to be tossed at somebody's leisure. The afternoon he left I stood in the cadet battalion parking lot with the words "Adios lieutenant" ringing in my ears, wondering what happened to the friendship as he angrily drove away in his packed car. He left in good physical shape to pursue another avenue of life. Even so, I experienced the loss associated with a compadre going down.

With ground school at last complete I concentrated on "aviating." One fine day a successful final check ride brought primary flight training to a close. Primary flight completions, one way or the other, along with next duty station, were posted on the squadron bulletin board. The next duty station indicated type of aircraft flown during basic flight training, which determined type of aircraft flown in advanced flight training, which determined category of aircraft one would fly in the fleet. The fleet choices for Marines were large many-motored things, little things with propellers, helicopters, fixed wing jets; right there at that bulletin board was where one first became cognizant of one's destiny.

Fully-articulated, rotorhead aircraft do nifty things, such as park right up there in the sky, or shift into reverse and back up in the middle of the atmosphere. Helicopters are unbelievably good at directly covering troops and moving things and people about with style, but they weren't why I was there. Neither were many-motored transport craft or small propeller-driven devices. Though grades were high and things looked good, I approached that board with closed eyes. With effort my heart rate slowed a little, a couple of deep breaths, then—eyes open—Naval Auxiliary Air Station Meridian. Ee-hah! Fixed-wing jets, yes-yes! Talk about tension release. I packed my trusty set of wheels, blasted off for basic jet training in Mississippi.

The city of Meridian bustled during business hours, but was rather quiet in the evenings. A friendly place with amicable people, where things were fine, and the surroundings Mississippi-green and pretty. There was no beach, no suntanned darlings running around with major portions of their physiology in view. Meridian women displayed incredible hair and smooth, pale skin. They wore dresses for the most part, emanated sophisticated heavenly scents, exercised exemplary manners, spoke a charming form of Americanese, soft with an enchanting accent, and demanded proper conduct. Well, at least in public.

After driving north out of the city on Route 19, making the right-hand turn onto the road leading to the station, and driving until fairly sure I had missed the turn, the NAAS Meridian brick gateposts and near buildings separated from the unbroken green. Officer and cadet quarters were new buildings set among rolling greens and trees around a little lake dubbed "Lake Fester," due to the lack of discernable means of drainage or water flow. They flew North American T2J "Buckeyes" at Meridian and though I don't believe the aircraft's appearance seriously titillated anyone's aesthetic senses, the thing was turbojet powered and no doubt had a lot to teach us about flight. Check-in. The place was even more relaxed than Saufley. Thumping people into military shape was fast becoming less important than thumping people into aviator shape.

Flight gear issue provided a "gee" suit (gravity suit) and torso harness. By means of an arrangement of bladders and connection to an aircraft system designed to inflate them, a gee suit assisted in keeping blood up toward heart and brain during accelerated flight, at least that was the designed intent. The other item, the torso harness, had fittings used to attach one to the seat of the aircraft and the parachute harness; the more significant of the two I suppose depended upon one's relationship of the moment with Our Lady of the Luck. Everybody in sight wore those things; nevertheless, to me they represented entry into an exclusive group.

More ground school, of course. The mechanics of flying required more attention, a certain brain acceleration to accommodate turbojet powered aircraft, constant awareness of the exhaust gas tube when on the ground to prevent conversion of one's background to cinders. The things shrieked, rumbled, extravasated a whole new set of noises and vibrations, looked singularly ungainly on the ground, but were smooth, responsive, graceful in flight. First solo in the jet was even better; the aircraft had so much more capability. Another small separation.

Basic instrument flight training included introduction to both partial panel recoveries and a new form of brain seizure. The instrument flight hood, a canvas sheet affair that pulled over the rear portion of the cockpit, was called a bag. Its purpose was occlusion of the view outside the cockpit, thereby forcing full attention to the flight instruments in simulation of IFR (instrument flight rules) conditions, which it did well. The partial panel plot was an arrangement whereby an instructor placed the aircraft in an unusual attitude, meaning some flight posture far removed from anything one would normally encounter, while the student was under the bag, usually with eyes closed at the instructor's request. The severity of the unusual attitude depended upon the student's point in training and the instructor's disposition that minute. The instructor, after placing the aircraft in some completely absurd flight posture, would fail a significant flight instrument, immediately returning control of the aircraft to a student with a seized brain.

"Open your eyes, you have the aircraft."

It was a command calling for restoration of the vanished world as one had known it, by use of remaining flight instruments. With eyes open, appendages on the controls, I'd squirm, make strange sounds while my brain processed all this shiny new data, then attempt to return the aircraft to some semblance of normal flight. I presume the instructor would have intervened rather than eject if things had gotten out of hand, but I don't know that for certain because it never happened. It didn't feel as though anyone would assist in that confined back seat anyway; one handled the situation, or was handled by the situation, no options.

Basic formation training, particularly while learning to accomplish a level CV rendezvous, also provided ancillary definitions for heart stopping and blood freezing. Logic behind this type of rendezvous was means of assembling a flight after launch off of an aircraft carrier that didn't take much time or distance to accomplish, or unnecessarily use wingmen's fuel. The flight's lead aircraft maintained a level turn, while joining aircraft used the radius of turn along a specific bearing to approach the lead aircraft. One could close on the turning aircraft by flying along the bearing line without use of appreciable speed differential, hence little power differential, ergo small difference in fuel consumption. When closing with the lead, one stabilized the aircraft's position, crossed under the lead aircraft, moved into any of several specific formations.

Now that's all true, it works well, however, I couldn't believe just working a radius of turn would allow everything to happen satisfactorily, augmentation with a little power ought to result in a satisfactory rate of things. The result: (how shall I say this?) a rather easily discernible speed differential. After wailing up the bearing line, I arrived in close with an astounding closure rate I'm sure caused the lead to want to be located anywhere else in the universe. But Naval flight students are dauntless, and though no doubt with closed eyes and prayer, the lead stayed right there while I accomplished some of the most spectacular formation joins you have ever seen.

That was one section, or two aircraft. Division rendezvous, flights of four with three of us simultaneously thrashing up the bearing line, were considerably more entertaining. As angels protecting fledgling aviators would have it, we all managed basic formation stage without damage to other than perhaps ego. My first solo rendezvous convinced me cockpit air conditioning probably wasn't installed for the convenience of aviators, more likely was installed to protect cockpit instruments and switches from an aviator in a state of overheat; it really didn't cool one all that much.

The aircraft were beautiful in the air, graceful atmospheric vehicles calling attention to the magnificence of flight, inducing awe while working and watching compadres worked those maneuverable little airframes. The white and orange machines overlaid green and blue environment with sweeping dynamic patterns, granted means of exploring an unexpected four-dimensional art form as we became more adept at various tasks and maneuvers.

A simple division rendezvous seen from the lead or the number four position can be remarkably beautiful, involving feelings of humans purposefully working together as aircraft string along in a graceful line, moving toward the lead machine. Early or late in the day, against a sky of cumulus and cumulonimbus clouds in early stages of development, in soft tangential sunlight that adds a splendid amber tint to objects touched, a well-executed division rendezvous could be breathtaking.

Banging along in the car, headed back to Pensacola after completing the Meridian phase of flight training, I wondered what had changed at mainside. The next squadron assignment was VT-4, located at Sherman Field on the Pensacola mainside facility. The squadron afforded air-to-air gunnery and carrier landing qualification. Start of the gunnery course was delayed two weeks, didn't matter, I smiled, revisited beaches and the previously mentioned company. Ground school commenced, smile, gunnery phase began, smile, gun hops, smile; gunnery pattern work is precise and just plain fun. Smile, smile.

An aircraft known as the "tractor," towing a banner a thousand feet aft along a prescribed route in a restricted area, set the stage for air-to-air gunnery pattern work. The restricted areas were specifically established to prevent people, aircraft, buildings, what have you from batter by sleek metal projectiles returning to the earth after having been launched at the banner. Flights of "shooters" would meet the tractor on the range, fly a specific pattern designed to provide access to the target without placing the tractor or other shooters in jeopardy. Meanwhile, the tractor flew a straight line and hoped.

Passing close abeam the tractor over a shimmering blue Gulf of Mexico with a two hundred fifty knot speed advantage, then flinging the aircraft up toward the perch, was a series of thrills, even in a T2. The perch is a position high abeam the tractor where a banner pattern run commences; working the aircraft down from the perch through the gun run was an excellent, rewarding study in precision and timing. I lost my first aviation bet, won my second during gunnery, the bets regarding who would score more hits. I don't recall hearing of aviation cadets who wouldn't bet on themselves.

Start of field carrier landing pattern (FCLP) phase brought more smiles. The pattern was a land-based way of learning procedures for shipboard landing operations, which of necessity must be more precise and different than land-based operations. There is also a different approach to landing taught in depth during FCLP, and though we all knew a little about the technique from training at both Saufley and Meridian, here the deal was real.

The first working FCLP hop stopped the smiles. I thought I could land the aircraft fairly well. The Landing Signal Officer (LSO) thought that with a great amount of effort, some day I might be able to return the aircraft to the Earth without damaging either too badly. It took another hop to comprehend things; subsequent hops found the smiles back.

The concern was a tendency to flatten the last few feet of descent just before landing, to minimize aircraft vertical velocity and begin the process of speed bleed-off, a routine practice in land-based aviation called "flaring." On long runways, flaring and aerodynamic braking are perfectly good techniques. When landing aboard ship, the idea is to get speed established, set up the aircraft's attitude, fly the glide slope down to landing with power rather than by use of aircraft attitude changes. The aircraft is flown right into the ship then trapped by a tailhook on the aircraft and arresting cables on the ship. A danger connected with flaring aboard ship is hook engagement prior to the aircraft's landing gear contacting the deck. The Naval service ensures landing gear on purchased aircraft can suitably accommodate these aircraft-ship landing collisions, but does not provide additional stress testing for slams to the deck from hook engagements while airborne. Flying into the ship's deck also is of benefit in the case of such rarities as hook skips, a broken wire, a pulled hook, missed wires, things along that line, all lumped under the heading of "bolter." As the aircraft hasn't quit flying, nor has the engine decelerated out of its fast response band, there is plenty of power available quickly, along with speed enough to get out of there before the aircraft gets wet. Once all this became evident, things were fine. FCLP training finished and we received a series of shipboard operations briefings. Everyone smiled, albeit nervously.

One morning, T2s containing one gent each in various states of alarm executed the previously mentioned form of rendezvous over Sherman field. The various flights headed out into the Gulf of Mexico seeking the U.S.S. Lexington, a distinguished old aircraft carrier whose glorious history earned it position as an impact object for fledgling aviators' first carrier qualifications. The division with which I flew descended, entered the landing pattern of a remarkably tiny ship I perused while setting up abeam. We were going to land on that teensy thing?

Holy shit.

There was a Fresnel lens on the port side of the landing area aboard ship that provided visual glide slope information. Its light appeared as a sort of amber blob from the glide slope, hence the name meatball, or ball. Just aft and a little to port of the Fresnel lens, where one would never ever see him if paying close attention to the ball as one ought, stood a highly trained aviator called a Landing Signal Officer, who assisted-directed other aviators in their approach/landing chores and enjoyed considerable clout in the ship's aviation circles.

I came out of my first ship approach turn, started down the groove holding my breath. Five hundred feet AGL as during FCLP and five hundred feet ASL at the ship, both mean five hundred feet above the surface. The ship's deck, however, sat there at around sixty feet ASL; that part of things looked different. My first ball call was gibberish that the LSO graciously acknowledged anyway. The aircraft rushed downward, I stared alternately at the Fresnel lens and the little piece of metal floating in the water we were about to hit.

BLOMPF!

We impacted upon the Lex while I was looking at the lens, I immediately shoved power to full, raised the nose of the aircraft, came out of alarm after the aircraft was comfortably flying. While making the clearing turn I looked back at the ship, it had grown a little.

The next pass was another touch and go. Two or three of those were called for to familiarize one with the working environment prior to an arrested landing attempt (read "familiarize as dominate one's apprehension"). I managed to sound like a human being the second ball call, flew the Fresnel lens, more or less maintained speed. I was prepared for the landing. Alignment could have been a little better; I hadn't noticed the stack burble on the first pass.

When abeam next pass, I lowered the tail hook for my first shipboard arrested landing. Would one of those little pieces of cable on the Lex really catch and hold this aircraft? Would the tail hook remain attached to the aircraft? Although Naval aviators had been doing this for decades, I still had a few little questions.

Working down the groove, attending to everything, suddenly I saw wave off lights. Wave off lights? Me? The pass wasn't THAT bad.

"Foul deck, aircraft in the gear," said the LSO.

Okay. It wasn't me. The aircraft landing ahead obstructed the landing area (us first-timers weren't yet all that adept at clearing arresting gear). I waved at my compadre in the wire as I went around, remembered to lower the hook when abeam, called the ball, and flew a reasonably decent pass to my first shipboard arrested landing. I am eternally grateful to whoever told me to lock the inertia reel harness, ensuring that my face did not become an imprint in the instrument panel as the word arrested was redefined.

Drenched in post first shipboard landing brain fade, I reduced power to idle while staring at the sea. After a while, frantic waving of a yellowshirt (flight deck crew) garnered attention. I turned only slightly red, reconnected with real time, and followed the yellowshirt's signals. It's possible the gent in the groove behind me also may have taken a foul deck wave off, though I don't remember anyone flying past.

Taxiing forward to the catapult, wondering how the Navy managed to expand the ship in just a few minutes, I was directed to the starboard cat. As you know, a catapult is a device that hurls things, in this case off of the ship. There are a number of things to be done in regard to an aircraft-catapult hookup. Once completed and the aircraft is "in the sling," both ship and aircraft are set for the launch. The catapult officer passed an engine run-up signal. I accomplished the run-up as well as doing everything else humanly possible in the cockpit before bracing, then tossed him a highball. The highball meant the aircraft and the aviator were ready for launch, and I actually thought I was. The cat officer stood between catapults, nodded as he touched his headgear in response to my highball, brought his arm down as if to touch the ship's deck, paused, smiled at me. See, he knew what was about to happen, and knew I didn't. His arm moved forward, as if tossing something off the deck. I was sitting in the catapult all bridled and tensioned like a good kid, left hand wrapped tightly around the PCL and the catapult hold lever, when ... Zangawhoop! Over the water, aircraft flying, fierce acceleration. Whang-ng-ng-ng bap!

My brain caught up with its skull before the aircraft started seaward. You see, there is nothing else quite like that. Well, perhaps drivers of top fuel and funny cars in the world of drag racing experience it, but under normal circumstances those people work only two of the physical dimensions. A cat shot is, let me put this succinctly, an unequivocal gas.

I laughed in wonder, turned downwind feeling fabulous. Everyone qualified and Trader John's, Trader Vic's, Pensacola, and Pensacola Beach received an extremely boisterous little group of gents that evening.

◎

Next stop in the pipeline was the Naval Air Advanced Training Command in Texas. I checked in at an NAAS Kingsville BOQ. My roommate was a friendly, relaxed, patrician lieutenant JG who looked at me as if reading a Venn diagram. "You own the white Corvette?" he said extending his hand.

I shook it, searched his eyes for some meaning. "Heya. Yeah. So?"

Turns out he owned an Avanti R2, the one with the Paxton supercharger. The issue of Avanti versus Corvette focused immediately and provided much amusement and mirth until he graduated a few weeks later.

Kingsville offered a thicker, even more businesslike environment; ground school was more specific, instructors spent much more time with small points, and maintenance crews, aircraft handlers, cooks, crash crews, admin clerks, everyone would do what they could to assist, if one asked. The basic air training command roughed in shapes, the advanced air training command was concerned with details.

Aircraft? The Grumman F9 "Cougar" in two varieties. The TF9, an F9 modified to accommodate a second seat with trimmings, and the student-coveted, single seat ex-tactical AF9, which one could fly after completing certain portions of the training program. The Cougar had been a fleet tactical fighter and still exuded a certain allure. It had fat (thick) swept wings and the centrifugal flow engine (as opposed to axial flow) was slow in response, but holy cow could that thing maneuver.

Familiarization and basic formation stages led to "C" stage, the Naval Advanced Air Training Command course in instrument flight procedures. Instrument flying is something every Marine/Naval aviator must do well, and definitely is not something to which humans naturally aspire. It involves hours of work that flickers not even one of your lights. It's no-thrill drudgery that can lull the most dedicated and well intentioned into a subtly disconnected state. But it is vital preparation for those infrequent but dire situations that can instantaneously light all your lights to max, sometimes to blowout.

We had heard horror stories concerning C Stage since beginning the basic jet program at Meridian. The stage was taxing, a series of intense studies in air work, procedures, application, behavior, discipline, headwork, the unexpected; it cranked along forever, giving the impression that it was what would be done for the rest of one's life. But just before brain blowout, it ended. The reward was a Naval Aviation Standard Instrument Card.

Next came formation and tactics, air combat maneuvering, bombs and rockets, low level navigation, a solo cross country RON. The student solo RON scheme allowed visit to any NAS within the IFR range of a tank of fuel. Imagine being turned loose the first time for two days and a night in a jet aircraft having only one seat. There was more air-to-air gunnery and another carrier qualification session on the Lex. Fly and learn, fly and learn; I was unmindful of the subtle change in my viewpoint, or of the mass of data accumulating in my head.

Upon return to the BOQ one evening, there was a little card affixed to my hatch, an invitation to see the Ed White uniforms representative. The card declared the fitting would require about ninety minutes. I sauntered down to the aforementioned cubicle where the rep had on display various uniform items, accessories, and a Marine Corps officer's dress sword with its elegantly simple Mameluke hilt. I picked the best of everything, of course. Then the rep mentioned charges. Er -, um -, charges? Other than specification and inspection, DOD is not involved with Marine Corps officer uniform items; the officer must purchase these on their own. Well, the Ed White uniform company certainly didn't want to see an officer ill-equipped or underdressed, and so offered several payment schemes. I picked the one most suitable and signed away.

It hit me suddenly. I was there, wasn't I? All the way through, right upon the boyhood dream.

One quiet spring morning around ten o'clock, ten hundred hours if you prefer, in a little second deck compartment at the NAAS Kingsville station commanding officer's structure, I was first commissioned an officer in the United States Marine Corps, then designated a Naval aviator. There were three present: the station CO, a Master Chief Petty Officer, and me. The little ceremony lasted ten or twelve minutes. The CO was not given to chitchat, doubt I could have said anything meaningful anyway. The captain shook my hand as a commissioned officer in the service of the United States of America—a wing wearing, no kidding, Marine Corps jet aviator for the first time. My heart pumped so hard I didn't have to use muscles to shake his hand.

Out of the building, the gold wings on my chest flapped away as my heart pounded, the brass bars on my shoulders dazzled in the Texas sun. I watched two Cougars in the pattern for a minute, checked the flight line area, and walked to the car. The shiny new boot jet aviator and the little boy with a dream regarded each other, smiled, laughed.

Chapter 4
Forty-Foot Platform

Hazard a guess as to first activity as an officer? A few days of leave, of course. I went home where the family treated me like visiting royalty, another separator. I looked up college friends but the internal distance moved was now obvious and conversations with them were halting. A couple of those old friends seemed to be edging on adversarial. Things had certainly changed, our paths were divergent, I was no longer part of that group. Okay, but how that diminished friendship was a little perplexing, another separator.

Time off, no matter how long the period, dissipates five minutes after it starts. I headed south, ensuring several east coast beaches were still there and okay before driving onto Marine Corps Air Station Beaufort, South Carolina, like it was mine. Conversion to an attack aviator, accomplished by the able aviators of VMA-331, would occur right here. The SDO (Squadron Duty Officer) that particular Friday afternoon was the squadron's junior aviator, until my arrival of course, at which time the boot position passed to me. He was relaxed, friendly, and obviously happy to have somebody around to elevate his status.

"You'll like it here," he said, "even if you are the squadron boot. Don't let that worry you, this place is good; flying is gooder."

We talked about anything as he led me around the flight line area, both of us paying special attention to the collection of Douglas A4E Skyhawks flown by the squadron. The little delta-winged single seaters looked distantly friendly, standing on their too-tall landing gear with slats hanging fully extended from wing leading edges. Shortly I was invited to cool my jets for the weekend.

Parris Island isn't far from MCAS Beaufort, so the next day I drove onto the island in a fresh tropical uniform, returning the gate guard's salute like I owned that place, too. The feeling lasted until my arrival at the visitor's center, where a formal sergeant unenthusiastically agreed to show me around. I didn't require an escort, just wanted to poke around the place awhile, but now I was commissioned and there are proprieties. Things were different as an officer. Normal activities seemed hidden from view and the place was startling. Things were in the same locations, looked about the same as when I was a recruit there, but nothing felt the same. Everyone, DIs in particular, exhibited extra-smooth behavior, people attended to me, gawked, clucked over, shied away, saluted, were painfully courteous, expressly avoided use of profanity. The perfect sergeant was stiff and formal as a human can be until he discovered I was once a recruit there, at which time he relaxed to only moderately stiff and formal.

According to the sergeant, my SDI was with a battery of 105 mm howitzers in the combat zone near Phu Bai. My JDI had been killed in a mortar attack in the same area.

Killed? My JDI? Dead?

The sergeant stood quietly looking away, allowing all the room in the world to deal with the information. That was the first time I gave any thought to SEA, at that it was only a reaction of sorrow regarding the death of my JDI.

We ended the little tour at the statue of Iron Mike. I drove off the island understanding the only people who really know what goes on there are recruits and their DIs. Parris Island wasn't home or anything, but like home, my Parris Island had slipped away someplace.

Wouldn't you know, first thing at the squadron was more books? A4 systems, procedures, specific weapons, deliveries, specific combat tactics—more data collections to assimilate. The squadron's strategic focus was tactical aviation in whatever form or arena; the working posture was contribute to squadron readiness or find something to do elsewhere.

Just after daylight one morning, walking down the flight line in the first-light chill completely elated, one of the squadron's salts and I were preparing to "aviate" about for a while, to acquaint me with the aircraft and the local work areas. I located the assigned aircraft, sure, just another A4E, but my first. After preflight I scrambled up the ladder and climbed into the cockpit. I knew what to do absolutely cold, but hadn't actually done anything yet, and though single-seat aircraft are the only way to fly, one really must get the bulk of things rather close to exactly right the first time. The do part, the difference between chatter and action, the sea of separation between academic discussion and actual accomplishment, can be profound.

My lead taxied by, picked me up, passed me the lead. After a little new guy stumbling around, I led onto the runway, completed the manual fuel control check, exchanged thumbs up with the escort, and advanced the throttle (excuse me, "power control lever"). The aircraft crept. I redoubled effort on the brakes, then released them as the aircraft moved forward anyway. Brakes didn't hold these aircraft at higher power settings. The A4 jumped off the runway quickly. I hustled to get the gear and flaps up as it accelerated into the cool morning, bashing along as it knew how, mindless of the boot sitting in the cockpit. What a remarkably alive, responsive, acutely maneuverable little weapons platform. Over the next few weeks, as I became accustomed to the machine, worked more toward the edges of its flight envelope, the aircraft transitioned from a mass of mechanical and electronic parts that flew rather well, to a comfortable, consistent, trustworthy vehicle; a mechanical friend, if you will.

Participation in a MEBLEX (Marine Expeditionary Brigade Landing Exercise) was announced at an afternoon AAM (all aviator's meeting) A few days later the squadron launched for Roosevelt Roads near San Juan, Puerto Rico. A MEBLEX is a part of training for an amphibious assault; the title really doesn't tell the story.

We launched off of verdant Puerto Rico into a crystalline blue sky, climbed out over a variegated deep blue to aquamarine sea dotted with a collection of island jewels. Once in the target area over one of those beautiful islands, we ran simulated ordnance deliveries on simulated targets. Usually there was time for a little extracurricular aerobatics and general flailing about for fun. The few weeks at Roosevelt Roads coalesced into rushing watercolors, a montage of friendly people, soft breezes, warm sun, sparkling clear

water, gorgeous environment, and quantities of tactical flying. It
was almost too good.

Often, one would see large freighters in sea lanes around Puerto
Rico. A friend and I discovered one of these huge things creeping
along the ocean one afternoon while returning from a MEBLEX
hop. It offered more temptation than two boot aviators in high-
suds little tactical aircraft could resist. We hauled by the freighter
at five hundred feet, moving at approximately five hundred knots.
So big deal. Anyone could have made a run way up in the sky like
that. We swung around for another pass.

"Take starboard," my friend directed on the squadron's tactical
frequency as we lowered the aircraft's noses toward the Merchant
Marine monster in the ocean below. "Turn apart after, make it
good."

Well, to a brand new cooler-than-polar-icecaps tactical aviator,
"make it good" is demand for a maximum zing, meaning park
everything about your brain and physiology but thoughts and
actions directly in concert with the elected activity. Now the A4E is
a transonic aircraft, but mostly subsonic transonic if you will; one
was obliged to do things just so in order to get the jewel up over
mach one. This day we had practice ordnance mounted directly on all
five pylons to simulate heavy ordnance, which had been dropped.
The aircraft were sans racks and drop tanks, and we had burned a
lot of fuel so they were also light.

Clean and light. Fast-fast.

Headed downhill at full power, the little scoots quickly
approached mach. Even as new hot shots that didn't know anything
yet, we knew better than to knock around people and things with
shock wave formations from supersonic flight. So, we backed off
the power about three one-hundredths of a percent, leveled a little
above the surface and merrily hauled toward the stern of the
freighter monster at the speed of heat. I shot by the starboard side
close, fast, looking up at a few wide-eyed downward stares; my
friend did the same on the port side. We turned apart twenty
degrees at the ship's bow, raised the aircraft's noses, aileron rolled
as we climbed back to altitude, completely confident in our ability
to put the aircraft precisely where we wanted them.

Next morning, before the sun showed up, the squadron
commander called us in for a little colloquy, the variety requiring a
rigid position of attention so the goo oozing from the deep gashes

of serious verbal laceration was absorbed by your uniform before reaching the skipper's carpet.

"They are AIR craft, gents," he said. "You both successfully completed several courses in aerodynamics. Recall the part about the atmosphere? I know it begins at our feet, we all live in it, but under normal circumstances, and understand these are normal circumstances, aircraft are flown above and far out of the reach of people standing on the surface, or on the deck of a freighter. Is that exceedingly clear?"

"Limpid, Sir!" Emphatic nods while answering in unison.

"When merchant marine seamen look down upon close-by aircraft, they become frightened. Their world starts to fracture. Their captain becomes unsettled, and in this case would rather enjoy watching as you were keelhauled. How would you like to be dragged under that freighter's length?"

Being run over by twenty miles of thick steel hull then passing through churning house-sized screws was probably a little more thrill than either of us required. We stood silent, contrite.

"What do you have to say for yourselves?"

We looked at each other, then back at the Skipper.

"Sir," I mumbled, "um ... "

"Sir," my friend looked at me, then at the Skipper. "We didn't hurt anybody or damage anything, Sir."

We actually thought about that before the run, a little confirmation never hurts.

"That seems to be true," he replied.

"I guess -, um -, er -." I really tried to talk, but it wasn't easy. My friend interceded.

"Ah, Sir. I think he's trying to say it was great, Sir."

"But we'll never do it again, Sir," in unison, naturally.

"You'd best not!" He ambled around his desk, took his seat, fidgeted with things on his desk a moment, looked up at us. "Hack," he announced. "You two are in hack for the duration of this cruise." His face showed he probably had done a few off-the-page things himself, but that sort of thing was decidedly un-smart.

We were being punished, but not horribly thank you. Hack meant we flew normally, but were confined to quarters outside of squadron operations. That wasn't too bad; the precise pass was easily worth a couple of weeks in hack.

"That's two weeks. If you again resort to such behavior, we'll do something official," he looked at each of us. "Got it?"

"Aye-aye, Sir," in unison again. Something official most likely put our wings in jeopardy, um -, no, thank you.

"Inform the SDO you're in hack, get back to business."

We exited his office without looking back, shook hands and breathed again, then proceeded directly to the SDO.

"Okay y'all bad-assed boys. No beaches, scuba diving, sailing, cruising. Your view in this tropical paradise shall be four walls and a boob tube," the SDO laughed.

It wasn't THAT funny.

"Don't worry about it, just don't do it again. I don't know anyone who didn't spend time in hack for similar things on a first cruise," he looked around, spoke softly, "including the Skipper."

Good to hear, of course, but the potential of "something official" had already caused our conversion to most angelic Marine aviators. We would remain that way for at least the near future.

The squadron resumed normal operations upon return to Beaufort. The little hesitancy and indecision about how to best approach any particular activity I had been experiencing was now gone. A few months later the squadron deployed to MCAS Yuma, Arizona, to put the final changes on junior aviators' weapons skills.

Positioned near the Colorado River among sand dunes somewhere in the vast southwestern United States, Yuma wasn't nearly as entertaining as Rosy Roads, but flying was first rate. Weather? There wasn't any weather; perhaps a little wind every five minutes or so. Yuma had about five iffy weather days a year for Marine Corps aviation, and those normally occurred long after we would be back in Beaufort. The local diversions were the officer's club, night clubs in town, and a little border town on the Mexican side, all of which fit into the minimum thrills category.

Zinging around the atmosphere in the desert-restricted areas was fabulous. Amazing velocities could be managed close to the planet's surface without much worry about sudden encounters. One afternoon not long after we arrived, a new guy brought back an aircraft with dings in the drop tanks.

"A Mesquite tree?" The maintenance officer raised his eyes questioningly. "One of my quality control people has declared the drops as assaulted by at least one Mesquite tree. Seldom do those things get more than about thirty feet high, now what about that?"

"THAT Mesquite tree must have been five hundred one feet tall," said the aviator, whose face reflected boyish innocence. "You know we can't work below five hundred feet AGL, I would never violate squadron policy. Even in the desert, even inside restricted areas where there are no people around, and nothing is taller than thirty feet for miles."

The Skipper put him in hack for the remaining two weeks.

Then early one morning a friend took off—okay so he took off, la-di-da. Well, he held the aircraft right on the deck until the north field boundary, then commenced a straight-up zoom climb inside the field boundaries. Tower personnel already had the impression he dragged drops on the runway, so no doubt they were somewhat taken with his little old straight-up climb.

Guess what? Well. Hack. That's what.

"Unruly, thrill seeking, undisciplined first tour aviators," the Skipper said at the traditional Friday happy hour that week as he tipped one toward the four of us, his bad-boy hack club. We held our breath, waited for a following verbal smack. "But damn can they fly."

Whap! Got us. Turned to stone, not even a moan. The last thing expected from a Marine Corps attack squadron commanding officer was a compliment to his hack club members. Goose bumps, heart heat up, frost on the epidermal covering. What a tribute.

Back at Beaufort, my status was elevated to combat ready. I had at last become a dinkum Marine tactical aviator.

So what about this Southeast Asian deal? After collecting information from as many sources as I could, including the squadron's classified materials section, I considered things for a couple of weeks, paraded up to the squadron commander's office, volunteered to go do my part. The information led me to believe the military had unwillingly inherited a rather serious can of worms from the CIA, that a hostile power was indeed in an aggressive expansion mode, that McNamara was much more interested in statistics looking a certain way rather than working with reality, and that members of my little club, Americans, were dying due to hostile activity. JFK had said to ask what I could do for my country. After having been specifically trained to assist in those kinds of situations, a means of service was discernible, so I originated a request for service in the combat zone. Was that not what the taxpayers' money invested in me and the congressional commission I accepted were all about? The right thing?

Apparently Pops-oh read and processed requests from his
junior officers. Orders to the SEA combat zone magically appeared.

Oh me.

Chapter 5

December

A Boeing 707 320C, owned or at least leased by Northwest Orient airlines, loafed along at altitude, whining and rumbling as it carried a group of uncommonly silent people over Seattle, across ocean in view of the coasts of Canada and Alaska, eventually to Tokyo. After remaining at Tokyo International for about an hour and a half while those bound for the combat zone sweltered in the confined cabin, the flight continued south over Okinawa, the Philippines, then turned west, toward Da Nang.

From the small seats of a commercial airliner cruising over the South China Sea, South Vietnam appeared sleepy, picturesque, mysterious. The Da Nang harbor and Hai Van pass areas were striking, the kind of deep aqua harbor and luxuriant green mountainous area one might picture at suggestion of tropical paradise. A few of the silent group strained to see; others slumped down in their seats. Everyone on board knew that some held only one-way transportation requests. Our Lady of the Luck and the Reap knew whom.

Landing revealed revetments, barbed wire, considerable combat equipment, atmosphere full of fine pieces of matter and smoke particles, noise, tropical heat, US military personnel armed with all manner of weapons, thick oil, engine, and verdure smells. We deplaned into the mass of equipment amid many C-130s wearing camouflage paint. The local area was busy and terribly dusty, felt unhealthy and seemed less attractive than it did from the air. I was the only aviator, the only person visible in a tropical uniform. NCOs directed troops; junior officers fended for themselves. I stood in the famous second lieutenant duh mode, trying to see everything. An Air Force lieutenant in a flight suit turned as he walked by.

"Hello," he smiled, "you lost?"

"Heya. Yeah," I laughed.

"Where do you want to go?"

"Oh, I think home." We both laughed. "Chu Lai, actually."

"What do you fly?" he asked.

"Alpha fours. You?"

"Fox one-oh-sixes, with the 48th Fighter Interceptor Squadron. Over there." He pointed across the field. "Get your stuff, we'll find a southbound C130 for you. Getting to Chu Lai from here is easy."

"Thanks. What do interceptors do here?"

He laughed again. "Not too much. We scramble occasionally against bogeys that turn out to be unannounced friendlies. Once in awhile we go north but not far. We're Da Nang's air defense, there isn't much to it."

We shook hands at the C130, wished each other luck.

There were many craters from detonated ordnance and burning structures on the fifty-mile trip to Chu Lai. This was not my first look at war-torn countryside. As an officer's brat in an occupied country after WWII, I played on dragon's teeth amid torn up buildings and bridges, negotiated huge holes in the Earth, and found many war souvenirs. However, this was active war; these structures were burning in the present rather than burned in the past. This was new war.

Though the Da Nang harbor looked inviting, most of the South China Sea didn't bring to mind the Caribbean, or enthuse one to the point of jumping out of the aircraft into a refreshing body of water. Chu Lai was located on the coast of a large cove, protected by a nice point to the north, a wide peninsula to the south. The area wasn't all that enticing, but the beach stretching up and down the coast, looking like a color separator added at the last minute, looked nice. There were two runways: a long concrete one to the west and a shorter one constructed using interlocking steel matting to the east. The combat aviator at VMA-331 mentioned a concrete runway under construction; it looked operational.

A hot and dusty world immured my tired body as I exited the Hercules. There were three squadrons of F4s located just off ten thousand feet of new concrete runway; there were also distant explosions.

"Where are the Alpha fours?" I asked a nearby corporal.

"On the east field, Sir." He was busy directing cargo. "I'll have the Lieutenant's wheels here in a minute."

So A4s worked off the mats? Oh well. Even in one hundred plus degree temperatures with full loads an A4 didn't need ten thousand feet of runway, but it would have been nice. I gawked at everything while attempting to ascertain the meaning of the distant explosions. I knew what they were all right, just not what they meant to the base. After a few minutes a jeep pulled up and I hopped in. Along the way, it bumped my gear and carcass through sand, kicking up dust in every direction, moving through thick burned and unburned JP5 smells to the east field, centered around an eight-thousand foot mat runway running parallel to the coast, three or four hundred meters inland.

Interesting, huh? I show up unannounced, with little status, thousands of miles from home in a rather undeveloped country amid people busy enough with their own work, who haven't a clue in regard to me or my working posture, and yet a driver and jeep show up to haul my gear and butt the last little bit to my destination. Of course the driver's job was to haul whomever, wherever, whenever as designated; even at that, it was pleasant, perhaps a little reinforcing, a point to which to hold in a new environment.

Matting of the east field was composed of steel alloy sections that interlocked to form an almost solid surface, such as a runway or pretty much any other kind of almost solid surface. I say almost solid because flexing of the matting could be heard, seen, and felt under any kind of vehicle, aircraft in particular. No complaint though; these mats were well laid over the sand and worked fine. But the Chu Lai mats were terra not all that firma, something one would never confuse with concrete.

Anything germane to flight operations was spread along the east side of the runway, west of a small ridge running about the length of the runway that precluded direct fire on the aircraft from the beach or sea, and direct fire on the living areas from the land side. Four squadrons' aircraft sat paired in revetments of sand-filled, fifty-gallon drums between the runway and the squadron areas, made up of three A4 squadrons, and an A6 squadron. Living quarters were plywood structures set in trees over the ridge from flight operations, nearly on the beach. The beach was a bone to tan colored sand strip varying in width, reaching far as one could see the coast in either direction. Group headquarters sat on a rise approximately half a click south of the living area, surrounded by related group support service outfits. The ten thousand foot concrete west field runway used by the three F4 squadrons of MAG-13 and other traffic was about three clicks west; the squadrons of MAG-12 were on the east field.

VMA-121's call sign was "December," the squadron known as the Green Knights, nick-named "Brand X," as they considered themselves the standard of comparison for competitive attack mission squadrons. Twenty minutes of talking to anyone who would talk, which was anyone not busy, convinced me VMA-121 was "my" squadron.

"You won't drop ordnance your first few missions," December's operations officer said as he briefed on in-country flight operations the next day. "Straggle along and get used to the place."

The place, as far as I was concerned, was I Corps and immediately adjacent areas, marked to tactical aviators with Tacan stations. To the southwest in II Corps at Pleiku, Tacan station channel 100 provided range and bearing information for one's navigational and locational pleasure. From south to north, I Corps proper contained: channel 50 at Chu Lai, channel 37 at Da Nang, channel 89 at Phu Bai, and channel 109 at Dong Ha, just south of the DMZ (demilitarized zone). By use of range and bearing information from these stations one could locate any particular target or chunk of real estate in or around I Corps.

"Was he serious about the ordnance?" I asked my section leader on my first flight, which occurred about my fortieth hour in country. What did the Opso mean?

The flight leader shrugged, rolled his eyes. Bombs and napalm canisters just hung on racks while I followed the lead feeling like a wedge, the world's simplest tool.

My second sortie was LZ prep, preparation of a piece of hostile real estate for helicopter assault or perhaps recon team insertion. The flight leader didn't see why I shouldn't drop on all that space below, so I did. Third mission was an intended strike, but we were diverted to a close air support mission that included hostile fire. Explosive ordnance was requested on the target, I delivered it complete with a strafing pass or two, even remembered to keep ejected casings from the aircraft's cannon off friendly heads.

"Okay, okay," the Opso said. "Welcome aboard. Now you can really get your ass in a sling."

I flew what we called a TPQ hop, missions involving an operator located on the ground in a protected area directing an aircraft along a route to a target via radar. The operator told the aviator when to release ordnance. The aircraft had to be exactly on airspeed, heading, and altitude, precisely on the centerline of the route of flight to unerringly deliver ordnance. The radar used wasn't precise enough for positioning an aircraft that accurately. We dropped tons of ordnance on TPQ targets with questionable effect at best, and creaking along following remote instructions in a straight line in the middle of the night at no knots was no thrill. The aircraft hung up in the sky at the slow airspeeds required by TPQ controllers but didn't like it. I didn't like it either as the reduced speed seriously cut into the flight envelope. Farther north, where SAMs could readily get at one, it was a little more thrill than really needed for a good time.

Case in point: One night a major was grinding along straight and level on a TPQ hop a little south of Gio Linh, tending to his instruments and the controller's instructions to make a good run.

BLAMahWHACKTOOEE!

A SAM launched from over the DMZ reduced his aircraft to unusable parts, transported him to oblivion. That incident caused heat and weirdness when decelerating to the slow airspeeds on subsequent TPQ missions close to the DMZ, adding context to the phrase "sitting duck."

On my first mission into North Vietnam, I nervously rolled in on the target about forty degrees off the lead aircraft's roll in heading. A stream of tracers reached toward the aircraft and, as I released ordnance, a few white wimpy puffs of 37 mm flak appeared not all that far away. I pulled off the target expecting flak to follow all the way to Chu Lai, surface-to-air missiles thick as bees, at least one hostile aircraft. Well, it's doubtful if SAMs were at that location. The light flak didn't get near us, much less follow us, and hostile aircraft didn't show that far south.

"Consider that a civil introduction," the lead said at debriefing. "Things get considerably worse up there." Considerably was a particularly acute word there as things turned out.

The north had some peculiar target areas. At any given moment in any of several areas, the ground, let alone the target, was hard to locate due to all the explosions in the atmosphere. Next time in the same area there would be no hostile fire, then a time or two later the sky would again fill with ugly erupting things.

I hustled through the distracting garbage in fast runs, with acute target tunnel vision, hoping my personal matter-repelling device was working okay. I put the ordnance precisely on the target, hauled butt out of there. Once in awhile we would surprise a target, get ordnance on before fireworks began, less often as time passed.

Frequently on night missions north, I'd see flares farther north, indicating our Naval brethren or Air Force tactical pilots were earning much more than flight pay, working targets under flares up there. It was always good to know they were present. Their handling of gnarly situations helped me handle gnarly situations, their courage added to mine; hopefully mine added to somebody's. Things seemed to work that way.

Work under flares over jungle-covered mountains was a little tricky. Though flares usually illuminated the general area, they left many points of interest to an attacking aviator in shadows. I'd start a run, the cockpit lit with nice rhodopsin-supportive red lighting, then as the rate of descent increased through something truly absurd, I'd hit the blinding white light of flares—endo night vision. Flares canted this way and that as they swung in their small parachutes, producing a false visual horizon in constant motion. I could barely see, much less use the gun sight pipper. Residual flare smoke trails obscured things and there was always the chance of skewering oneself on a burned out flare casing hanging on a dark parachute in the flight path. The target, sometimes position of friendly forces, the terrain, and all the rest of what was going on had to be kept in mind. Weapons switches had to be set, the delivery calculated and executed, the aircraft flown, the rest of the flight-required attention, and so forth. Hideous weather and the horrible beauty of assorted weapons fire gracefully floating up to kick our asses into oblivion were just a couple additional complexities often tossed in to ensure a suitable level of interest.

It all could be taxing, certainly. But working these situations with a sense of style and good form, while keeping the aircraft in one piece and assisting your wingman and the friendlies below in remaining intact, was exhilarating, satisfying work. But as Solomon's ring reminds, nothing lasts forever.

Time. Rushes of seconds. Monday? Sunday? Did it matter? Yesterdays, today, tomorrows squished into a time-tube blur. Sunrise—day sorties. Sunset—night sorties. New aviators arrived, old ones left. I flew with people I knew and people I didn't know. People I didn't know died in combat. So did people I knew.

Performance with the aircraft despite circumstances, a willingness to consistently give your best, and at least halfway get along in the squadron were part of a short list of things emerging as important. Exclusive little squadron cliques of the world disappeared; there were capable combat aviators, there were other people.

Journalists appeared from time to time, seemed disappointed at finding aviators stationed on the exotic South China Sea not suntanned to a fabulous bronze after playing continuous beach volleyball. Reckon they didn't have the picture; at any given time the old volleyball group was probably distributed all over the peninsula. Squadrons were tight groups, no question, but not in the way journalists seemed to expect.

Most aviators at Chu ran friendliness and exuberance on the surface, with cold isolation and sometimes a little hostility underneath. Warm and light just after coming off a gnarly mission was easy, you made it back, things were okay for the moment. But there were other gnarly missions to fly, each with the possibility of not returning. People were killed, sometimes I knew them; sometimes they were friends with whom I sweated through flight school and our first squadron. I packed up a friend's gear for shipment to his wife, what a privilege. Have I mentioned cold?

Surface friendliness and underlying isolation solved the problems of letting down somebody, somebody letting down you, of attachments or significances. My scheme was acceptance of a person as a sovereign human being with a set of individual characteristics, without becoming involved with the person. The affinity arising from being with a group in a situation was there of course, as was demand for group and individual performance. In those senses I cared about us all. But personal friendships? Nah, too much anguish. The good guys for me were people with whom I would fly north anytime regardless of circumstances. There were a few obvious bad guys and a huge sea of people—everyone else.

Large quantities of nearly irrelevant pap were handed out to justify things and get us into the environment, but the American government and public's apparent opinions of our efforts demanded truth, the real version. Riots, strongly stated disapproval of us, the general go-this-way-one-minute-that-way-the-next sentiment expressed by the American people, or certainly their press representatives, were of no assistance to anyone I knew in the combat zone. It all knocked holes in reasonable cause for the death and destruction around, which eroded logic used to put life in jeopardy for the good of the country. Had we relinquished existences for anything worthwhile?

No one provided good information, elucidated tactical purpose making any sense at all, ergo, there was no way to tailor individual moves to a U.S. or large organization team effort. I focused on the Congressional Commission in the service of the United States that I accepted and a desire for us to remain alive. The offer of commission did not state "fun all the time, eight to four in the United States, you'll definitely live through it, or comprehendible by all people." And the offer had been declinable.

After reset to superficial affability, high proficiency at tasks, harmonious alignment, and internal distance, I wanted partners in war—combat compadres and nothing else. I did my best, expected others to do the same; it seemed that or perhaps none of us would live through it. Right or not, the process was well underway in only a short time. Some shiny people with previously happy faces became subdued, with faces reflecting guarded noncommittal on a good day.

The A Shau valley was a frustrating place. Ta Bat, A Shau, A Loi, the three small landing strips on the valley floor, were thumped to shambles, leaving as targets suspected troop concentrations, enemy munitions, and supplies areas, as well as stretches of road and a bridge or two. We'd go in there to lacerate a road, perhaps disjoint a bridge, only to find the road or bridge repaired or something new constructed within a few days. Some of those remote but well-traveled roads became comically serpentine around huge craters.

There were reports of a big yellow bulldozer in the valley at different locations. I thought I glimpsed it once through thick jungle canopy off the valley floor, but couldn't locate the thing. TACAs spent a lot of time looking for that bulldozer; I don't recall anyone getting it.

The little landing strip at A Shau was decorated with the carcass of an A1 "Skyraider" shot down during the overrun of the Special Forces camp there. The machine's aviator had been heroically rescued by another aviator in another A1; daring-do indeed. The old hulk was there last time I flew into A Shau.

"Slim To," a good friend with whom I flew in the world, joined December. That nickname came from an incident with a particular girl early in our training command days. The woman, who made a point of dating only majors or lieutenant commanders and above, was certainly easy to view and could easily be termed a highly desirable companion. Cadets were nothing to her. In spite of that, my friend angled toward getting to know her; she slammed him pretty badly. The nickname came from my answer to his question one evening when we were out on Santa Rosa Island, feeling no pain whatsoever.

"Think she'll go out with me tonight Buddy?" Laugh, snicker, laugh.

"Doubtful, aviation cadet," laugh, "not enough poop on your shoulders. You are slim to none with her."

"Slim To None" was picked up by nearly everyone, ran for a while before shortening to "Slim To."

Soon after his arrival at December, we resumed the relationship we had established back in the world.

"It's time," he would say when we flew together, "time to ride, PH."

The first time he said that I stood quizzically looking at him, which caused him to laugh. "Get a King James and read the Book of Revelations, chapter six, verses seven and eight," he said. "Especially the 'power was given unto them' part." I located a King James Bible, not a difficult task:

Revelation 6

7.   And when he had opened the fourth seal, I heard the voice of the fourth beast say, Come and see. And I looked, and behold a pale horse: and his name that sat on him was Death, and Hell followed with him.

8.   And power was given unto them over the fourth part of the earth, to kill with sword, and with hunger, and with death, and with the beasts of the earth.

"Well," I said next time I saw him, "you mean the situation or us?" I thought he might be equating aircraft or us and the pale horse.

"A little of both." He looked at me longer than usual. "There is something about you, buddy."

I laughed. "Well, I'm here of my volition, that certainly says something."

"No. I mean it." He was quiet a minute. "That blonde and blue stuff does make you pale. And son," he smiled, "sometimes the look on your face scares even me. But I'll just call you PH. How about that?"

"How about that?" He got his nickname from me, complaining about a little reciprocity didn't seem correct.

Look on my face? What look? Probably I should have done something about the one that scared him.

◉

"Let's ride, it's time to ride, PH." After figuring who covered out, who covered back, who ran first in the case of missions north, off we'd go on a mission. Our mission count climbed; he became increasingly nervous.

Regarding mission count, there was no significance to number of missions flown in the SEA combat arena by Marine aviators. We flew sorties until we couldn't for whatever reason. With any luck, the primary reason would be normal end of the tour. A tour was thirteen months and the least number of combat missions that I heard about in one tour was two. The most was three hundred thirty four.

Approaching one hundred missions, Slim To went to the Skipper via the Opso and asked to be removed from the flight schedule after one hundred missions. He was convinced anything over that would be fatal to him. He returned much lighter, explaining they understood and that he would be transferred to group after one hundred missions. He flew his hundredth. The Skipper did as agreed, done deal.

"Whew," he said while organizing his gear for the move to group, "I was afraid I was going to get killed."

Whew. He seemed okay again. I went off to fly something up around Khe Sanh and returned to find everyone available flying. It seemed every infantry outfit had contact. My wingman and I launched as soon as the aircraft turned around. Joyride placed us as needed for close air support. We headed back to the Khe Sanh area near Hill 881, where the FACA told us we worked NVA in concrete bunkers.

Now how in the world ...? When did they construct those? There weren't buildings, roads, anything around for miles, except guns. We returned to Chu Lai with bullet holes in each aircraft. As the activity began to unwind, I went to toss one down and get some sleep. Slim To's gear was still in the hootch.

"So where's Slim To?" I asked the small group of tired aviators sitting on the beach, working on settling down so they could sleep.

"Haven't you heard?"

The tone of his voice told me: endo Slim To. I felt that horrible sliding feeling, emptiness, loss.

"He flew today, didn't come back."

Some of my switches clicked to off. I took a huge pull on my cognac.

"His aircraft hit the trees flat, broke up in the jungle. There wasn't a beeper."

"What got him?" I was in a daze.

"Mission one-oh-one," a soft voice answered.

After a long pause somebody else spoke. "Klondike (the FACA) says twelve-sevens. Infantry advises they'll get to that area in the morning."

Tears. Arm up for a silent toast.

The Reap wasn't going to stop. Maybe it would get us all, maybe it didn't matter. I mean, bodies die, eventually. Was sooner better than later?

The little group on the beach drank a toast. All that could be heard was the soft lapping of the South China Sea. Even the airfield just over the ridge went quiet for a few minutes.

Slim To received a posthumous Purple Heart, should have been awarded the CMH. He could have slid off to the side, let the thing go by, but that wasn't Slim To. The situation pointed at him. He didn't duck, took the deal straight on, gave all for us. What's your definition of hero?

Most in-country missions were direct support of friendly forces, the main idea being to keep them alive. Sometimes we worked with a forward air controller on his feet down there, sometimes with a helicopter or other combatant down amongst it, and sometimes with FACA/TACA aircraft that moved around their assigned areas, applying themselves as needed, a good idea that worked well. As a rule, the FACA/TACAs appeared after things developed, placing themselves in the position of having to catch up tactically (no offense to the FACAs or TACAs who did remarkably good work in thin-skinned, minimally armed, slow aircraft right in front of the guns). Though not necessarily completely in touch with all facets of a situation on the ground, a FACA/TACA overhead added a large-picture view, immediate coordination of support, and early warning of potentially disastrous things creeping up on the unit.

CAS (close air support) required precise ordnance positioning; there was no appreciable margin for error. An aviator's choices were: hit the target; miss the target and accomplish nothing; miss the target and damage friendlies; and a rare fourth choice, hit the target and damage friendlies—a last ditch thing by request before certain destruction. I think the consensus among aviators I knew was if one had to go anyway, one may as well take a collection of the enemy along. Perhaps it was better to be blown apart by friendly air than die while being slowly skinned, tortured, and demeaned by a group of contemptible pain and horror specialists.

Most combat aviators with whom I flew were remarkably adept at putting ordnance through windows (or holes in structures anyway), in doors, in a specific clump of vegetation, et cetera. Nape was a bit skittish because it tumbled so badly. I had to nearly scrape the canisters off the aircraft with the ground to ensure precise delivery. One was obliged to know one's fusing stuff, though. Ordnance fusing required time to arm or it wouldn't initiate a proper detonation sequence. The space between too close to arm and too far away to get the desired hit was sometimes skinny.

Also, it was essential that surface detonations match in number items dropped. For example, three explosions after four explosive items were dropped meant, if nothing was done, some friendlies somewhere would later receive that fourth blast as one huge booby trap or mine, or many smaller ones. A combat aviator was obliged to be well versed in delivery methods, arming times, fusing, and ordnance types. Situations involving tactical air were normally fast moving, often complicated with unusual facets of terrain and weather, such things as diversely positioned friendly unit segments, and of course, countering fire from multiple locations. One had to be knowledgeable, adept, adaptable to continuously changing conditions, and had to clearly see and utilize that which was present.

Chapter 6

Serpent

My wingman and I checked in with a TACA one afternoon in support of a Marine Corps unit that had encountered a small group of structures that metamorphosed into a heavily armed monster of a place as they approached. The unit was outgunned by a considerable margin. The NVA didn't normally engage without significant fire superiority anyway, the daytime engagement was an additional indicator of the Marines' peril.

As I rolled in, little green balls of light floated up, turning into streaks as they rushed past the canopy on the starboard side. The NVA often used tracers that burned green, appropriately a color used by ancients to indicate death. The sight pipper touched the target. I checked airspeed, waited an instant for the altimeter to unwind another couple of hundred feet, and pickled (dropped) several hundred pounds of destruction.

"Oneofftargetsot." Gravity loading of the pull-off squashed my voice.

"Really," my wingman replied to this statement of the obvious with an oh-thank-you tone to his voice. " Two's in."

Troops in jeopardy normally preclude the luxury of a target attack from just any old heading. Absolutely not done is placing friendly troops in even more jeopardy with a sprinkling of fired casings from the aircraft's cannon, or skipping jagged metal fragments haphazardly in their direction. VC and NVA understood that aircraft flew the same track over the ground when working CAS targets and were truly obliging at filling the airspace around the target approach.

Dash two flew through the attractive green and orange streams of deadly little balls of light on the same line I had just taken and called off the target. I rolled in on the same old heading. About two thirds of the way down the run, all too familiar little colored balls of light floating up toward me turned to streaks as they intersected with the aircraft's flight path.

Thunk, thunkunka-clunk-bang!

Oof.

Rounds hit the outboard port wing. The impact transmitted through the airframe wasn't too horrible, nothing about the aircraft changed. We (the aircraft and I) were in too close for aborting the run to make any difference, so we pressed on with visions of the aircraft disintegrating as I attempted pull-off. Well, it didn't. It flew normally, completed a routine four-gravity pull-off. I waited for the gee monster to step off me before speaking.

"Watch it, Two, took a couple," I said happily, not real happy about taking hits, but pretty amped about still being there, able to talk.

"Where?" my wingman barked. "You okay?"

"Firm. Port wing tip. It's cosmetic."

"You sure, One?"

"Firm, Two."

Two now had the immeasurable pleasure of again running the gauntlet of fast moving little items in the sky. I thought about the infantry down there, what they must be going through. They were gaining the upper hand, pushing enemy off the low ridge as they worked toward the structures. A few thousand pounds of bombs has a rather remarkable effect upon even the most aggressive tendencies. There was little fire next run. The aircraft flew fine and Two drew even less fire on his subsequent run. The TACA called us off as Marines overran the structures.

The damaged Scoot attracted little attention back at Chu Lai, just another down aircraft in need of maintenance. Later, sitting on the beach among aviators with a little cognac, somebody said, "That was close, man. If the NVA shot a little farther to the left, you wouldn't be here." Yeah, well. If.

○

On another CAS mission, this time as wingman, I set up to roll in on the tree line the lead just napalmed. I watched as his nape hits burned out.

"Good hits, One, break, drop a pair of napes, Two," the helicopter pilot said directing placement of my ordnance. "Hit fifty meters at twelve o'clock from the far edge of One's burn. There's more of them up there."

I let the pipper settle down a little short of the target area, looked for friendlies, and finally saw a few of them huddled in little dents in the ground behind rises just to the south of the tree line, busily engaged in returning fire. The pipper superimposed the target. I released the napalm, pulled off.

"Good hits, Two. Shit! They're running into the open! Dash One, can you strafe now?" The percussive rattle of his door gun augmented the helicopter pilot's words.

"'Firm, One's in," the lead calmly stated.

Bodies tumbled as the lead's rounds reached the running group. The helicopter pilot sounded ecstatic as One pulled off. "Great, One! You got a bunch of them!" The door gun continued to pepper his transmissions. "Ready Two?"

"Two's in."

I rolled in on the running mass; more of them fell to my guns. Then, as One started his next run, they jumped into a ditch. I couldn't believe it. Now that was embarrassing. I mean they may as well have just shot themselves. Jumping into confined space vulnerable to air attack while there is an air attack in progress is one way a tactical leader can wipe out the remaining segment of their outfit. That is what occurred.

Neither of us was even a little pleased about the fish in the barrel bit, but leaving the group to kill more Marines and hammer up more locals wasn't the thing either. You know how things sometimes shape—we were handed the situation, we dealt with it, there wasn't anyone else. The helicopter relayed only seven Marines were killed. He figured we had over a hundred confirmed enemy dead, another fifty or sixty probable. He was still excited. I couldn't feel a thing.

The lead and I met on the flight line after returning birds to the chocks. Slowly we walked toward the yellowsheet desk in the maintenance line shack. He stopped abruptly then looked toward me, though it was obvious he was far away.

"God damn," he said.

We stood awhile, silently looking at nothing.

"Yeah," I exhaled, "I think maybe so."

It was just one of those damned days. Upon reaching the ready tent we heard that one of the most gentlemanly, graceful people I ever met had just died near Xepone. His wingman reported hits that knocked off pieces of the aircraft, which exploded as it impacted on the guns that hit it. The gent took the guns and their crews with him. Lord knows what he went through as he spiked his mangled aircraft on the weapons that killed him. Single seat aircraft are private places.

It was also a day that killed another of my close friends, one who I had been with since preflight, a member of the hack club. After taking heavy automatic weapons fire on a CAS mission, his burning aircraft crashed into the jungle, fireballed on impact—no 'chute, no beeper. He and I had been in some hairy situations together, always threaded through them okay. So what happened?

Both gents were capable combat aviators. Maybe their cover was weak. Maybe scans dropped for an instant. Maybe it was just their time, I don't know. It's true that some people flew combat missions without stepping into situations well, simpler for them to remain uninvolved I guess. But these two were maximum chargers, cube-gleamers—the best.

I was feeling weird enough from the mission, but adding my two dead friends to the whole thing just shoved me toward hyperspace. I didn't talk for two or three days, again.

Chapter 7

Mileage

December prepared for rotation to Iwakuni to cover contingency plans and return to TO (tactical operating) strength. As it began to look as though a day of departure may actually arrive, interesting expressions appeared on many faces. Exit from the combat zone for a few weeks ought to be cause for wild celebration, but the feeling of leaving unfinished work to others placed thick clouds over the Iwakuni sun. Smiling, happy-masked faces chattered constantly about getting out of the combat zone, things that would be done. It was just divertive jabber. The issue of tactical people running up to paradise for a few weeks while other tactical people remained to receive bullets in their direction every day seemed a Damoclean sword hanging heavily over most discussions.

One day around noon, a great gaggle of A4s flew into Chu Lai and the squadron from Iwakuni settled into the areas just vacated by December. About an hour later, December's A4s launched for Iwakuni, via the Philippines and Okinawa.

Walloping sheets of cool clean rain pounded Iwakuni, lashing at aircraft as each section arrived. I could barely see the plane captain's pins-in signal. I shut down the aircraft, executed a relatively controlled fall down the ladder, and ran through the shattering crystal to the squadron area. The arrival party, dispatched prior to our departure from Chu Lai, and several replacement aviators stood soaked, laughing in the soft afternoon freshness, waiting for us. It didn't look as though Iwakuni had seen incoming fire for quite some time.

Japan was healthy, civilized, attractive, restoring some civilized veneer for the moment. But the combat zone hadn't disappeared; we were going back. Sitting on a bench under cherry trees, however, viewing Soroban Bridge (an aesthetically pleasing, handcrafted five-span construction over the Nishiki River), the combat zone could not be seen or heard. A little imagination (and squinting) conjured finely dressed swaggering men wearing swords, accompanied by richly dressed women moving across the arches. Samurai, Bushido, a civilization founded by warriors and lords, taken apart, redone by merchants and treachery. Perhaps that was the right thing, I don't know. Proud, trained Samurai of pure blood did not make themselves evident.

I managed visits to Tokyo, the Hakone pass, Kobe, the Mia Jima shrine, Hiroshima and the Peace Park. People were courteous and sophisticated. Shikoku and Honshu are densely populated islands, and though individually restrictive, the constant formal social behavior lent dignity to everyone. The civilization is old, well lubricated with refined manners and customs. The exception to continuous smooth conduct was the Hiroshima Peace Park, where at the ground zero monument, local people young and old made clear that an American combat aviator was not the most welcome of visitors. As I thought about how the forty-foot weapons platform and I easily could have accomplished much more than Hiroshima or Nagasaki all by ourselves and what I had been doing farther south for the past few months, I felt quite a social distance open. Another separator.

The squadron deployed to Naha AFB on Okinawa to sharpen new arrivals' weapons skills before returning to country, the deployment brought out an interesting phenomenon. For the most part, the seasoned aviators who had been attached in Japan had been desking it for a while. That meant there weren't any combat aviators. Most of the non-combat aviators seemed to be looking for a one-for-all, all-for-one tight little squadron bunch thing, not realizing those had all fallen victim to the Marine Corps individual replacement tour practice applied in SEA. The combat vets, wanting to get along well and make everyone feel welcome, were distantly friendly and not interested in becoming markedly involved. Some new people were perplexed, maybe even a little resentful, but at the time they had less of a picture of combat squadron operations at Chu Lai than have you from this account.

Further, many newly attached senior officers expected automatic placement in positions of leadership by virtue of time in the air wing; however, these senior people were in the position of juniors in terms of the job at hand. Most of them were unhappy with that. Combat training in a peacetime environment teaches plans, tactics, various strategies, and techniques. Of course the training is essential, but even with stringent simulated combat conditions, it does not teach combat. There isn't a substitute for the experience. Ten trillion hours of grinding around friendly sky, working weapons exercises with your buddies on both sides, did not indicate performance under fire. Nor did dropping zillions of practice bomblets on friendly target ranges within fifteen feet of, or even directly on, the target markers. Most combat aviators didn't buy automatic knowledge or competence, having had that experience often work out badly. We all knew of perfectly capable peacetime leaders and aviators with nice looking paper qualifications who functioned poorly, perhaps even disastrously, in the combat arena. Combat aviators wanted a little demonstration of paper-qualified people's actual performance in the real environment before placing their lives in the keeping of the untested. Thus, the squadron went back into country with two mutually exclusive subsets of aviators.

Chu Lai hadn't appreciably changed. December had settled into the departed squadron's areas and quickly picked up a share of the wing fragmentation orders. War was ... flying was ... *it* was as though we had never left the place.

A senior aviator joined at Iwakuni flew into the ground on a flight north; his wingman had no idea what happened. Another removed himself from flight operations after two missions, which didn't make him a bad guy or even raise any eyebrows. It was actually a considerate thing to do with doubts concerning his capability. Combat flying demanded confidence, concentration, performance; no one I knew would fault somebody for not doing it if they genuinely couldn't after giving it a real shot. People who could function well but didn't, or people who couldn't do well but insisted they could, were entirely other things. It wasn't possible to work a combat situation acceptably while covering for an incapable partner, and the type of incapability really didn't matter.

Some new senior people required instant decorations, use of the combat arena for career ticket punching, paper career development.

Single mission air medals were handed out gratis to certain folks, some Distinguished Flying Crosses were awarded for exceptionally ho-hum performance. Other services gave non-aviators DFC awards for such as dying in an aircraft on the ground when it took hits, causing many of us to wonder what Distinguished FLYING Cross meant. No one I knew was against anyone receiving an award for dying in a grounded aircraft, but a DFC for a non-aviator in the cargo section of an unmoving aircraft when it was attacked? And the CMH, our country's highest, awarded to a high ranking officer for taking a couple of light hits while his incompetence, deficiency in matters of combat, and poor use of tactics resulted in the killing of most of his unit? Disgusting. Worse. Fucking disgusting.

There was requirement for new awards:

- The Congressional Medal for Exactly Nothing, with invisible combat clusters.

- The Silver Quasar for Sitting on One's Ass, with combat cushion pin.

- The Distinguished Crisscross for Destructive Effort and Egocentric Intent.

- The President's Magnanimous Award for Dissimulation, Back-stabbing, and Avoidance of Responsibility.

- The Effulgent Medal for Personal Use of Taxpayers' Property and Money.

Administration of the awards system largely nullified exceptional effort and knocked down morale of gents doing really astonishing things. An inordinate number of awarded decorations had nothing to do with valor or service above and beyond the old call.

On the other hand, not all awards were bogus, there are numerous deserving award recipients out there who managed extraordinary things; some should have received much more than they received. There are also many deserving of awards, who accomplished truly heroic acts but received only a hard time, both there and here, for their efforts.

Too often, decorations or the lack of them in the part of the war I knew depended upon what people represented in terms of publicity or internal value, or whom were one's associates. Awards became another meaningless facet of the war, another thing corrupted and of no value. I was having difficulty locating anything shiny at which to look, much less to which to hold.

A remaining old friend and I sat in the sand near my hootch one night, slowly working through canteen cups of something or other while attempting to calculate the odds of a mortar attack's first hit impacting at a point between us. The conversation moved to gone friends.

He's in the world, he's MIA, he's dead, he went home; he bought it up north; something blew his wing fuel cell; he went FAC, his position was overrun; he turned to avoid the village off the north end of the runway with a fire after takeoff and never separated from the seat; flak got him; he disappeared out of the pattern at Da Nang; he's home with his beautiful wife; they found him with most of his skin torn off; he transferred to MAG 15 in Japan; a SAM got him; he's home; he's in the Hanoi Hilton; he's home also, he got out and is driving airliners; nobody knows about him, his wingman never saw him again; he's at Balboa, I heard he's healing up great; he was medevaced to Okinawa; he was found decapitated; his aircraft exploded over the target; his aircraft exploded when it hit jungle.

After a while, we quietly stared off into different portions of the universe. A little more time and we silently walked off in diverse directions.

"Are you hit, One?" the Air Force TACA asked. We were working a target just north of the A Shau valley.

"One's off, negative Helix." Did I look bad on the run? It wouldn't do for a Marine aviator to be anything less than totally amazing while working with an Air Force TACA.

"The twelve-point-seven fire looked like it went through you, break, Two. Drop forty meters at three from One's hits."

"Roger, Two's in," Two responded, cool as ever. I hadn't seen automatic weapons fire on my run but it was glaringly obvious on Two's run from three different locations. I flew through that intense a level of fire without noticing?

I don't know when precisely, but after a few missions north I developed "target tunnel vision." Now, there is target fixation, or locking on a target to the exclusion of everything else, which could easily mean a hit on the target with the aircraft. Target tunnel vision, on the other hand, means concentrating on the aircraft, the target, and the ordnance as one thing, while attenuating all other things, but not completely excluding them.

Moderate to heavy flak on one of my first missions north caused a certain casualness of ordnance deli as smoke and fire in the atmosphere around captured my attention. Little and big pieces of metal went bashing off in all directions from those fascinating explosions, which were numerous and nearby. Target defenders used barrage fire tactics around targets, putting as many pieces of metal, explosives, whatever up in the air as they could. Attacking aircraft had the great privilege of navigating through those garbage-filled chunks of atmosphere.

The North had more small arms and automatic weapons, large caliber anti-aircraft guns, surface to air missiles, fire control and surveillance radar, and opposing aircraft upon occasion. Fire control tracking devices required continuous alteration of as many things as possible in regard to the aircraft's course through the atmosphere, to deprive hostile radar of a tracking solution. The custom of unpredictably flinging the aircraft around the sky to avoid tracking solutions was called "jinking."

Some aircraft had active and passive electronic counter measures (ECM), though not Marine Corps Scooters. We jinked a lot, turned off things electronic, like the Grimes light (anti-collision beacon), navigation lights, transponder, Tacan, et cetera, when headed north. One had to know tone's wingman to properly work north at night, and no one directly followed anyone.

Most aviators I flew with recalculated book 450-knot deli sight settings for ordnance deliveries at faster airspeeds, in order to minimize exposure to little people with big guns. Going too fast was no good either, as ordnance wouldn't separate from the aircraft predictably or follow a calculable ballistic trajectory. Each type of ordnance had a non-negotiable, you-had-better-be-within-it deli speed range. Outside of that speed range none of the advertised ballistic parameters was applicable. For example, napalm did strange things over about 520 knots. You could drop on a target in the A Shau valley, only to hear about your canisters impacting near the Philippines three days later. Well it wasn't that bad of course, but one definitely did not want to attempt deli of ordnance faster than it would deliver well. I wouldn't have considered "hip-shooting" bombs, rockets, or napalm before combat; I learned it could be done with startling accuracy.

"Good hits, Two, you got a gun," the TACA sang out before Two called off. "One, looks like nine o'clock at a hundred fifty meters from Two's hits will get the others."

"Roger." I set up Snakeyes, reset the gunsight for a ten degree run. "One's in."

Inside a great weapons platform, I had speed, agility, bombs. The gunners below were prepared, waiting with multiple guns set up for crossing fire. Mixing the small front form of the aircraft with a little hilly jungle background as far as the gunners were concerned seemed like a good idea, hence the set up for a shallow dive angle. I saw double streams of little colored balls of light reaching for me as I crossed the target. They passed far enough aft to allow a semblance of normal breathing.

"Okay, One, you got 'em," the TACA called as I pulled off.

Two's last run drew only small-arms fire. The TACA sounded happy as we departed for Chu Lai, and I was glad we were all okay and had accomplished something. My wingman on that mission was relatively new in country, talked extensively about the mission with friends once back at Chu Lai. I didn't say anything, other than to greet or respond to somebody. Was I talkative like that when fresh in country? I guess miles were piling up on me.

Chapter 8

Streamers

One afternoon on a CAS mission with the squadron commander, I rolled in and discovered target defenses were serious about knocking us out of the sky. Nothing new there.

Bangety-bip! Bop-boom-bam! Thunka! Whap! Bap!

The aircraft took hits just before I fired my rockets; that wasn't new either. I launched the pod of rockets, pulled off a little more gingerly than usual, the airframe began to shake, exhaust gas temperature moved to ridiculously high, oil pressure was diminishing, the engine suddenly sounded and felt like a thrashing machine, the fire warning light was entirely too red. Now that combination of ingredients *was* new.

"Bird's hit!"

No doubt my voice was completely calm as I turned for the sea, three or four miles away. The Skipper joined, the controlling Klondike FACA offered his squadron's exquisite helicopter pickup services, but I elected to continue to Chu Lai. Jumping out of an aircraft still at least attempting to fly didn't seem the best idea, particularly in view of what was waiting down there. At the least I could get way the hell out over the South China sea before ejecting, perhaps I could even get the aircraft back to Chu Lai. It wasn't as though we had all the spare aircraft in the world.

The next flight of A4s checked in with Klondike just before the Skipper and I switched to squadron tactical frequency. They were ready to cover us but I was still flying and the target was still shooting—a tactical air no-brainer. Later I learned the guns were silenced after a run or two without poking more holes in friendly equipment.

Injured Scoot and I remained enormously feet wet en route to Chu Lai as I continuously evaluated the aircraft's performance against chance. The engine, surging between sixty-five and ninety-two per cent regardless of where I positioned the PCL, sounded like it was tossing pieces against the fuselage. The fire warning light brightened as we went along, the exhaust gas temperature gauge pegged high, oil pressure continued to diminish, fuel flow was alternating between none and all the gauge would show, and the hydraulic flight control system was lightly jerking the aircraft about.

Yippee-kie-yay! Hot doggies!

"Skipper, I'm going to chain off everything except the drops, what do you think?"

To chain off something in an A4 is to manually release the item. I wanted everything off the wings to reduce the coefficient of drag, but wasn't sure what systems still worked, hence the chain-off. I knew I needed less drag and realized that I might have to land on the drop tanks. I had no idea if the landing gear elements were damaged also.

"I think there's nothing like a little cruise down the coast," he said, "and I think you're smart to keep the drops. You're in the machine, only you can make the moves. If it were me, I'd chain the ordnance. All I can tell you is it hasn't caught fire and blown up yet."

A little cutting humor and a stated belief in one's capabilities are worth everything in such a situation. I set up everything, checked the Skipper's position.

"Okay. Off they go."

Roger," the Skipper replied, "clear."

I chained pylons one, three, and five, left the drops on two and four. The aircraft immediately became more stable, felt a little better, but all the symptoms still pointed toward ejection. Though certainly ready to eject, I wanted to get the aircraft all the way home without endangering Chu Lai with a burning hunk of shot up tactical aircraft.

My call was to run the tune, man; big-band swing with heavy metal accents, fabulous percussion, dissonant harmonies, contrapuntal melodies. If things stayed together and we could get abeam Ky Ha, the helicopter base just north of Chu Lai, I'd give landing some thought.

"Watch your airspeed," the Skipper cautioned.

"I know, Skipper. That's all it has."

Was the Skipper shaking his head when I looked at him, or was it just me shaking as the aircraft made its desire to get down onto the Earth clear? He was right there in a nice, slightly acute parade position on my port wing. When he saw me see him, he loosened to a tight cruise; it was good to have him out there.

A fire warning light most definitely messes with mental processes, especially when it sits there, continuously flickering, winking, and laughing at you. I was ready to exit via the Escapac rocket seat the instant the Skipper told me the aircraft was burning. When the warning light approached the brilliance of the sun, I asked him about fire. He politely informed me I wouldn't need the radio to hear him, should that be the case.

We staggered down the coast, me breathing one million times a minute, alternately flying what remained of the aircraft or readying to eject as the forty footer vacillated between flying and setting up to bash against the planet. The little Scoot stayed together though; hydraulics settled down, the Skipper saw no fire although he did mention things looked a little black around the tailpipe. Perhaps the largest factor was the aircraft felt like it would get us there. Can't tell you why or how, the little weapons platform just felt like it wanted to go home, and knew how to get there. The Scoot was reasonably stable abeam Ky Ha, fuel had burned down to less than half of the internal tank capacity, and despite the damaged engine's lack of thrust, we had managed to gain a little altitude with which to play.

"Okay," the Skipper said, "if you're unsure, turn east and punch, right now."

Once I started an approach the only option was to complete it. I had altitude and speed enough to make the field should the power plant fail, but that was it. If anything came up I couldn't handle, the aircraft would bash into something down there, and toward the end of the approach I'd be outside the ejection seat envelope, meaning there would be no bail out capability.

Decisions, decisions. However badly, the Scoot was still scooting. I have never been able to abandon something showing that much heart, so the wounded forty-foot platform and I turned inland — the tune played on.

"Here we go." I rolled toward my hastily predicted boost off approach initial point.

"Rog-err," the Skipper acknowledged. "Stay high. You sure as hell aren't fast."

He declared the emergency with Chu Lai, called for the crash crew, took care of the radio work. All I had to do in that respect was change channels—little thing, big assistance. I commenced a boost off approach to the concrete runway. The boost off, or no-power approach game, was played with altitude and speed. If you ran out of either, just affectionately pat your little old goose goodbye; it was definitely cooked. Remaining high all the way in, I let the aircraft get fast while dropping the nose toward the field, anticipating the engine failure that finally occurred a little over a mile off the north field boundary.

Then came the familiar turbine unwinding sound. I flipped the manual fuel shutoff, moved the PCL around the horn (to off), deployed the RAT (ram air turbine, an airflow driven electrical power generator), unplugged the hydraulics, and lowered the gear manually. No hydraulics, no flaps. Accordingly, I reset my landing pictures. Things looked pretty fair.

About four days later, the three landing gear indicators at last turned from barber poles to down symbols, meaning all three landing gear elements were down and locked okay. I breathed again for a minute. Oddly, I thought about a little girl who hadn't been in mind since I was nine or ten years old. Why hadn't we said good-bye when the family left Europe?

After another six days or so crammed with marvelously interesting, truly thrilling moments, the main mount tires squawked on the runway just as I ran out of airspeed, altitude, and ideas. The tires touched down about a foot over the end of the concrete—fifty or so miles of run, twelve inches of slack. I held the nose wheel off until it fell through as speed diminished, tentatively tried the brakes which worked fine, braked judiciously, turned off early. It seemed cool to position the aircraft out of the way of operations. When I stopped, its locomotive capability was history for a while.

End of that tune, reverberation.

That magnificent bashed-up forty footer brought us all the way home. I do hope you never hear noises made by a powered airframe during a power off landing. It seemed every component groaned, rattled, clunked, squeaked, squealed, or wailed.

The crash crew materialized as I turned off the runway in an enormous silence. I saw them about halfway down the approach, then either got busy or they disappeared, I really don't know which. Their sudden appearance exactly where needed was a mystery, but a truly wonderful trait. People in silver fire suits crawled over the aircraft searching everywhere for fire, checking for hot brakes and spots, and leaks of any kind. They quickly pinned the landing gear, chocked the main gear, popped the canopy, then saw me move. The gent readying the escape ladder looked up at me. I waved him off, didn't need it. If I'd shown some signs of life sooner, they probably wouldn't have popped the canopy. Moving just took a little time. The whole crew looked up, gave a huge shut down signal. I laughed, but habits being habits, I touched the PCL to be sure it was around the horn as I exited the cockpit. A silver suit walked to me as I swung down off the refueling probe.

"Good looking tailpipe, Sir," he chuckled as he pulled off his headgear.

I waited for it to clear his ears. "Heya. Thanks for coming to the party."

Crash parties are either satisfactory events or complete debacles. This one was a nice little deal and I was happy the gents in silver suits were present. We walked back, looked into the exhaust gas tube. He smiled, I shuddered.

The aircraft took hits that smacked up the fuselage not far from my left shoulder, tore up the port intake duct, slammed into the compressor section of the engine. Turbojet compressors are designed to capture and compress air, so of course it gobbled up the pieces and passed them, along with pieces of itself, through the burner cans to the turbine section. You can imagine the effect of four or five, six-hundred grain chunks of solid metal, moving at somewhere in the vicinity of twelve hundred feet per second, colliding with compressor blades turning at 11,156 rpm, moving diametrically at close to a thousand feet per second. The turbine section spun away as designed, throwing its pieces and the rest of the mess out the exhaust gas tube, which didn't mind seriously hot gases but obviously wasn't too keen on broken chunks of metal. Thank goodness the Pratt and Whitney J52P6A was a tough little power plant.

Wouldn't you know—I was greeted with verbal hits from several senior officers for flying the aircraft home? "You should have ejected," one said. Hindsight specialists, whose situational evaluations come from comfortable positions of viewpoint far outside the situation. The Lord must dig Monday morning quarterbacks, there are so many.

"Well, when it's you, make your call." Pretty salty response, eh? I wasn't entirely thrilled at being verbally knocked around for returning a needed aircraft. The gent who disagreed with them was the one who counted. The skipper was also right there on my wing through everything except the boost off approach.

"You know? That two hundred knot shit made me nervous," he said later.

"Didn't want to go too fast, Skipper." Laugh, laugh. Easy to do after everything works out cool.

The aircraft came up after some adroitly accomplished sheet metal work and a change of the power plant, CSD, and hydraulics pump subsystems. Maintenance people work their own forms of magic.

Eventually every aviator I knew at Chu Lai was affected by absurdities of various command elements. Constant justification demanded of actions taken in combat, continual nagging and judgment from non-aviators, non-flying aviators, and noncombatants; the blessed rules of engagement, inflexibility and narrowness exhibited by some non-flying commanders who didn't seem to grasp tactical reality. Maniacal frenzies for specific paper statistics heedless of real situations were fierce. Ridiculous pressure was placed on aviators for such as downing aircraft for things such as a Tacan (navigation aid) malfunction or for an aircraft suffering hits in a combat zone. This silliness pushed us into an e-man-for-himself framework; any sense of squadron accomplishment or team effort vanished. The only team was you and the aircraft, perhaps you and your wingman, sometimes a couple of sections together, against all comers.

Too much mid- and high-level leadership appeared as self-serving quarrelsome, old thinking, out of focus amateurs in hot competition with each other for paper career positioning. These commanders didn't work men they understood in real situations they understood, they worked their own appearance on paper, hurt all of us, and unnecessarily killed some of us. They exhibited little regard for damage done to the group, others, mission capability, nor did they seem inclined in the least to presume responsibility for their decisions. Their poor performance could always be blamed on an unfortunate subordinate in a defenseless position. We needed professional tactical leaders in whom we could believe, but with too few exceptions, that isn't what was present.

A majority of people worked well though, took care of their duties admirably, and presumed responsibility for their position, often with vigor. Squadron maintenance people serviced aircraft, filled them with fuel, loaded ordnance, and kept the birds operational. Administrative people filled out engorgements of forms, kept our hours, and handled tons of paperwork. Support people managed whatever was necessary, taking care of thousands of large and small details so aircraft were prepared, the missions launched; all we had to do well was the "aviating" part.

The squadron's administrative, operational, logistics, and support people were great—there could have been no tactical aviation without them. They'd laugh at you when they found film containers, loose pistol rounds, or candy bar wrappers in the cockpit, but any taboo items would either disappear or be returned without question. They'd look at you like you were from space when you tried to tell them the aircraft "felt all wrong" when executing this certain maneuver, but they'd figure it out and fix it. After a few combat missions an aircraft usually had an idiosyncrasy or two. Maintenance people would meet you at the yellowsheet desk and ensure you were aware of them prior to your signing for the bird. They didn't get much blood in their faces, thank the Lord, but they were there, working with us, repeatedly accomplishing near miracles to get another aircraft up, bleeding with us when a compadre went down, helping aviators in ways about which they probably don't know.

It was good to come off a sortie without a wingman and have a bright-faced plane captain scramble up the aircraft's ladder with his chatter. Are you okay Sir? How's the bird Sir? Where'd you get the fuckin' bullet holes Sir? Is everything all right? All of that while replacing the safety pin in the ejection seat curtain, flipping your straps back, taking your brain bucket and kneeboard—a little warm concern amid the obdurate insanity. It was worth a lot and those people deserve much more glory than they received.

⊙

Early one morning a good friend and I flew a mission north. We had managed such foolish things as the flat-hatting of beaches on the way home from missions and the spending of a little post-target time hunting the wily MiGs in the north. This mission objective was a point target (as opposed to area) just south of Vinh; we elected a low-level approach with popup deliveries.

Popup deliveries assisted in getting ordnance on a target with decreased warning to the target and the approach was flown low to avoid detection. Despite aircraft speed and position under radar coverage, all those people with phones and radios could report one's passing. Likely somewhere there existed somebody who could plot the aircraft's track. My friend and I usually worked a tangential approach, popped up at an initial point, plugged the target, then retired posthaste. Nice tactic.

As my friend popped up to port, I placed many points of the compass between us. Being first on a target was a privilege in a sense as first runs stirred up things, while subsequent runs received heavier, more accurate fire. My friend and I flipped a coin before the mission to see who ran first. After a nice popup and roll-in, downhill he went.

Thuppeta-thump! Krump! Bum-boom-blamah! Bomp!

Flak chased him as he descended. Now that was new. Flak working downhill? And worse, the ugly explosions were closing on him.

"Break NOW," I shouted on the radio as I popped up. "You're tracked."

He released ordnance, broke to port, kept his nose down, raced for the coast.

"-sofff!" Enunciation gets little attention when there is a fistful of gees working on the aircraft. The gee monster was standing right on him.

"Okay. In." I was in one-gee flight at that moment, then got busy with my own deli as puffs and splotches appeared all over the sky. His ordnance exploded on the target. Enemy guns flashed. As the aircraft steamed rapidly toward the planet's surface, I steadied the pipper, checked alignment and aircraft state of balance, released the ordnance, and jinked through a marvelous display of murderous intent.

"Whrr-rrr yo-ugh?" Now the gee monster danced on my head as I jerked toward the coast, headed for the surface. I didn't care where he was; I wanted to hear him talk, to know he was all right, right then. I was looking directly at a SAM as it launched.

"Past the crossroads, straight for the coast," he answered. Clear enunciation, the gee monster was off his case. He was back to one-gee flight, hauling butt for the coast. Good to hear him, but the smoking telephone pole coming uphill like a fast freight train repositioned me in pump.

"SAM up!" I jerked the aircraft toward the Earth, maneuvered the nose to get approximately perpendicular to the missile's flight path, wanting that thing to have to calculate at least a quintrillion changes per second.

"Shh-ut!" The gee monster had jumped on him again.

The SAM continued upward, appearing downward from my inverted position, passed a little closer then I really would have liked, its flight path straight as an arrow. Yes-yes. Straight in this case meant ballistic flight, indicating we weren't targeted by fire control radar, the missile was fired visually as an unguided missile, no doubt with the hope its internal radar would acquire one of us. Or perhaps the maneuvering broke the fire control lock before the missile's internal radar had us. I didn't know, really didn't care much; it did not get us. Now one of those things got attention, got handled, that was that; many of those things could get a little strenuous. I nearly burned out my eyes looking for more of them.

"It's ballistic. I don't see more," I said. Then I saw another one zinging off to the moon, some distance away. "Belay that, there's another one up ballistic, to the north. They don't have us."

The forty-footer and I hauled for the coast, low, fast, leaving the gee monster in the target area looking for things to squash. "Where are you?"

"Feet wet," he answered. You?"

"Almost. Ah, tally. I'm a couple of miles or so at your four thirty when you roll out." He was easy to see as he turned south. We swooped down the coast to Chu Lai.

"There are no SAM sites at that location," a debriefing android stated in one of the debrief trailers we were privileged to use after certain types of missions. He then looked at me and asked, "And how can flak be set to detonate at continuously decreasing altitudes?"

Invalidation from a non-combatant, non-aviator, non-participant recording device in a body, unable to conceive of more than one gun firing at intruding aircraft, really didn't warrant a response.

I turned to my compadre, wishing the gee monster would show up and just squash the whole debrief mechanism across the table from us.

"Shit." He looked at me tiredly.

I then turned back to the debrief zombie. "Why don't you go up there and see for yourself, Dorqueface? You've got all this paper and shit in this air-conditioned, safe area trailer, so you think you know everything. Don't listen to us. We only go out to those places on your paper every day and do and see real things while you sit on your ass trying to imagine things to talk about."

My friend stood, the debrief mechanism involuntarily ducked though there was no action directed towards it, and we exited the trailer. Stupid invalidation is an isolating mechanism that generally leaves residual heat. We walked along smacking our kneeboards with earphone cords as we headed back to the squadron area. One couldn't even pass along information without being minimized, nullified, demeaned.

I lead a section on a mission along the western border to work targets of opportunity. My wingman was a major who was new in country and we were to work with a Helix (an Air Force TACA) near the A Shau valley. We checked in on the Helix's frequency as he was identifying targets in a hostile area. He marked one for us with rockets containing white phosphorus.

"Roger the smoke." I set my master armament panel for bombs, received no response from Helix. "Want them on it?" I asked.

No response.

"Say, Helix?"

No response.

No static, no hiss, nothing—no damned radio.

I gave the old nordo (no radio) sign to the major, then passed the lead. He parked me in an orbit, went off to unload his ordnance. Figured my fuel back with the load of bombs while watching his hits, I'd burn down to an acceptable weight; there was little cause for concern. The major came off target, joined, took the lead, passed hand signals for me to follow set up for a hot run, then pointed at the target area. After confirming I understood what was happening and had the target tally, he moved into a high cruise (a covering position), I executed a run, dropped everything on the target.

That major knew his stuff. After working with people who used anything as an excuse to RTB, here came this knowledgeable field grade gent, competent, willing to accept responsibility for his actions. It was good to see, we needed many more of those.

Chapter 9
Doppio

Augering around the sky near Phu Bai one evening on a TPQ mission, working basic airwork skills and looking around with not much in mind, the TPQ controllers voice crackled in my headphones, "December two-two, turn left to base minus forty-five, verify altitude at base plus twelve."

I turned the few degrees the TPQ controller requested, replied, "Two-two, steady at base plus twelve."

The base reference scheme was an unimaginably clever construct that delineated daily, codified variables for airspeed, altitude, and heading, at the whim of somebody, somewhere. One could easily locate "S," "A," "H," followed by the appropriate numbers, or just the three number specifics grouped together somewhere on the ready tent chalkboard. That day, references were 220 knots, 10,000 feet, 315 degrees. Now imagine how difficult it must have been for an NVA monitor to check a radar screen for my new heading, do a quick calculation using the controller's instructions, and report the base reference heading to somebody. High level, secret, devious stuff, oh yes. Hopefully the scheme confused somebody other than friendly controllers and aviators.

"December two-two, release two bombs, on my mark."

"Two-two, wilco." The armament panel was already setup.

"Standby, standby—mark!"

Click, bombs away. Suddenly, licking flames of rockets launching flashed on the dark surface below about sixteen miles southwest of Hue, not where I was placing ordnance.

"I have an active target," I rolled toward the flashes. "Rocket attack in progress to the north, about sixteen miles southwest of Hue. Site tally, permission to engage."

Rules of engagement required clearance to fire on something as obvious as an enemy rocket attack. Friendlies didn't use 122 mm rockets. Hue was outside the rocket's range and on the other end of the rocket stream were the friendly forces receiving the rockets.

"Unable, December two-two. Contact Joyride," the TPQ controller replied.

I changed frequencies, talked to Joyride while watching rockets detonate on their target.

"Cannot grant permission, December two-two."

"Who can?"

"Contact Panama."

After argument concerning the right to be who I was, where I was, Panama denied my request. By then the rocket site was lost in the dark, all the rockets launched to do their grisly thing.

Command directives didn't embrace new situations, happening right now differently than before; they worked only with precedent. What when there was no precedent? All I could reach were juniors with little knowledge and no authority. Had I been able to quickly reach somebody with experience and authority, I may have saved lives that night. Why wasn't somebody available? Why didn't I just paste the rocket site anyway?

My flight leader and I worked NVA positions in a tree line along the northern edge of a river; presently there was considerably less tree line. The sharp popping of automatic rifles firing in concert could be heard every time the FAC transmitted. A few runs resulted in bodies floating in the river near the target, some of which began to swim toward the opposite riverbank. The flight leader rolled in on the swimmers. Amid the small arms fire splatter in the water, a thousand foot geyser shot upwards, leaving the river surface boiling where the bomb struck. Many bodies disappeared, two continued to swim.

"One's off," the flight leader called.

"Two's in, guns," I replied.

Not feeling anything, I reset the sight for the internal 20 mm cannon, flattened out the run to let the pipper drift up on the swimming figures. How sporting was engaging swimmers with a tactical aircraft? Compadres, now permanently part of the landscape because of people like the swimmers, came to mind. This wasn't sport; they would just try to kill more of us. The pipper touched the swimmers, I eased a little forward stick to hold the rounds on a point target, fired a short burst, maybe five or six, but HEAT rounds are pretty serious when they impact. The two figures evaporated.

"Good shooting," the lead said.

"Grazie. Two's off." I couldn't feel a thing.

Emotion and combat flying. The former had to be trapped, dealt with when finished with the latter. Elementary, huh? Sure, so easy to discuss out of the situation. Gents who didn't do that became dangerous to others, ineffective, or didn't return to the world. Aviators I knew at Chu Lai behaved mildly compared to those in movies I have seen concerning such situations. There was quiet nonparticipation and some boisterous conduct while under the influence of alcohol. Apprehension was visible to anyone caring to observe it but wasn't discussed. It was contagious to the point of self-destruction. In the air these gents were quiet, no-nonsense, precise tactical aviators. There was no room for anything else.

The most appropriate mechanism for me was to become the centrum of the machine I flew: an ultra-complex human system within, attuned to, and managing a complex machine system. That had the advantage of overlaying excellence and professionalism on the destruction I was dealing with. The more professional, the more effective. The more effective, the more excellent. The more excellent, the less I felt. The less I felt, the better destructive device I could become, the longer I could live, and the more worth I had to my kind. Sound a little dangerous?

As a rule, elimination of threats in combat equates to destroy the enemy's will to fight, or destroy the enemy. This enemy was arrantly motivated, sometimes with ancillary pharmaceutical products, essentially eliminating any chance of displacing the will to fight. They strapped on satchel charges, ran at us until shot to pieces or until they blew themselves apart. Option one down, leaving moral issues.

Issues of humanity, morality, and ethics should be forefront considerations of those committing talented people to real horror shows. Once in an environment, one is there. Horrors don't cease for combatants because command structure and political factions located in comfortable remote environments are adversarial, confused, ignorant of the situation, disorganized, indecisive, unresponsive, unclear, narrow of viewpoint, or self-serving. Continuous requirement for individual viciousness in order to survive the combat arena also does not diminish. I doubt you'll find this written anywhere else, yet in that terrene environment it seemed nonetheless a commandment:

"When in combat thou shalt not stand around moralizing while thine enemy kills thy close-at-hand buddies. In such situations, thou shalt do all in thy power to keep thy close-at-hand buddies and thyself alive and in good working order."

Mental framework most suitable for me involved no emotional response, no doubts; only clear actions that enhanced survival potential. I used aircraft checklists to attune to the tasks or disconnect emotions, your preference. The pair of NVA in the river was a real threat to my group. The situation—and my actions—were beyond discussion.

Chapter 10

Sterling

There soon came orders transferring me from the squadron to group. It may have been a favor, I don't know. I really didn't want to leave the squadron. My raison d'être was flying tactical aircraft, leaving the squadron took me away from that. I felt less valuable, more isolated, but so what? The USMC didn't want to hear that. Its interest was an organizational slot filled without protest. The amazing number of dollars invested in me as a combat aviator didn't seem pertinent.

The ancient slot game, you know it: a slot must be filled by a name, any name with paper qualifications that can be vaguely construed as acceptable will do. Once in a while an individual with some understanding and capability would fill a slot. Things worked well, but only because of an exceptionally determined individual, not the result of a slick, well-grooved system. Logistics specialists attempted to run combat operations; combat specialists were obliged to run administrative shops. It isn't at all difficult to determine an origin of the preposterous functioning about which we've all heard.

I went to MAG-12 as the junior aviator and arranged group tasks to run in automatic mode. Thanks to an excellent gunnery sergeant and two fine sergeants, I continued flying via sniveling. "Sniveling" was the practice of wangling onto a squadron's flight schedule, used by group aviators wishing to continue flying missions. I think it was so-called because of the quality in a groupie's voice while begging for those missions. In normal context snivel is a nasty word, but querying squadron schedules officers and operations officers for missions didn't seem nasty at all

I checked in with "my" gunny daily. He obliquely, oh so politely told me to get lost; he'd find me when necessary.

"Nothin' for the Lootenit to do today, Sir," he'd say.

With a smile reserved for junior officers, he would produce coffee, talk for a few minutes, escort me to the hatch, and wave as I walked away. I never discerned whether the gunny was emphasizing "lieu" in lieutenant or alliterating the new designation "loo attendant." But he seemed friendly and in just a few days we had a large chunk of mutual trust in place. It looked like the gunny was getting everything done with facility. I may have done things differently, but not really any better, so I monitored from a distance to avoid putting dings in his system.

A couple of times a week, I checked with the two sergeants, both assigned to me, but of course they worked for the gunny, as did I. They always smiled pleasantly while telling me everything was fine, and everything always was fine. Those three gents had their moves flat down, which reflected well on me also. I conducted regular courtesy visits, stayed out of their way, flew as much as I could.

"Sir, I need two things," the gunny said one day.

I took the coffee, nodded as I slurped, was all ears. He was actually going to ask me to do something.

"I need wood Sir, for this new section here," he said pointing toward an unfinished building section. "Now there's wood in Da Nang, but the supply lootenit up there won't copperayt with me."

Along with the new word, he had every kind of situational detail I might possibly need. I used his phone to set up a meeting with a wing logistics officer, who had some time that evening only. Damn. How could I get up to Da Nang that afternoon? Wing people seem to be forever busy. If I missed this opportunity for wood, Lord knows when the next might occur. Made a call to MAG-13 to check on its C117 flight schedule. The Hummer (C-117) was going to Da Nang that afternoon and with just a little hustle I could ride it, perhaps even bring back some wood.

The Gunny's second request was a meeting with a lance corporal who punched out a couple of colleagues. Apparently the two punchees grabbed some personally posed pictures of the lance corporal's wife, enthusiastically showing them to anyone who would look. The gunny wanted somebody "official" to talk to him "unofficially" about keeping the pictures to himself.

"Hell Sir, you know what pussy does to young agents. Enigh don't wanna article fifteen 'im."

I nearly dropped my coffee at that word. Not *enigh*, the other one. Enigh must be a young agent. "Let me talk to the people he pasted, Gunny."

"Sure Sir. That would be fine."

The pair showed up looking apologetic and frightened in just a few minutes, squirmed, looked at each other nervously the entire time, made clear their desire to get out from in front of me that instant. Both bashfully admitted they probably would have done the same in a reversed situation. They didn't exhibit hard feelings, weren't hurt, and weren't after the lance corporal. The thing began to look less complex. They seemed happy to leave the little space the gunny set up as my office.

"Okay, Gunny. Have those three shake hands, watch their faces, if you detect hostility, keep working on them. I'll get with the lance corporal at ten hundred tomorrow." If I didn't get moving, the Hummer would leave without me, we would acquire no wood. "How are we for wheels?"

I almost said, "Have the troika shake hands." Lord knows what I would have found upon return; the gunny may have had them pulling a sleigh. Wheels showed up in about two minutes. I made the flight, arriving at Da Nang after a ride up the coast with reciprocating engines slightly out of synch the entire trip.

The supply lieutenant at wing logistics in Da Nang was my recruiter, commissioned via a program that converted perfectly good, reliable, valuable staff NCOs to second lieutenants with superior retirement arrangements. Good for the new lieutenants, but the program had some less than thrilling effects on the ranks of staff NCOs; their years of knowledge weren't immediately replaceable. Part of his deal was a tour with the First MAW logistics shop.

"You're my star recruit," he said.

"You're my only recruiter, Nugget." I made sure he could see my silver bars. We howled about that, then along with his staff sergeant, commenced toss down of a few. The wood deal was arranged during the following rather lengthy conversation:

"So how come you were screwing my gunnery sergeant around there, Lieutenant?" I asked. (I used "my," but in reality *I* was the gunny's new lieutenant. After all, "my" gunny had me in Da Nang happily acquiring wood for him!)

"I didn't know it was you," he answered, "and I didn't know you really needed the wood there, Lieutenant." He downed another shot. "People stockpile wood and sell it. You wouldn't believe the black market shit that goes on around here." (The black market. Money over people, conceived and driven by human-fucking excrement.)

He paused, looked at me a minute, then added, "And I ain't gonna apologize to you for that, but he'll get righteous treatment next time."

We each attempted to smoothly put away another shot, laughing like idiots. The staff sergeant sat quietly, reinforcing one or the other of us as we talked. I believe he consumed twice as much alcohol as either of us, yet he easily maintained the more dignified bearing.

After a while I caught a zero dark thirty flight back to Chu Lai on an Air Force C130. I thought about the first time I flew the Da Nang-Chu Lai route as the aircraft moaned down the dark coast. Now things were more familiar, probably still didn't know a lot, but could pretty much picture friendly and enemy units on the indistinct land. The Hercules crossed ridiculously close to the approach end of Chu Lai's concrete runway at five thousand feet, dove abruptly, flared madly, and turned off the runway with six thousand feet remaining.

"Holy Mackerel," I said to the pilot.

He nervously explained the Air Force listed Chu Lai as an unsafe facility due to hostile fire; he executed an appropriate landing. Funny about perspective isn't it? The gent was definitely upset about being near Chu Lai, and all things considered, I was home safe.

The lance corporal showed at ten hundred straight up. He seemed a decent sort who really missed his wife. I declined a view of the offered pictures. Where memory of women was more than enough to keep me slightly daffy, pictures were too much. I asked if his wife knew who saw her photographs and his face turned port light red.

"I never thought of that, Sir! God! She'd kill me!"

We talked about respect for a special woman and he agreed to discontinue flashing her pictures around. I'm happy that worked, freely given mutual agreement is so much cooler than forced agreement or threat of punishment. The gunny came in after the lance corporal departed with another coffee. He handed it to me all smiles. I must have done the right thing.

A few days later we got wood; tons of the stuff, enough to cause the gunny to clap me on the back in his happiness. Ex-recruiters tend to more than make up for their sins you see.

"Damsir, this calls for one," said Gunny.

Voila! A special bottle of at least fifteen-thousand-year-old Scotch suddenly appeared along with two canteen cups. We toasted most anything at all.

"How's the Scotch?" he asked.

"Umm," I intoned while slurping. Fine single-malt Scottish whiskey at ambient air temperature? There isn't anything like it.

"Did he show you the pictures?"

"Well he offered, I thought that would be out of order."

"That's good Sir, but you shoulda seen her. Best boobs I ever saw. An' the poses. Gahdam!"

Women. Woman. Darling. How was she doing? Was she okay? Her exciting smile, star-flecked eyes, model face framed with satin hair invaded my mind and everything crinkled up inside. Lord she was beautiful. Would I see her again? If I lived through this, if she didn't find somebody else, if we had something left in common after this, if the planet didn't disintegrate, if this, if that, if . . .

Gunny and I put our feet up on crates, leaned our chairs back against opposite corners of the little space, and talked about this and that as we did in some of the scotch. It wasn't long before we fell asleep.

Now all things considered, life wasn't what one could term terrible at that point. Minimal, perhaps Spartan, after all, we were in a combat arena. Most life forms adapt to an environment at least to some extent. I flew missions as often as possible, remained out of the sergeants' way, convened with compadres often, drank quarts of Marine Corps coffee, walked the beach forever, even slept once in a while. But life is dynamic and in the Marine Corps, particularly in combat, things change drastically moment-to-moment; one ought never to presume a given situation will exist for long.

Case in point: Group received a quota for a forward air controller, a normal Marine Corps thing in a combat zone. I was the junior aviator, a clear no-brainer; it could not have been easier for the group administrative section. I was ordered to a FAC position with the Seventh Marines.

The Marine Corps had an idea a combat qualified aviator or two assigned to each infantry battalion would assure the infantry of the best possible service regarding matters of air support. Certainly a valid concept, but the position wasn't on an aviator's most sought after positions list, even in peacetime.

There is a book the Marine Corps provides each new member at the recruit depots called "Guidebook for Marines," which contains an appendix of "Common Military Terms." In this appendix "forward air controller" is defined as "An officer (aviator) member of the Tactical Air Party/Team who from a forward position controls aircraft engaged in close air support of ground troops." The phrase "from a forward position" does not provide any clues whatsoever as to that into which one will be dipped out yonder.

The thought of not flying chilled me completely, the thought of going into a hot field with a combat infantry unit after what I'd seen caused sweat and shallow breathing. I worried, wondered, sat on the slight ridge overlooking the flight line for an entire night. Going out with the infantry worked into me acceptably after a little time, but my knowledge of surface jungle combat was miniscule.

In the sky, in fast moving armed aircraft, even up only twenty or thirty feet I knew enough to be completely comfortable most of the time, lightly to moderately tightened up maybe up to eight or nine per cent of the time, and in full pump oh, say one per cent of the time. But the ground? Down in the weeds and bushes? Oh shit, oh dear! I didn't know enough to get through that and there was no way to get training before I went. What a training program. OJT with real bullets and blood.

My last combat hop was a road reconnaissance mission in route package one, flown with considerably less restraint and more zeal than normal. It might have been the last hop of my life.

Chapter 11

Utopee Yah

I left Chu Lai dressed in stiff new jungle utilities that were totally unlike Nomex flight suits. The grace knife strapped in my left armpit the whole time I had been with the air wing went along. It was comfortable under flight clothing, remaining largely unnoticed until I made some unusual body movement. But under jungle utilities the thing was an ever-present metal object. Ill at ease anyway, I arrived at First MarDiv headquarters feeling like a boot again. I stood nervously in the tactical air control party (TACP) offices on Hill 327 with one hand under my flak jacket touching the knife, waiting to see the division air liaison officer. The knife was a constant; touching it seemed to help. Wonder if Napoleon was touching a grace knife under his gear?

A convoy headed to Hill 55 from Da Nang airfield had dropped me near the medical battalion at the foot of Hill 327; the walk up to division CP was startling. I was accustomed to eye contact, greetings, and general friendliness from people with the air wing. Here people moved eyes away, avoided contact as best they could, spoke only in response to direct communication, used guarded word formations, and curt phrases. Social interaction on the way to division offices placed a real wall between those gents and me, one I wouldn't have positioned there. Stop me if you've heard this one—another separator. It would be that way for the tour with the infantry.

First MarDiv elected to position on Hill 327, while the VC/NVA chose to exercise combat tactics elsewhere, perhaps because the division was sitting near the military crest on the east slope. Just over the summit on the west side, listening and observation posts provided information regarding hostile country to the west. But daily survival situations occurring on terrain below the division CP to the west weren't observed by anyone but participants. Fast-witted people lived; others died out there, every day.

I didn't know anything about such scenarios at the time, or about the level of brutality required to survive a guerilla environment. There is gentlemanly, there is war, they don't line up—never have, never will. Post war or post battle, a victor may exhibit gentle traits at his option; certainly not during combat.

"Hey Buddy," the division Air Liaison Officer greeted. He was my first CO, my hack skipper of a thousand years ago in a totally different existence. "Good to see you."

"Good to see you Colonel, didn't know you were in country." He looked safe and fine, and was cordial as always. At least we could relate.

"Into every life," he paused, "oh you know the rain bit. But this will do your career good. You'll have both air and ground combat experience when you finish the tour."

Yippee-kie-fucking-yay.

He seemed genuinely concerned, his large-picture viewpoint, matter of fact discussion of issues instilled a locus for my scattered, vectorless outlook.

"I need you at the first battalion of the Seventh Marines," he said. "They're not too far out, covering our front door."

One Seven's CP was located in the hostile country I mentioned to the west. Perhaps the colonel's smile was because he wasn't going out there. I learned later, after a little first-hand experience, he had given me the choicest of his options.

"Aye, Sir. What's the best way to get there?"

The old UH34 chugged out to Hill 55, upon which was the regimental CP for the Seventh Marines. The trip accommodated a procedure calling for check in with the regimental Air Liaison Officer before posting to the assigned battalion. The door gunner grinned at me forever, I didn't know why, but it made me wonder about a few things—my chances of living through this for example. I spent the time thinking, not the best thing to do in that sort of situation, and watching the countryside. The view from the helicopter brought to mind missions I flew in that area, and some nasty tactical situations at locations easy to see.

Well, I wasn't going to Dong Ha, Con Thien, Gio Linh, Khe Sanh, or near the rock pile. Maybe I'd live through the night. See, I didn't know anything. Flying all over I Corps hadn't shown me that the whole damned place was hot to the infantry. Seemed like one area was just as bad as another in its own way; the only real inconstant being the time they became warm.

Hill 55 appeared, a reddish-brown island separated from a vast green sea by a black ring, compliments of flames people who cleared brush in a most expedient way. The helicopter spiraled down, landed. The gunner flashed his smile as I disembarked.

"Good luck, Sir!"

That certainly seemed genuine. "You bet, same to you."

I asked the helicopter aircraft commander about the door gunner as we trundled toward the operations bunker.

"Fixed-wing saved his ass a time or two when he was infantry down around An Hoa. He figures you've been there. See who you could be to him?"

I exhaled, "Hope I did some good."

"We all want you fixed-wing guys and your ordnance around, you know that."

I guess I sort of knew that; it was still nice to hear. But now I was another deathwalker, a high-priced shooter, for the most part.

The HAC gestured at a bunker next to the one toward which we were headed. "The one shop is over there. Good luck."

"Thanks for the lift. Good luck to you."

Jungle utilities on Hill 55 weren't new, starched, or even clean from what I saw walking toward the administrative section bunker, and it rather obviously did not matter. What a sight: me in crisp utilities and jungle boots with shiny black leather. I was new, green, a first lieutenant—everything bad in a package, lacking only the clipboard and pencil. Like it or not, on anyone's part, I was there. I had to figure things out in a hurry.

Sandbags riddled with small arms holes covered everything. Some bags and structures had taken explosive hits from larger weapons. This was definitely not Hill 327, not a place you'll ever see in a travel brochure. Many sets of hard eyes followed my walk. Not hostile eyes, hard eyes that had seen things out of the range of decent. Considerably removed from my most comfortable riding position, I checked in with the one shop, calling on the regimental 14 actual, whom I knew from Chu Lai.

"Here's the deal," said the major. "Talk directly to division for support unless your battalion participates in a regimental operation, you'll get more immediate response that way. Time is everything out here. Even a few seconds can make all the difference. If you need anything from me call, but with luck we won't be talking much. If I were you, I'd ditch the revolver. Don't carry a forty-five, carry a rifle. Definitely do not wear wings, don't wear rank. Look like you don't care. You're air support for a battalion now. You haven't even been to your battalion yet, but you're already a priority target for snipers and every other damned body that can shoot or throw explosives. Watch your ass all the time and I'm not kidding. Learn everything you can from the oh-threes, and learn fast. NVA kill aviators first out here buddy—any way and anytime they can. Questions?"

Um-ah, well-ahh, umm. Oh me. Oh-oh, oh shit. "Umm, guess not, Major."

"Okay. The next thirty-four will lift you to One Seven. Call me. Let me know you got there. Good luck."

I sat against empty ammo crates near the LZ, attempting to assimilate this new environment, and remained unnoticed until about an hour later, when the other UH34, which would deliver me to Hill 10, was inbound. Once the helicopter landed, I rushed across the open space and jumped aboard. The machine departed immediately. I was the sole passenger so the doorgunner pointed out various items of interest as we made our way to my new battalion's CP. In just a few minutes, Hill 10 emerged from the surrounding green, looking more like a slight bump in the Earth's surface than a hill. The UH34 spiraled down onto Hill 10's LZ. I pushed off my gear and offloaded my carcass as the wheels touched down. The helicopter departed quickly, leaving me standing on an apparent edge of the Earth

Hill 10 was rough looking, scarred from explosions, with defensive bunkers all the way around. The perimeter was flames-cleared with four rings of liberally laid out concertina wire, separated by fields of scattered barbed wire over tanglefoot, extending around it. Tin cans, which alerted any attempt to breach the wire, dangled at short intervals from various levels of the thoroughly staked wire. The LZ lay on the east side of the hill.

A figure walked down from the crest to greet or shoot me, I wasn't sure. As he got closer, an austere face emerged from between a well-used flak jacket and a ragged helmet cover hanging loosely over his eyes.

"Welcome aboard." He shifted his M-16 to the other hand, speaking quietly. "Don't move towards me, let's get out of the LZ. We take sniper fire in the daytime now and then. Take your own gear. If they think you're an officer, they'll probably try to kill us now."

I almost mentioned being an officer, but it seemed better to listen, not demonstrate complete idiocy until absolutely unavoidable. He led me over the hill to a sandbagged, thoroughly beat up strongback. Gesturing me in, he pointed to a rack, where I dropped my stuff. I didn't know who he was; it didn't seem judicious to ask. This environment was different than anything I had known, made me want to be invisible. During an impromptu show-around he explained that he was the FAC I was replacing, everyone out there knew who was whom, no one wore rank, he ran at least a medevac a day, the booby traps were a son-of-a-bitch, the hill took some kind of incoming most nights, the hostile snipers taking potshots at nearly everyone were less of a problem now, and that I had better be prepared to shoot back.

"I know what you've done in the aircraft," he said as we walked back to my new home. "I know how you feel about that. This is different. You can walk through afterwards and see everything and everybody you did. You can't hesitate and expect to live. Neither can you add a fistful of power and fly the fuck out of there. You have to work whatever is there as long as it is there, or you die, or people you were covering die. No shit, people get killed out here if you drop your part of it. This is going to hurt you, and it will change you."

Fabulous.

"Welcome to Hanworth," the battalion administrative officer said using the battalion's call sign at check in. "The executive officer will brief you, then you'll meet the CO."

The XO exhausted about a minute, the CO approximately two, cordial treatment by both. Three minutes packed with information.

I wandered around the hill and worked on getting located in the place. There were 81 mm mortars and 106 mm recoilless rifles, tanks, and a battery of 105 mm howitzers reinforcing the battalion. And snipers. Bravo and Charley companies were headquartered on the hill, Alpha Company was posted to the north on Hill 22, and Delta Company worked off of Hill 41, located a few clicks to the west-southwest. The battalion TAOR bordered on hostile country to the west.

"Happy Valley," a depression running between the westward ridges, was a route into the Da Nang area now blocked by the battalion. North, east, and south boundaries interlocked with Marine units, but the NVA didn't care, they came from everywhere. To the east was "Freedom Hill," Hill 327, with the division Command Post located high up on the eastern slope. The battalion's charge was a portion of the perimeter defense of Da Nang, which lay on the other side of Freedom Hill. Much farther over 327 lay the world, a mystical place that eluded specific memory.

Lean, silent, grim-faced Marines of One Seven were glaring contrast with the soft, densely foliaged, colorful countryside around Hill 10. They were practiced combat people. I was a combat person, not exactly a new concept, though this arena was decidedly different. Feeling much out of place and missing Chu Lai badly, I stumbled around aimlessly for the forty-five minutes or so until dark. There wasn't a hint of a tactical aircraft anywhere. My new jungle utilities and chunky muscularity didn't blend with the faded and tattered utilities over slim, spring-steel business muscles on hard-faced, hard-use bodies of combat infantry. I had to be a ridiculously easy target to locate through a telescopic rifle sight.

Mountains to the west set the sun early, the area darkened quickly, I couldn't sleep. Who was flying what back at Chu Lai? How was this unfamiliar lack of sounds significant? The FAC I was replacing clumped into the hootch.

"I know you're not asleep. Come over to the COC bunker, see how things work."

I followed, unsure of myself in the new environment. The hill was dark, not as dark as when flying over ocean under a thick overcast at night, but close. About halfway to the COC bunker I felt a deep sense of immediate danger, started to say something.

Crack!!! Snap-Pap-Pop!!! Pop!!! Crack!!! Pop-Pap!!! Snap!!!

Green streaks flashed, slashed passed both sides of my head close enough to feel. Sharp sounds smacked against my ears and spirit. My involuntary response was to retract everything, including legs. I collapsed. Lying in the dirt breathing heavily, still feeling the fast moving pieces of metal zipping past, I listened to the hill take the short burst of rounds. A brand new razor-sharp iciness cut outward in shimmering pulses from my stomach.

BLAM-aa-ah! BLAM-aa-ah!

Two rounds went out from the snipers in the tower on top of the hill. Another burst of incoming rounds impacted in trees a few meters away. Two more rounds went out from the tower. I lay in the dirt, silent, confused, my stomach pulsing like a wildly idling top fuel engine.

"Hey," came from darkness through the ringing in my ears, "are you okay?" Feet clumped toward me, I nodded as I sat up, unable to speak.

"Come on," he pulled me to my feet. I stumbled along behind into the COC bunker.

"Scare you?" the watch officer asked.

I just looked at him, still unable to speak. He explained it was a common occurrence.

"Some Charles will burn a magazine in the direction of the hill figuring he has to hit something, then he'll *di di mao*, run away. He'll stop pretty soon though. Snipers have Starlight scopes now, and they've killed a few of 'em. Nothing to worry about."

Sure. Nothing to worry about. "How do they get through the patrols?" At least I could talk again.

"They don't. They live here. Drive water buffs by day and try to kill Marines at night."

An EE8 rang. One of Bravo Company's patrols thought the snipers hit the shooter.

"How did they see him?" I asked.

"Flashes, most likely."

"But AKs have flash suppressors."

"Ha," the watch officer smirked, "you'd better get hip fast, Airedale. Flash suppressors don't hide shit from the target."

As it turned out, flash suppressors didn't hide much from much. Muzzle flashes were visible off surrounding brush, rain, smoke, dust, low clouds, fog, unpainted skin, et cetera. The FAC lead me to the TAC party area of the bunker.

"The VC force some of these people to fire rounds at the hill on certain nights," the FAC told me.

I looked at him a little funny I guess, judging by his facial response.

"They give local people a weapon and a few rounds, tell them what to fire at and when to fire. They do torturous shit I don't want to talk about if these people don't do what they want. The bastards get what they want or the villager's family members die horribly. You'll see some of that shit before you leave here. It's guaranteed to make you sick."

Those rounds were much too close. I had no means of returning fire. I'd never felt so helpless and a weapon went with me evermore. I have no idea why the ball rounds between the tracers missed my brain-housing group. Our Lady of the Luck, I guess.

The departing FAC and I sat on the hill between mortars and recoilless rifles the evening prior to his departure. He was headed for southern California, where he'd rejoin his sweetheart, leave the Marine Corps, and fly for an airline.

"What do you think about this war?" he asked.

"I don't know, something doesn't seem right," I replied. "Feels like a money thing to me, you know, the upper cluster makes money, certainly not us. I haven't really thought about it yet though, been busy."

He nodded, looked back to the west. "Yeah, I know what you mean. Something is definitely out of order, but it's up too many levels to see from here. We could have stomped this whole country by now, but we sit waiting for some fourth-worlder to try to kill us." He paused, took a breath, looked around. "It might not even be out of order. It just may be the middle levels accomplishing their stupid-shit cover-up, suppress, control, manipulate everything moves, I don't know. A little straight information would help, wouldn't it? Fucking lies."

His head turned first one way, then the other as he scanned the area, then a slow, measured discharge of breath.

"Whatever, you'll get busy. This infantry war just grinds along all the time. It's not like a target, where you get more than you can imagine in a few minutes then you're outta there. These people get unimaginable light-to-moderate shit all the time." He looked behind us to the east, then toward Delta Company's hill off across the paddies to the west. "They get max exposure too, but not like some targets I've worked. This weighs on your mind more." He spoke more softly. "When you were a kid, did you ever think crap like this actually happened on this fucked-up planet? That men could really do this shit to each other? Or to the damned civilians, the women and children?" His face reflected deep sadness as he shook his head. "Those pieces of shit out there don't have respect for anything."

I answered by not answering, not yet having seen what he had.

"They are sick animals buddy, and they'll kill you if you're not fast. That's what they do. Kill us. It's never safe out here. Remember that. Never relax out here. Get your senses peaked, keep 'em that way."

A mortar crew began setup for a fire mission. "You're on your own out here; remember that, too." He looked at the crew, back at me. "Just a flare shoot."

The mortar crew yelled the traditional, "Fire in the hole!"

Chug!

The round departed and shortly a flare popped to the west, a couple of clicks off the hill. Over a party on a ranch in the States those 81 mm flares would be pretty.

I looked at him, "Well. No prize, you're too short."

He continued looking at the flare, shrugged. "There aren't any prizes out here. Just life, if you're good, and lucky."

A firefight fired off at the base of some low hills in Charley Company's area. We ran to the COC bunker, where we found the gents in the bush not needing a thing. That particular night they had everything thoroughly handled.

Chapter 12

On One

Introduction to combat field operations was a supply run on tanks to an observation post in some nearby mountains. Tanks aren't to ride, I thought as we mounted the steel monsters. And yet, they are powerful, heavy mechanical monsters that are indeed a pleasurable, mildly exciting ride. This was a routine affair, including a little sniper fire that didn't seem to bother anyone but *moi*. A Marine scrunched behind the turret returned a few rounds, turned to me.

"Don't sweat this crap, Lieutenant. They can't hit shit."

"That's not what I'm worried about them hitting."

His seventeen or eighteen year-old bright blue eyes danced in a field of freckles as he smiled. "Yeah? Okay. They just do this to fuck with us, Sir." Yeah? Well it did, as far as I was concerned. I settled in as an apprentice to the infantry trade, asked Charley and Bravo Company commanders if I could get out with more of their patrols. A few days later at first light, I lined up in Charley Company's area with the rest of a patrol. The freckle-faced kid I met on the tank walked up behind me, snapped a round into the chamber of his M60, set his ammo belt the way he wanted it, grinned and nodded at me, his face phrasing a silent question past me, to my radio-bearing corporal.

I'm sure you've heard about officers, how suspicious and dangerous they are in general. And an aviator? Holy shit. One of the things I learned with the battalion was how alone a Marine FAC can be in the field. Nobody talked to me except TAC Party, and that was address of the rank—all business, nothing personal. Disconcerting at times, it was the way. How to be of service to people who wouldn't define the tasks? I figured I'd go out with patrols until knowing enough to do the job on my own, perhaps also acquiring enough MOS 0300 skill to be an asset in some of the ugly situations I heard would occur.

Two nights previous, the TACP corporal and sergeant patiently went over my gear. I haven't the foggiest as to what I may have done to deserve special treatment by the sergeant and corporal of the TACP, but I'm happy about it.

The Marine Corps dictates a list of items one will carry in combat. The list is generated with every conceivable situation in mind, except firefights. Most of that specified crap slowed one down, interfering with the ability to move the weapon around well and greatly decreasing the chances of getting through a firefight. One carrying all that shit probably would set up those around, and themselves, for the Reap. For example, take the poncho. The poncho is a nice piece of gear in the rain (I imagine you've heard it rains in a tropical rain forest). However, rain impacting against a poncho can be heard by any old hostile from quite some distance, certainly enough to allow for arrangement of a little old surprise that could no doubt kill about half the outfit in seconds. But the Book says...Yeah well, pick the book or pick your life and the lives of those around you. I'm sorry to say the Book was that far out of alignment with new situations. In all likelihood those around would make the decision for you, regardless.

The two gents tailored my equipment to the current surroundings and mission. They showed me what not to carry, what to tape, how to walk, how to use dirt and greasepaint, how to sling a rifle so it was always pointed well and ready, and how to set up a knife so it could be drawn quickly. They passed a swarm of things worth knowing.

"Don't look at anything alive," they said. "Look through or off to the side a little, Sir. If you look right at it, it'll know you're there."

"How do you initiate ambushes?" I asked.

I knew there were innumerable ways to coordinate execution of an ambush and that the idea is to arrange something simple, a signal or procedure so ambushers initiate the thing together. It seemed appropriate to know how One Seven fired off the things. The two gents looked at each other for an instant, then at me.

Oops. Perhaps inane questions were why most of these gents didn't talk to officers.

"Sir," the corporal returned quietly, "there's no count here. You go right then, you always know when. Everything goes on one."

The sergeant interrupted by first clearing his throat. "It's bad if you're slow, Sir. You go on one here. There's no count like in training. It's always for real. You need to come out of the gate at max. You go as fucking hard as you fucking can, on one."

They were patient and thorough, which I believed had a lot to do with their still being alive. They exchanged my new flak jacket for an older one and thrashed my new helmet cover.

"FNGs get hit more often," they explained. "You want to look like every other one out there, Sir. Like another hired gun who's here forever. The radio will draw enough fucking fire. We don't need to give them any officers to shoot or try to capture. And Sir, you need to fuck up those boots some. They look too new."

The corporal spoke up. "Sir, you have to understand that they want to fucking kill you. They want to kill us all, and they will fucking do it if you let them. No shit Sir, there it is."

No shit Sir, it's right in front of you. I believed him, began to worry about doing something stupid that killed somebody else. They led me to a clear area on the hill.

"See Sir," the sergeant talked as we walked along. "Like this."

While moving gracefully and quietly as a member of Viola Farber's ballet company, he talked about balance, center of gravity, awareness of the location of all body parts, and awareness of surroundings. Quiet, agile. Step toe down first here, heel down first there. He talked of booby traps, trip wires, and weapon positioning. In ten minutes I was walking with a renewed measure of confidence, feeling almost okay for the first time on the hill, and so I laughed. They laughed too, but I imagine it was at having to teach somebody who ought to know how to manage something simple as walking fifty meters.

"I'll tell you, Sir," the corporal stated on our way back. "We don't get too much contact during the day, but you never fucking know what will happen. The motherfucking nights are the bitch. Those little bastards are everywhere."

Okay. So nobody talked to me socially. The little data exchange instigated by those two was easily worth many social interactions. I may never have put it all together of my own observation; it was many patrols worth of lessons passed in a couple of hours one evening.

◉

The patrol lined up, exited the wire and spread out to maintain about seven to ten meters between men. I was in the last third of the column, watching, listening, attempting to see everything as Marines twisted through rice paddies ahead. There's a feeling to that, having to do with courage, strength, danger, trust, being a critical part, knowing you'll be covered as best the group can manage, a small group going against something unknown, capability, interdependency, purpose, actually doing. May not relate well; it's deep good feeling.

The sweep was a good first patrol. The point and two others quickly killed a sniper they found in a tree. I heard a few caps bust, got down, it was over. The sniper was a pretty girl in her teens that looked like anybody's girl next door, lying there with her chest blown apart. The whole thing brought my sister and the fortune of being born in America to mind. She was serious enough: the point accumulated another ding in his helmet and Bones received a round through his Band-Aids. Teen-angel war. Puppies killing puppies while sour dour old infirm dogs sat across the water barking at each other over nothing.

◉

The next patrol introduced me to firefights. I was down in the bush with rounds cracking and snapping all around, trying to somehow get the flak jacket material to thin so I could get lower while attempting to locate positions to which to return fire. The freckle-faced kid put out volumes of fire with his M60 while I lay there as confounded as I have ever been.

"I can't see them," I said as the fire died down a little.

"It's almost always like that, Lieutenant." He tapped his helmet. "Use your radar." He looked up the trail in response to a shout.

A voice screamed, "Get it out there right now!"

"All right Sir, shoot with me. Cowboy up," he barked as he turned to his gun.

Cowboy up? It was an unexpected comment in that arena, but a perfect thing to hear right then. Guess we had a better picture of each other than I had thought. Four magazines later I realized the 5.56 mm rounds just didn't punch through thick brush; the rounds from the Steel (M-60) certainly did. Regardless, the rush worked, the patrol got three confirmed, and nobody in green was hurt. What an experience.

The time-tube blur was worse in the field. Multifarious moments mashed into meaningless memory mush. The current instant was yours, whatever happened hadn't cut you out; the next few time units were the thing, length of units depending upon surrounding circumstances. Time units ran as hours most of the time on the hill, sometimes even a day. In the bush, or in a sudden situation, they squeezed to minutes, sometimes seconds. And in intense moments, down to the discernible little chunks of time between heartbeats, situational heartbeats—not semi-comatose, cruising-on-the-couch-with-the-tube heartbeats. The interval of time between the sound of your weapon reporting outbound rounds and the visual recording of impacts of those bullets striking target could seem a few lifetimes.

Terrain of One Seven's TAOR around the hill ranged from rice paddies and open country, to high grass and thick brush in any direction, to densely foliated hills, serious jungle, and jungle canopied mountains on the western edge. Each had rhythms, smells, peculiarities that had to be worked well. Booby traps in thick grass weren't the same as in the jungle or on rice paddy dikes, neither were enemy positions or mannerisms. Though small unit tactics were small unit tactics in a general shape, terrain required variations one needed to know. The smells and rhythms of things could be remarkably informative if one could read them. Sometimes the terrain rhythms, smells, and peculiarities gave warning.

"Don't go in there now," the bush would say. "Feel that? Smell this? If you go in there today, you'll get your asses kicked."

Often the point would stand or squat perfectly still a long time, checking out every possible thing while the rest of the patrol quietly covered him so he could do a decent job. Sometimes when in free-fire zones, we would waft over to a better feeling area and call mortars or artillery on the funny-feeling area. On one occasion, the called fire mission produced secondary explosions and many groans. On another, 81 mm mortar fire triggered about a beehive's worth of swarming RPGs, that punched holes in three tanks on the road between Hill 10 and Hill 41. The latter involved the TAC Party, three sections of F8s, and two sections of A4s to clean up enemy that had tunneled under the TAOR to construct a rocket storage area and were now spilling out of the ground.

When flying, I sometimes knew that fixed wing air assisted calling in forces; seeing it work from the requestor's point of view that day convinced me it was wonderful. A number of Marines continued breathing who likely wouldn't have otherwise. The action also cleared up little feelings of incertitude regarding TACP worth to the battalion.

Out again with a Bravo Company platoon getting the lay of the land, learning who and what was where in the TAOR, when toward the end of the day the platoon leader turned us inbound. Suddenly I found myself in the dirt as bullets cracked and snapped overhead. A cold intense rush of energy cut through me, forcing the wind out of my body. One instant was quiet, the next the atmosphere filled with popping, fast-moving little pieces of metal. Something about shooting came to mind. Okay, so I'd die like a Marine, returning fire. There was a period of confusion on my part. Then we were running through trees and brush toward an unseen enemy firing at us. I ran along blasting away at winking muzzle flashes that quickly disappeared. We ran down, found nothing, headed home. Firefight number two, no one hit. How several hundred bullets managed to traverse a small space housing many human bodies without hitting even one of them was beyond me.

"Welcome to spontaneous poor ambushes," the Bravo Company commander said to me after the patrol. "You wouldn't be standing there if it had been a good one. The platoon sergeant tells me you're charmed. He thought the 'bush sprung on you, but you got up and charged the fire without getting hit. Nobody got hit. That's good."

"Was that why the silent treatment?" I asked.

"Probably." He rubbed his forehead. "That and new. Nobody wants to get used to you in case you get killed, and they don't want to trust you yet because they don't know if you can hack it. If they trust you, they're used to you. If you get killed, that'll fuck them up some more. It's a bitch. But yeah, they probably couldn't believe you didn't get it. You better watch that John Wayne shit."

John Wayne shit? It was the only action I knew how to take in the situation; the other choice was lay there and die. "That's all I knew to do."

"Well it worked pretty good," he smiled, "but watch yourself. There are usually sharpshooters set to pick off hard chargers. And another thing ..."

The company gunny poked his head in the tent, nodded at me, and spoke to his CO. "Excuse me, Skipper," he said. "Perimeter's set, guns'll be on five and eight." He paused as the company commander nodded.

Five and eight referred to defensive bunker numbers. The custom on the hill was placement of machineguns in the perimeter after dark in different positions each night. On high-risk nights the guns moved several times through the night.

"Skipper," the gunny continued, "I've got to get another mike-sixty barrel for patrol eight. It's a 'bush and I want that barrel replaced now. I think it's close to orange, from the deal last night."

Patrols went out every night from each company. The gunny made reference to patrol number eight, which was to set in ambush that night. The machine gun really had to be in excellent working order.

Essentially a good weapon, and certainly one esteemed by gents with whom I was in combat, the M60 had this little thing about melting barrels during long bursts. An M60 action could comfortably manage a five-hundred-fifty round per minute cyclic rate of fire; the barrel could accommodate a rate of two hundred rounds per minute for up to two minutes, or fire at the rate of a hundred rounds per minute for ten minutes. Yeah, well go ahead and count that in a firefight where everything around you is being blown apart, two minutes is forever, and you really must have the damned gun output up to around twenty rounds a millisecond. We all know about metal and heat, it seems nonetheless unreasonable to equip combat machine gunners with weapons having to be babied because barrels can't sustain intense combat level of fire. That was the case, however, and when the barrels turned a smelter red-orange from overheating, endo the barrel. That meant whoever was depending on the gun was deeply immured in egregious doo-doo.

Speaking about babied weapons, how about equipping combat units with rifles never tested in the combat environment and that worked for only about a half minute in that environment? Nice engineering, testing, and procurement wouldn't you say? And the dead because those rifles were suddenly worthless assemblages of fucked metal and sorry-assed plastic? Acceptable losses? Think the letter from the President said that?

Here kid, take this piece of garbage with you. We know the combat arena requires a reliable weapon to survive, but that's the best we can do. Hope you live through it.

Mod two of the rifle worked acceptably or this wouldn't be in front of you, but early model weapon malfunctions killed people and trust. Now, why would you suppose combat people question everything?

"Did you check with the armorer?" Bravo's skipper asked.

"Yessir. I need a little help there, Skipper."

"All right." The company commander stood, motioned me to follow as he spoke to the gunny. "Be right back, Gunny."

A Marine Corps battalion armorer manages, maintains, issues, and sometimes customizes devices that keep Marines alive in combat; treat them nicely. An armorer is everybody's friend, particularly in combat of course, and they are normally good people. Even so, every once in a while, usually when firefight issues are abnormally numerous for a battalion, somebody like a company commander may be obliged to walk down to an armorer's empire and tweak one just a tad in order to assist in a review and possible restacking of task prioritization, shall we say.

"So what I was saying," Bravo Six continued as we walked the dark hill toward the armory, "was you don't want the NVA to know you. If they know you're air, they'll put some effort into killing you. They don't like air much and they watch every fucking thing. No one will want to be around you if you're a designated target."

He stopped in front of my place. "Think about that, and do something about your hair."

"My hair?"

"It's fucking blonde, man. Easy to spot and easy to remember, even high and tight, even with your helmet. See you later."

So rub greasepaint in my hair? Shave it off? What?

He rattled the hatch on his way back with the machine gun barrel. "Take some," he handed over six old Mark 26 fragmentation grenades, "you always want to have a few of those with you."

The booby traps were a son-of-a-bitch. There were the infamous punji stakes in many varieties of traps, also some creative things done with trip wire, broken glass, and barbed wire. Occasionally there were mines, but most booby traps in the battalion's TAOR were cleverly concealed grenades. They were in holes, chest high, set in chains, overhead in trees. Some bounced up when tripped, some were just there under or near things. One could hear their distinct muted, almost mortar tube sound nearly every day. Then about twenty minutes later a medevac helicopter whupped over to pick up the pieces. Booby trap detonations at night were usually enemy killed by their own traps. Once in a while a patrol ran across evidence of this. Deadly to all, the local populace didn't escape the things either.

POCK!!!

A Marine went home minus parts or in one of those sorry fucking bags. There was nothing you could do.

WHOAUMPF!

A Marine lay bleeding, sometimes screaming, usually the pieces blown off by the trap were evident, they wouldn't go back on no matter how hard I tried to think them back into place. I can't begin to describe what it's like to watch human beings go through that. Some would try to recover their weapon, or get their damned radio back, try to stand up to go on; their spirits wanted to go on, they just didn't have enough remaining body pieces. They would try to keep going, try, look up with a face that said, "Oh God, why can't I do that? I was just doing it a minute ago. I want to do it now." The look on their faces when they realized pieces were gone was too much to bear—another fucking facet of the fucking heartfuckingbreaker.

Sometimes I wondered if I should ask the gent if it would be better if I just shoot him, administer grace to a down compadre? Would that stop the pain and shock, the violation and horror he was feeling? Would he say yes? Would it assist him? What would I want him to do in a reversed situation? What could I do to assist?

Not one thing. Nothing, nada, rien, nulla, nichts.

Oh, cover him and his pieces, get him out, but there really wasn't anything anyone but the Bones could do for him. There wasn't anyone who could be gotten to for having done that to him; there wasn't even anyone around to properly notice. Injustice, pain, anger, horror, sorrow, tragedy, violation, grief, hate, violent intent stuffed in compartments somewhere inside. Firefight after firefight after booby trap after dead Marine after maimed Marine. All of it collected, increasing numbness, impossible to feel accumulating in there.

Incoming mortars, which nearly reduced me to blathering idiocy the first night I experienced them at Chu Lai, became increasingly less frequent while I was with the battalion. Most 106 mm recoilless rifle crews generally had return fire on the launching tubes before the first rounds impacted, with 81 mm mortars on target right behind them. Damage from mortars wasn't the worst thing out there, providing some decent overhead cover existed. In the open, however, they were no fun at all.

A few days later I went out with a platoon sweep. "Gettin' to be a habit, Sir," Freckles smiled, as he and his a-gunner followed the TACP representatives again. The patrol was routine to the point of uneasiness in most of us. My internal iciness flickered and flared throughout, causing constant shortness of breath and nervousness. It was late in the day when we turned inbound.

KAH-POCK!!!

The slack rose a few feet, disappeared in low brush; the booby trap blew off the lower portion of one leg. He was screaming. As I called in the medevac, the ambush sprang. Bullets smacked all around, the fearsome sound came up, rock and roll, oh Baby.

Let me break this a minute, focus on the point in front of this group. He was leading a group of his compadres through hostile country, in a position of great risk, at any time only about a step away from Lord knows what, while doing his best to pick a decent path, keep the platoon off booby traps and mines, locate enemy, and hold everything together. His closest ally was the slack, covering from about twenty-five feet behind. Suddenly, the slack was hurt and screaming, the slack position was vacant, there was no immediate cover, and fifty feet of dense vegetation stood

between him and his compadres. Just as suddenly came a hail of
bullets from everywhere. What do you suppose he thought and felt
as hundreds of bullets shredded his body?

Two people in front of TACP went down in rose-colored spray,
covering us with the warm sticky squish of blood and pieces from
them. Bullets were everywhere, tearing up vegetation, kicking up
dirt, leaving our ears ringing as they smacked passed much too
close.

Know how animals freeze in sudden light and humans pause at
abrupt sounds? In this situation one may be similarly inclined,
however, if one pauses, one is dead. The natural reaction to
determine what is happening must be overridden. One must get
down that instant and return fire quickly as possible.

"DOWN-NN," Freckles screamed, returning fire.

I knocked my RO down, or he knocked me down, or we knocked
each other down, I really don't recall. We spent the next few
minutes putting out as much fast moving, copper-jacketed steel
alloy as was humanly possible. Freckles and his a-gunner worked
closer to us. I grabbed the radio, shot, and screamed for gun ships
to accompany the medevac. I could hardly hear, but division had to
know what was going on. I must have told them five hundred times
the place was hotter than Hades. Incoming fire was met by a
waxing roar of outgoing fire. Freckles emitted a loud stream of
primitive sounds that interpreted as, "Fuck the fucking barrel, I'm
counting. Keep the gahdam belt straight!"

An eerie wail came from somewhere, the sound interpreted as
Bones got it. A bandoleer of full magazines landed next to me,
compliments of Freckles' a-gunner. He was giving us ammo and
directing us to cover the machinegun.

Machine gunners and a-gunners instantly become extremely
popular people during a firefight, for both sides. We wanted
Freckles there, healthy and shooting; they wanted him and his gun
off the planet, that instant. Cover a machine gunner driving the shit
out of the gun to keep us alive? You betcha. No problem.

Poison of the combat zone had been seeping into my
bloodstream for close to a year. It accumulated in my mind and
heart until it reached critical mass: I could kill anything. At that
moment I wanted the patrol to live, if that meant killing everything
else out to Alpha Centauri, so be it. I scooped up a handful of the
magazines, tossed the bandoleer to my corporal, became the
quintessence of a Marine Corps combat rifleman, putting rounds

into everything non-Marine presenting itself. I fell a little short of quintessential with a frame of mind not particularly oriented toward consideration of stringent fire discipline.

"Hanworth one four, Hanworth one four, how copy, over?"

The words came up from the grass. The language was normal human, so I knew the voices weren't located near us. How I heard the radio over the firefight noise, I will never know. I grabbed the handset, screamed particulars to the helicopters, and continued to put out as many well-placed bullets as possible. The helicopters arrived on station. I briefed them in about three quarters of a second, using guttural sounds they somehow understood, while supporting fire plummeted from the gunbirds.

"Goah," I shouted toward my corporal as I nodded toward an area. The gibberish meant I was going over there. He nodded while continuing to shoot.

"Kohdagahn!" That meant stay with and provide supporting fire for the machine gunner, which he did.

I hauled the radio to the area closest to the wounded I could see, while issuing a stream of primitive sounds meaning get set for the pickup. I was definitely in "the pump," a state akin to pump, but much further along. It's a nervous, perceptive, high-energy state; as far as I know one must look right into the Reap's pasty white, black-hole-eyed face to enter it. Once there, one may experience atom vision, see protons, perhaps even electrons.

The platoon sergeant, knowing what to do without need of the funny noises I was using to communicate, signaled to cover the LZ I had just designated by my position. Freckles and the other machine gunner poured fire at locations sniping at the helicopters. An older Marine, say around twenty-five, sprawled next to me waving his arm toward the area in front of us as he looked up questioningly. The clear area was the only reasonable LZ around. No doubt the NVA knew that, too. The area had to be checked for booby traps and mines, but we were still taking fire. Right in front of me that minute was the highest order of being, a brave unselfish Marine willing to put his life on a line for the good of the platoon. I nodded my head, pointed, and grunted sounds meaning "mines, traps." Peculiar amid unbelievable weapons sounds of a firefight was the amount of brief but well-understood two-way communication accomplished with nearly mindless grunts, screams, barks, et cetera. It was as though we were all hooked into the same thread, using the vocalizations as indicators of timing for events we all knew were necessary. A high functioning, exceptional state of togetherness I have missed since. It seems the threat of immediate death is one of a few things that can get a group to that level. That's a damned shame.

The gent handed over a smoke grenade, squiggled across the clearing, pausing every few feet as he checked the ground. Now that really was hero stuff. He was out there in a clear area, crawling along looking for mines and traps while bullets cracked and popped all around. Everyone covered him. Anything even slightly suspicious received a withering volume of fire, the advertised line being that particular gent absolutely will remain untouched. And so he did. In a couple of minutes, though it seemed like a month, he flashed thumbs up from the other side of the flat spot. Almost immediately, I heard noises behind me as the wounded were lined up for pickup. Talk about teamwork!

"Ooay," I hollered into the handset. "Dyoohabtallee?"

"Roger Hanworth, we have you in sight."

Though gents in the helicopters understood this guttural communication also, the situation, and I, settled down enough to return to more normal language.

"Winds are zip," sudden apprehension. No wind? Oh-oh. Sunset. I re-hooked with the full environment. The sun had set and incoming fire had stopped. I much wanted those helicopter crews and the wounded out of there before dark. I really wanted all of us out of there, but two helicopters wouldn't hack it in one trip and splitting the group was in the category of "Have you fucking flipped?"

"The LZ is clear, we've been cold a few minutes. There are six or seven down here for you, here comes smoke."

I flipped the smoke grenade into the LZ; heard people behind me carrying the wounded tighten up. Puke yellow smoke threaded upward toward the helicopters.

"Got the smoke?" I asked.

"Ayefirm Hanworth, tally the LZ."

"Mind the trees, come on down, cleared to fire."

They had us in sight. No other friendlies were close, so I gave them a *carte blanc* to shoot. The lead helicopter spiraled into the little LZ, blowing yellow everywhere while I prayed for no more incoming. Covering birds swooped around the area, watching both the medevac birds and us.

Red smoke was decreed for a hot LZ, yellow was available; none of us needed smoke. I popped it because the gent who cleared the LZ gave it to me for that. Didn't matter about need it because when somebody shows that much courage and heart, the little old smoke grenade they handed up gets used, even during bright daylight on a clear no-wind day in the President's LZ at the White House.

Smoke canisters were not my idea of a heavy-priority item in the battalion's TAOR anyway. Magazines filled with comforting little 5.56 mm rounds or more grenades were priority items, thank you.

The LZ remained cold, request by prayer approved. Four badly wounded and the four dead—the point, the platoon leader, his radio op, and the Bones—all went out on the two helicopters. There was almost nothing left of the point; some truly courageous Marines went out there to bring in his remains. By the way, the point, the Bones, machine gunners, anyone with a radio, anyone looking like authority was often among first hits in an ambush. That day Our Lady of the Luck, the combatant's darling, extended some courtesy to the TACP corporal carrying the radio, the two machine gunners and a-gunners, and me.

The two gents blown apart right before my eyes flicked in and out of thoughts all the way back to the hill. Two live, anxious gents ceased living, their bodies torn to pieces as we watched. The corporal and I still had some of their internal squish all over us; it just as easily could have been the corporal and me. That old sliding, life-changing feeling made the walk home seem like I was watching from some distance.

Freckles, also covered with blood, came over when we were back inside the wire. "Dammit, Sir," he seemed unsure if he should continue, but he did. "Lieutenant, you stay down out there when you talk on the radio. They'll kill you when they see that, Sir."

Hell, they just tried to kill all of us, but he was right. I got busy returning fire, then working the medevac, popping up and down like a puppet. I didn't think about getting down once the medevac was underway.

"You're right, thanks for covering me," I said stupidly while I thought about the gracious smile Our Lady of the Luck bestowed. I still had a lot to learn, fast.

The TACP corporal stared at me. "Good job," I said. What a numb-nuts comment. There should be much nicer things said at a time like that. He looked at me funny, started to say something, but never did.

I needed the name of the gent who cleared the LZ; that action warranted decoration. I was looking for him when everybody just walked away from each other. I don't know what I was expecting, but it certainly felt lonesome watching people shuffle away in all directions.

"Kee-riest!" The watch officer's intense face and defensive body posture put me in the creature from another universe category when I walked into the COC bunker to check with the TACP watch. He stared a long time. "Blood on the moon tonight. That must have been good."

If I looked anything like Freckles or the TACP corporal, I could understand his horror, however, his shock wearing off came too late. My isolation switch had flipped. Everybody in the place stared while I stood there, suddenly unable to speak. There was dried blood and goo on my face, fried blood on my M-16, more blood on my hands, sleeves, and the chest of my flak jacket.

I had been in close situations in the air and on the surface, but those previous adventures seemed more a matter of first evading something, then returning fire to it. The deal was avoidance and destruction of the thing in question, but at least I existed. This particular firefight felt like we were all dead, had no existence, as though we had to remanufacture future life. There was nothing to avoid; it was right there upon us. We had to counter the destruction in process and overcome the source of that destruction to keep living. It gave new meaning to the phrase "back from the dead."

A firefight moves involved people apart from those not involved, is yet another separator—and not a little one at that. So if one did a few of those, how far away from normal people would one find themselves? How about if one did eight? How about seven hundred sixty eight?

Though I didn't realize this until later, an instant in a combat arena altered basic structure. Focus shifted from self to how self may be of benefit to those around; from I to we, from how may I extract from, to how may I contribute to any given situation? A change for the better I believe, and though subtle at the time, one with impact upon my life. Less beneficial, but a change nonetheless, concerned my sense of belonging. Up to that moment, I had a sense of being part of something, a nation, a corps, any of several groups.

I haven't had a feeling of belonging, of being an integral part of anything since.

Chapter 13

Academy of the Elite

Awake in a sweat, alert—firefight in Charley Company's TAOR somewhere—I crashed off the rack. It wasn't good. AK sounds were synchronized and continuous, M-16 sounds were erratic. I grabbed my combat gear and hauled to the COC bunker, nearly decking the watch commander.

"Oops, sorry. Need air?"

He shrugged while regaining balance, continued to talk on the EE8. He didn't have enough yet with which to work.

"It's one of Charlie's, Sir," the watch corporal said as I passed on the way to the TACP radios. "No comm."

We looked at each other. No comm was bad; so were the firefight sounds.

One cannot indiscriminately run air into an area because of a real feeling in his heart that Marines are dying. With the concerned group unobserved and unable to communicate, there is no way to determine tactical reality, ergo support fire could easily kill those one wished to assist. I wanted to beat my head against the bunker bulkhead, to scream, to be out there. But without a sense of tactical reality, a unit cannot mount a reaction force and hump through four or five clicks of rice paddies, jungle, and ambushes at three in the morning with any expectation of arriving in time to accomplish much of anything.

Division wanted to know what I wanted. I only knew Marines were dying, and so requested a flare ship and gunbirds. The explosive chatter from across the rice paddies grew to a roar. Alpha Company wanted an explanation as they had an ambush set to the north of the firefight. Snipers couldn't see the firefight through Starlight scopes, too much intervening plant life. Recoilless rifles and mortars wanted fire missions and the Arty FO showed up wanting to know how his howitzers could assist. Everyone in the COC bunker stood morosely waiting for a tactical picture to take shape.

Charley Company's six actual called the watch officer. The patrol's RO went off the air in the middle of a sentence and there was no means of contact, no units close enough to figure out what was happening or to get to the patrol quickly. TOD: 0310. The firefight waned; the hill went on alert.

Division one four diverted our air support to Dodge City, an area in the third battalion's TAOR. "A real sandwich," declared the voice at the other end of the line. Wing was doing the right thing with the assets available to them. The Charley patrol couldn't communicate and all the aviation support in the world wouldn't have been able to work the area well. Still, it felt lousy. Wait, wait, wait—silence from the field was really tedious.

At TOD: 0345 one of Alpha's ambush sites fired on several enemy to their west, who returned fire while continuing to move northwest. The Alpha patrol thought they hit several of them.

TOD: 0447. A Charley Company patrol at last reached the now silent firefight location and reported the patrol in question dead to a man. Suddenly unable to overcome gravity, my heart sank to the Earth's core. Daylight revealed many enemy dead also, which was unusual as NVA normally hauled its dead away. It would have been much more acceptable if whatever spooked them had accomplished that sooner.

Despite all the support—aircraft, artillery, snipers, tanks, weapons company, and willing combat infantry—a small group of teenagers was literally blown to pieces in a jungle one night because the damned radio took the first hits. That handful of gents was suddenly alone against a much larger, determined NVA force. Only the Lord has a complete picture of what occurred out there.

Perhaps your country has the best equipped military in the world and maybe you are equipped with the finest, but ultimately infantry combat equates to you, the few people around you, the immediate situation in its entirety, and the terrain. It requires courage, knowledge, resilience, capability, adaptability, excellent instincts, and a powerful spirit. Even with that, once in a while you are favored to stand in place and just take what's coming.

Our Lady of the Luck, the combatant's darling.

I located Charley Six Actual just after daylight. "I want to go out there," I told him.

"Now what in hell do you think you can do?" he asked.

"I don't know, something. Shit."

A patrol was going out to pick up the pieces of what had been Freckles' squad. I got used to his smiling face, his damned gun always being there. It would be different now. I was probably alive because of him.

"Can't do it. You're air around here. Can't risk it. They're dead. Get helicopters to extract the bodies and don't fuck with me right now."

Of course he was right. Upset, too. I banged my fist on the 105 ammo case he used as a table. "Damn! Damn! Damn!"

He banged down his fist and bellowed, "No shit!"

"Let me know what else I can do." I stood to go.

He nodded, "Fucking war."

Hill 10, the hill. I walked to the crest overlooking the battalion CP and saw a neat stack of Marines in bitten plastic bags near the battalion aid station. Covered by a tarpaulin, they sat silently waiting for return to the families that started them. I could hear a stiff official representative talking to a bereaved set of parents back in the world.

"Sorry folks. Look, we used up your son, but here's what's left. Thanks for letting us use him."

I could picture the parent's asking why and the resultant shoulder shrugging as the representative replied, "Folks, I don't know."

The dead Marines got that way linking with what they thought were other Marines. The two wounded survivors reported encountering enemy dressed in new American issue utilities and equipment, and speaking English. They obviously knew how to link.

Somewhere there existed pieces of garbage passing for human that made money when what they really needed was their waste-filled throats slit.

Out near the river a platoon-sized patrol had just finished a light exchange of rounds with a few enemy. The squad with which I was working swept along a trail to move stragglers and flankers toward a blocking force. The gent ahead stared through me, eyes wide open. I turned to see a giant NVA swinging a gargantuan AK47 toward us.

The NVA was moving fast. His face was flushed and showing surprise and he was off balance. The ammo pouches strapped to his torso were crooked, his knife sheath was sticking out horizontally from his belt, his pith helmet was coming off, and his trousers were covered with mud. The AK he was rapidly moving to line up on us had a muzzle orifice that looked like the entrance to the Mediterranean. I spun my weapon overhead, squeezed the trigger as the muzzle pointed toward the man.

Behrr-rr-rr-rr-rr-rr-rr-rr-rr-rr-rr-rr-rr-rr-rr-rr-rr-rr-ah-ah-ahh!

Trill the "r"s, like the Spanish in *ferrocarril*, you'll get the sound. M-16s with the selector switch in the rock-and-roll position were pretty serious about dispatching little fifty-three grain bullets that really smacked when encountering fleshy tissue.

My first round popped out his left shirtsleeve about thirty-six feet as it smacked through. The next splintered the AK's forestock as it knocked the rifle off target in slow motion. Round three drove the weapon against the man's chest as it smashed into the receiver just ahead of the stock. He dropped the weapon. Subsequent rounds punched through hands clutching chest. He looked toward us in complete disbelief, his eyes closed, head dropped. Round after round smashed into his already dead carcass, breaking little pieces away, splattering blood everywhere. Other weapons joined in converting the man to paste. The body was a red smear from waist to neck when finally it came to rest.

I continued to fire long after the weapon expended its ammo, long after everyone else ceased fire. I may have fired that rifle the next two million years if somebody hadn't touched me on the shoulder.

"It's good, Sir. You got him." The gent's words and touch broke the spell, allowing me to return to the living.

"Damn. Burned my hand." Duh. Mumbling about something obvious was important I guess. I held the muzzle on target by gripping the barrel abaft the front sight ramp instead of using the forestock—a taintless technique taking a back seat to shoot-right-now. I tore my T-shirt, wrapped the strip around the burn, changed magazines, and waited with the squad to see what else might turn up. After awhile we ambled over to the dead NVA.

"Dumb shit shouldn't have crossed the trail," somebody said as I arrived at the remains.

Suddenly viewing it from far away in hyperspace, the blown apart body lying there seemed to be at the other end of a reverse telescope. The guy took many hits, I'll guess at thirty or so, seventeen of which were mine. Then, as if the scene simply shifted, we were walking back through the wire at Hill 10, hours later.

If that little freeze-up number had occurred during a kicking along firefight it's likely I, and probably others, would have not made it back alive. Still don't know what that was and I spent considerable time the rest of the tour worrying about it. Good news is it never happened again.

Chapter 14

Converter

Firefights are men changers (women and children too, if they're that unfortunate). Life-altering, brutal, never-to-be-forgotten lessons rather obviously presented. The things are studies in death, pain, and waste. They convert men to monsters for a time and may not be recalled or redone. The results are not negotiable. Though wounds can be patched, bodies take the hits. The totality of incidents is recorded in memories that cannot be erased. The dead are dead; they will never again be seen. Violated spirits remain, as does a remembrance of heightened perception, energy, and function, coupled with the desire to return to that level from time to time.

Holy fuck! In a fraction of a heartbeat. Click! Firefight mode. Shoot, quick. Move. Shoot again. Quick. Get that guy, now. Now get that one. The noise. Unbelievable noise. Marines hit. Numb. Look around. No emotion. Can't see shit. Shoot. Damn! Drop to the ground. Earth explodes. Pieces of dirt, brush, rocks flying, slamming. It stops. Stop shaking. Nearly bought it that time. Get outta there. Quick! Is he still there? Good. Shoot at that bush. Get that guy. Quick. Change magazines. Get down. Shit. Bullets everywhere. Where is it all coming from? Get those two guys. Oh, shit! Close. Whew! Oh-oh. Move, now! Where are the rest of us? Holy shit! There's two NVA over there. Kill 'em, quick! OK. BOOM! The world explodes. What was that? Is the weapon okay? Area clear? Move! Now! Look around. Shake off the dirt and shit. Can't hear a thing. Shit! Watch the grenades. Shoot that guy. Fast. Shoot. That bush moved. Shoot. Now! Get over there. Now! Cover him. Whew, he made it. Uh-oh. Get those guys. Oh fuck. Shoot. Change magazines. Shoot. Where are they? Shoot. Are they everywhere? Hearing starts to come back. Shoot. Shoot. Change magazines. Where is everybody? Get that one. Oh, shit. Shoot again. Fuck! Mount the bayonet? Oh-oh! They ARE fucking everywhere. Shoot! SHOOT! Change magazines! Shoot! Shoot! Change magazines! Shoot! Ah! There's Marines. Don't bunch up! Can't cover worth a damn bunched up. Rounds cracking through the brush. Fucking close. Where did that come from? Shoot. Change magazines. Shoot again. Where are they? Shoot. OK. There's the corporal. There's Bones. Firing's stopped. Senses peaked. Don't unwind now, there's more out there somewhere. Be careful. Check magazine. Be alert. It's over for the moment. But it isn't safe. OK. There's more Marines. Not safe yet. Oh God! Look at him. They shot his face off. Who's screaming? Oh shit! His arm's gone. Still not safe. Not safe. Not safe.

Nothing gets healed in a firefight. Personal problems remain unresolved. Firefights do not "make you a man" or qualify you for much of anything. They offer a means for individual definition in terms of function and emotional capacity, and acquaint participants with the remarkable effects of pure adrenaline. The word "sudden" is redefined while a cambering of mental framework occurs. Survivors are truly fortunate; however, much hard work is required to recover a semblance of normalcy and many unforeseen choices lie ahead.

Firefights require teamwork, honesty, concentration, and demand a quality of ethics unknown by those who haven't been in one. That's too bad really; seems that level of conduct should be required of each of us so that we might survive well together.

Pulling the trigger on a human attempting to do the same to you or your compadres leaves residuals. The occurrence is unlike anything I could have imagined. There's exhilaration at getting through standing that lasts a few moments, and a blackness that comes over your heart that lasts for years, perhaps forever. Too much of this can easily position one in a dark place from which he may not return.

Your targets, human beings such as yourself, with children, wives, sweethearts, indecision, doubt, courage, and emotion, blow apart right there in front of you and do not get back up. Neither do your compadres. And it is fast.

Blouwbang! Your target is dead. No moan. No scream. No move. No chance to say or do anything clever. The Reap honored your endo processing, picked that ex-human up that instant, right there.

Through the years, like it or not, the more delicious and revolting scenes replay thousands of times at odd moments. With a little time and thought the experience provides a sense of how far from constructive life a great number of us have strayed. One thing about amazing destruction is the gained view of constructive.

Firefights are converters that accomplish damage, convert live people to dead people, nothing else. Any participant involved in enough of them eventually also will be converted. Firefights bring no awards, rings, recognition, status, women, money, fat contracts, signing bonuses, or even acknowledgment for participation. If you and your compadres manage firefights well, are good at what you do, and Our Lady of the Luck is in the mood, you get to keep your life.

Perhaps firefights are necessary in this world of tears from time to time, for reasons of continuance, survival, forced expansion of territory, or something. But they are not winning things, they are force things. People who get through them may have their lives afterwards, but not the same lives they had before.

No doubt you have seen films attempting to portray this kind of activity—do not believe them. If one chambered rounds or cocked weapons as frequently as in films, live rounds would be all over the deck, rather than available for working targets. There is entirely too much thrust toward manufactured dramatic attempt and clever comments. I don't remember anyone talking during a firefight; people used plain old base-level grunts, growls, screams, and barks. The texture, tonality, and urgency of the sounds conveyed the message. Movies also utilize a little glorious music to focus emotions on other than the simulated death and destruction. When you're really killing and maiming people attempting to do the same to you, the violence is the music. It's a cacophonic, explosive soundtrack, punctuated by the sounds of humans in various states of effort or injury, with a definite rhythm, pace, and key.

In a real firefight there is no jump to the next scene. Unlike the movies, you must stand there seeing, smelling, hearing, and feeling it all. Sometimes you have to wipe a guy's internal fluids and goo off your face. You soon learn, however, that the stuff won't wipe off a hot rifle barrel after it's cooked on, nor can you get it off utilities and webbed gear. Neat holes in otherwise intact bodies are a film's concession to audience sensitivity. The only neat holes I ever saw were from small fragment slivers. The reality is that bodies are torn apart when struck by bullets. Pieces break off or are ripped away. Bones shatter and tear. Organs and muscles explode. Wet tissue and body fluids spray over everything nearby. Sometimes it wasn't possible to identify the ground pile of meat lying there. Neat, pretty, glamorous, romantic, or at all dignified cannot be applied here.

I'm not after anyone; I just want you to understand that nothing on a movie screen is like combat. Authentic combat footage doesn't present the whole story either. If you haven't been there, you don't know; and that's good. If you've been there, look around, take a breath, touch anything with which you are familiar, settle back into your easy riding position. Here's to you. Glad you're still around.

There were different types of firefights. Some would begin with fire returned towards a couple of incoming rounds seeming to come from a sniper. These would often turn into total mayhem in no time. Others began with our firing upon one or two apparently isolated enemy. Soon, though, the surrounding countryside would start sprouting hostile weapons and all hell would erupt. We couldn't see much in the way of targets during these and they rarely lasted too long. On occasion, there were firefights that involved only a light exchange of bullets, amounting to little expended ammunition. But people got hurt and killed nonetheless. Then there were the assaults: any weapons, any tactics, full-tilt deathwalks. These things were real casualty producers and could crank right along, requiring close personal engagement with the enemy using knives, bayonets, rifles as clubs, entrenching tools, hands, feet, elbows, knees, teeth, helmets—whatever was available.

Ambushes were the lowest, most vile type of firefight. Killing those who have no indication you're present is disgusting stuff. Getting hit by somebody you don't know is present is even more loathsome. Maybe ambushes are necessary, I don't know. They have eliminated many humans and other creatures through the years, but are unclean and wicked, and leave blackness on one's heart.

An effective ambush wasn't even a firefight. The world would go instantly from uneasy to shocked confusion. If your training and conditioning were good, and you weren't a first target, or if the ambush was poorly set up, timed, or executed, at least something could be done. If training and conditioning were poor, or if it was a really well executed ambush, chances of getting through it were slight. If one were a primary target, training and conditioning probably wouldn't matter at all. Cleverly set up ambushes were brutal, leaving no time or space for anything. The correct choices for ambushes were to either avoid them or be the ambusher.

A firefight demanded unbroken concentration, attention to detail, and a mental flow that took in and considered everything, then quickly calculated a solution. If something went unnoticed, or if thought processes moved off point for even an instant, the chances of living through the thing reduced dramatically. Even with that, Our Lady of the Luck had a lot to do with what was received by whom.

After a firefight, some stood shaking or staring into space shedding tears. Others would look at the ground or the sky for a period. Some were angry, some seemed far away. All were changed.

Soon after the shooting stopped, the environment slowly returned to normal. Birds chirped cautiously at first, then began chattering as usual. Little creatures resumed doing what little creatures do. The place calmed, replacing the deathly silence immediately following a firefight with the small quiet that exists when the world is considerate and observant.

Life trundled along as if nothing of significance had occurred. The distant sun shone unconcerned. The wind swiftly dissipated the screams and sounds of violence. Mother Earth seemed unaffected as her surface absorbed the blood and tears. Plants, animals, and the whole damn physical universe could not have cared less and the Lord did not intervene, having already granted us the integral freedom that comes with human life—the freedom to choose anything available, anytime.

After a firefight one could clearly discern that only human beings attend to human beings. And tragically, only a small number of them do. What a shame. Lives are of consequence, the dignity of any life is important.

Chapter 15

Privileged View

Body bags, loathsome plastic constructions to confine bodies, prevent anatomical pieces and goo from dribbling all over the place, were not the subject of discussions I remember. "So-and-so went home in a bag" or a similar comment was about the extent of body bag chatter. Initially I tried to treat the bags as sacks of just any old material, but that didn't work. Lifeless bodies are considerably heavier than they appear, and the lack of high frequency vibrations from complex material designed to house that which vibrates at high frequencies, is eerie. Partially filled or funny shaped body bags were too much, really.

Not many people talked about the wounded either; somebody hit seemed to transition from a present time personality to a past tense abstract. You'd hear things like "Yeah, I knew so-and-so until he got hit." I think so-and-so ceased to be real when hit, whether he perished or not. He would become an abstract locked in time, a symbolic representation perhaps even without the original personality's name. If the wounded stayed up or returned quickly, the real-time relationship continued with just a small break; if the wound took the person away for more than a few hours, the mind would dull any anticipated hurt by abstracting the real person. After a while, it seemed anyone leaving the immediate arena for almost any reason, including going home, became abstract.

Abstraction, symbolic representation, is merely a construct with which to play in a normal environment. The version thrust upon one in a combat environment seems more a form of avoidance, defense against pain if you will. It is a system in which objects have only contextual significance within the moment.

A particular sergeant was with TACP for a while. He was good at getting things done—a fine Marine. As excellent in the bush as he was on the hill, the TACP depended on him. One day while on patrol with a company, somebody just forward of him encountered a booby trap.

PAH-WHOCK!

In an instant, the sergeant lost an eye, a hand, and a foot. His lifestyle, his dreams, nearly all the base data he set up with which to work his life, was unexpectedly altered. His excellent effort for us rewarded with a portion of a tab accumulated by another, asleep in front of him. I'm unable to recall the sergeant's name. I can see his face anytime, though I must return to the days at Hill 10 first. But there's no name.

As it turns out, there is quite a collection of nameless combat faces in my memory, some with tags such as "Freckles," or a gent particularly adept with M79s, called "Basher." That isn't disrespect or minimization toward any of them, quite the converse actually, just the mechanism we employed. Likely I'm a nameless combat face in some peoples' memory.

The night of the Tet Offensive in 1968, the most violent explosions I have ever experienced pulverized my pseudo-sleep, acquainting me with the business end of surface-to-surface rockets. I ran, that is to say flew over the surface of the Earth, to the COC bunker to get air support amid explosions, hot metal, death, brilliant flashes, deafening sounds, heat, concussions, metallic shrieks, pieces of metal zipping by. I made it to the bunker that shook with each blast.

Rockets were suddenly present, with not much to be done about them. They could destroy people in diggings or in a normal bunker as easily as they could people in the open. One could be doing all the right things, yet be smashed into teensy little pieces all over the area. Surface-to-surface rockets didn't feel like man weapons to me; they were insentient, freezing-cold human killers.

One afternoon as I came off COC watch, a rare occurrence for an aviator on Hill 10, snipers rang down reporting a VC or NVA sitting on a water buffalo, drawing a map, about a click west. I went up to have a look. My binoculars clearly revealed the lone Charles with his AK slung over his back, carefully looking, marking on a piece of paper, looking some more, returning to his piece of paper; he must have had copies of the patrol schedules. Anything obvious was always suspicious, so we checked around carefully for other developments. At that moment, it seemed the Charles was singular. The newly posted COC watch officer agreed with the sniper's request to disburden the water buffalo. Bravo Company owned the TAOR containing the VC, and didn't mind a little sniper activity at that location. An alert was passed around the hill and to Delta Company on Hill 41. An angel-faced corporal wrapped himself around his issued sniper's piece.

BLAM-ah-ah!

One shot.

Smack-OH!

One less Charles.

A head shot at something near a kilometer.

Terrorism is a word definable by use of any reputable dictionary. But like words such as thunderstorm, ocean, and moonlight, real comprehension requires direct experience. One morning on a routine patrol, cruising the "friendly" side of the TAOR, we walked into a hamlet to discover villagers huddled in the central square. Some were crying, some just staring into space. The platoon dispersed while several Marines attempted communication, but those people were upset to catatonia. Remains of two men of the village were located in a small clearing behind dwellings. There were no signs anywhere, of course. No young to middle-aged men or older boys were present. Those who may have been were likely now part of the "cause," voluntarily or not. The remaining villagers certainly weren't going to say anything, as they were probably told their children, themselves, the rest of the men, perhaps the whole village, would be next if they stepped out of line.

Here's a little scenario for you: A Vietnamese citizen, old Nguyen Plain Friendly Guy let's say, is in his home for the evening relaxing with his family when the front entrance bursts open. Armed men hold him at gunpoint, force him to watch while they set up to brutally violate his wife. Perhaps they knock his little girl around or something equally disgusting while thumping on Nguyen. They may intimidate the son, but probably don't injure him because he may be of later use. While Nguyen is in complete shock, he is told to go to such and such an area the next night to pick up a weapon with a number of rounds, which he will fire at Marines later that evening. He hesitates. They cut a strip of flesh off his wife, promising more horror or death to him or his family if he doesn't immediately oblige them.

Tactics varied. I'd heard about women and girls tortured, violated while other villagers were forced to helplessly watch; sometimes children were the victims of hacked fingers, eyes poked out, flesh cut or torn as in skinned animal. It was brutal, horrible, vile shit that made me sick at heart. The way Vietnamese citizens were slammed around by nearly anyone with bad ideas and some weapons convinced me of the wisdom displayed by our forefathers when ensuring our right to bear arms.

News of that kind of horror made a young boy with a hand grenade, or a teen-aged girl sniper, much less difficult to comprehend. What a choice for young men and women: do as dictated and probably die horribly or don't and surely die horribly along with causing the death or mutilation of some of your family members.

One afternoon, while covering a group of compadres working through a village from where fairly significant fire was drawn, a child appeared. A little girl of about six exited a dwelling, casually strolled toward the compadres standing nearby discussing a next tactical move. There were grenades attached to her, easily seen from my position but unseen by the group. She drew closer. I knew the damned grenades were going to blow any second and transport my compadres and the child to oblivion.

Okay. No benefit of council, situation moving right along, what happened next was pretty much up to me. What to do?

Shoot the child to keep her away from compadres? Take her out without pain? Should I holler to alert them? That would compromise my position and likely draw immediate fire. Might possibly be the last thing I ever do.

Should I shoot near the child to turn her away from my compadres, which also would alert them before it was too late? That would also give away my position and possibly scare the child. Keep in mind this little girl will not survive this incident no matter what I do; somebody has already positioned her for the Reap.

How about doing nothing, perhaps rationalizing the deaths of my compadres with some fortunes of war crap? Doing nothing was an alternative, however unpleasant. But presuming that my compadres would allow me to live after discovering my lack of action, that alternative may well have been my ruin.

Damn! What? The little girl was two steps from killing or maiming my compadres and there was no more time for thought, no more time to wait for something to intervene. I was out of everything except action. Make a move; do it now!

Yeah? Well, I dropped a perfect sight picture over the little girl, wanted to kill her quickly, without pain, but couldn't. A child? Innocence? How? Fuck no. I shot near her to turn her away. My compadres got down, the grenades detonated, and there was one less little bright human on the planet. I was colder than liquid oxygen.

If I lived through combat, the little girl, everyone involved would be in my dreams thousands of times—another face of the heartbreaker. I could have taken her out without her knowing or feeling anything, the administration of grace to a little girl who was dead in any event. It's probable that my elected path resulted in her being frightened just before she died. What a fucking big brave Marine thing. Lord, what will you do with me?

See, there was no hostile fire, no raging firefight, no confusion, no one next to me screaming and dying. I wasn't covered with gore, wasn't facing immediate death; I could focus on the one issue and override the normal, more intense combat response. Tell me what is correct action toward an enemy that does such things?

A general reconnaissance patrol trundled through countryside around Hill 10 for a few hours with no contact, no nervousness, not much other than the walk, the combat zone's version of a constitutional. We heard M-16 fire a few hundred meters away at our two o'clock, after a little radio chatter cautiously closed on the suspect hamlet. Another Bravo patrol stood over a dead VC official, who had been relieved of accurate sketches of our positions and the previous day's patrol routes, a set of water colors complete with brushes and paper, a relatively large sum of Piasters (money), several documents in Vietnamese, a Chicom 9 mm pistol, and his life. He took hits in the lower left leg, chest, and head. A hit in the face exploded his skull, causing his eyes to sit at weird angles and exposing what was left of his brain. Though the pistol indicated a position of authority, villagers didn't seem to notice him as they passed by and the gents in green gave him no more attention. When the ARVN showed up to take the body away from the flies, we proceeded back to Hill 10.

Sitting on the hill a little later with the dead whomever occupying my thoughts, I tried to remember who I was, what I had been in the world. There was only preparation for combat and combat. I was born for this?

One night incoming trounced me out of a trance-like state, shrapnel tore through the strongback, explosions were close, everything shook, pieces of metal whizzed through the place breaking things, blowing things apart. I lay there listening for artillery's return fire, wishing they would hurry up. At last artillery returned fire, the explosions stopped, I laughed. The enemy missed, we continued to exist, I could go back to sleep. There was nothing else about which to care.

Entranced in morning mist after coming off a quiet COC watch, I stood watching the last of Bravo Company's night patrols come in. My reverie was soon interrupted by dog tags clanking behind me. Dog tag noise? Not here. That was somebody-in-the-rear-area-playing-Joe-Combat stuff. Couldn't be a combat Marine.

"Good morning Marine," a high pitched, exuberant voice nearly shouted.

I turned to a remarkably clean-shaven face regarding me. The youngster wore new utilities and boots, a brand new flak jacket, shiny brass bars that didn't dazzle in the Southeast Asian mist. He looked like he'd been in country about five minutes. I say youngster but he wasn't much younger than me. New guy would be more appropriate.

"Heya. How are you?" I replied.

Anger flashed across his face. "How am I what, Marine?"

Oh shit, here we go. He wanted a "Sir" behind the greeting. Oh we just cannot have this disrespect from the troops. I looked like everybody else out there, good for me. I guess not so hot for new lieutenants.

"Mornin', Skipper." The Arty FO offered an elegant, perfectly timed exit from the situation as he greeted me *en passant*, heading for the COC bunker.

Skipper in Marine infantry talk generally, though certainly not always, refers to one holding the rank of captain. I had been promoted to captain a few weeks earlier, something that would have attracted minimal attention in the air wing, but was of considerable significance on the hill. There were immediately discernible changes in attitude and conduct of those around me, and though people still didn't talk to me just for fun, they greeted and acknowledged instead of looking away or suddenly finding they had something pressing to do elsewhere. If someone did talk to me, people gravitated toward the conversation, rather than nervously scrambling away. It was a vast improvement over the previous situation.

"Heya, Artillery," I answered. "Delta got two on Charley ridge last night, not much else."

"Good to hear," he nodded, looking at the new lieutenant's shiny bars. He quickened his pace as he continued on his way.

The new guy showed a face only a bewildered second lieutenant could display. "Skipper? Sir?"

"Yeah." I didn't care for the potential sniper fire his bars might bring any more than the FO. "Let's get off the flat here."

I walked toward my banged-up strongback faster than usual, with dog tags clanking along behind. Actually, the strongback was banged up when I arrived three million years ago; it was seriously mangled now.

"Well, damn! I - I -"every second lieutenant in the world has stammered like that a few times at the least.

"Relax, welcome aboard." I don't know how many times I stammered the same way. "It's not healthy to flash rank out here. If you notice nervous people trying to get away from you, chances are it's because they're anticipating the sniper fire those bars could attract. No doubt you'll also want to tape your dog tags, or get those little Ken Nolan rubber frames." It looked like he was lagging a frame or two. "To make them clankless." His face showed he caught up. "Where are you going?"

"To Alpha Company, Captain."

I nodded, "Got time for coffee?"

He nodded, "Yes Sir, thanks."

A little dab of C4 always did a nice job of brewing the C rats mixture labeled as coffee. Once lit, the stuff burned hot for longer than one might think. C rats coffee is coffee only due to lack of availability of anything else. His facial expression showed he wasn't used to the gruff stuff yet. We talked a bit, or more correctly, he talked. The lieutenant had volunteered for combat while at Quantico, Pops-oh graciously obliged him. He was of a well to do family, had an engineering degree, a sweetheart, and couldn't wait to take home a little honor to his people. After coffee he ran off to finish his check-in.

I just sat there a while.

He was a decent sort, displaying no evidence of the edge he was going to need, but really, how could he? He'd never in his life needed that edge, probably didn't even know of it. The edge of a blade is a kind of thing you desperately would prefer your family and friends never know about, much less be obliged to employ. The lieutenant could still talk about himself like he was with college friends in a student beer joint. It felt to me he considered this another OCS exercise through the hills at Quantico. He was still completely human. I hoped he could listen to his platoon's combat veterans and put together a real picture, real fast, something he cheerfully acknowledged when I told him. Later, in the afternoon, he headed out to Alpha Company.

"See ya, Skipper," he waved as his jeep pulled away to join a short column going to Hill 22.

"Good luck to you," I returned the wave.

There he went, another bright nice guy headed into a world of shit. Our Lady of the Luck doesn't care about bright, nice guy, world of shit, or much of anything we're concerned with; she manages a show of her own.

The following week I went to Hill 22 to liaison with Alpha's Six Actual concerning an air strike in his TAOR. After completing the op business I inquired about the lieutenant. The Six told me that he'd been assigned to the first platoon. On the first break of his first patrol, the lieutenant casually flopped down under a tree alongside a trail at a stream crossing, like he'd probably done a thousand times in his life in the world. Apparently his RO screamed a warning, which the lieutenant dismissed. A booby trap did what the damned things do and the lieutenant was dead when the Bones got to him.

⊙

"Blow the shit out of this fucking place, Skipper," one of Alpha's tough guys quietly directed as he heard F4s arrive on station, high above us.

He was referring to the village sprawling across the flats below that had claimed many Marine lives. The surrounding area was increasingly hot. Friendlies had been evacuated months earlier, but the village population was increasing; no children, woman, or old folks were seen there. Alpha Company favored removal of the village.

That I could do, with a little assistance from the air wing

The machine gunner who was set up directly in front of us, spit over his gun, then looked at me. I nodded to him, thinking about some bright faces I saw that were gone now, then turned to the 3.5 gunner.

"Hit the center of the joint, hold for my signal," I said.

He acknowledged with a head nod as I took the handset to brief the F4s.

"Run on a heading of 3-5-2, pull off to starboard."

I picked a heading of three-five-two because it provided lengthwise access to the village area, making life a little simpler when delivering ordnance; cleared the aircraft through mountains and set up things well, should one of them take a hit; ran the aircraft parallel to our position so they could work sans additional worry of our position relative to ordnance impact; and made directing ordnance delivery around the target area easier for me. Running the delivery pattern starboard kept the flight away from even more hostile country, and that particular day winds weren't of significance.

"Be cautious of the mountains on pull off," I told them. "Drop bombs in pairs first, I may change that, depending upon what you stir up. We're cold, doubt it'll stay that way. Stand by for a Willy Peter mark."

I tapped the gunner on the shoulder. The 3.5 sang its abrupt whooshing tune, mangled brush behind it. Tough guy immediately went over and stomped out a nascent brush fire then laughed, perhaps at putting out a potential fire to protect an environment that hid things that killed us. The WP round blossomed in the center of the village. The shot could not have been better. I thumped the gent on the helmet for the nice work, motioned people down, and then gave my attention to the aircraft.

"One, do you have the smoke?"

"Firm, Hanworth."

"Confirm you hold us tally."

"Firm, Hanworth. We see you down there."

"Okay One. Cleared hot, hit the smoke."

"Roger, give me a couple of seconds," he had to come around a few more degrees to get on the run-in heading, "One's in."

BAH-KAH-BLOUWEE!

The center of the village erupted. The platoon was silent for a moment. They watched the F4 execute a really shit hot pull off, then burst into cheers. Tactical Marine air and tactical Marine ground forces; anybody know how you do better?

"One's off," he replied.

Beautifully off. I wished he could have heard the cheers and felt the emotional lift from the platoon.

"Sweet, One, sweet, break. Two, hit three o'clock at fifty meters from One's hits." Automatic weapons fire erupted down in the village. "Okay gents, target turned hot, automatic weapons. Repeat, hot target."

"Roger, hot-target. Two's-in." A little automatic weapons fire didn't slow down Two.

My spirit, heart, and eyes were with the aircraft, while my body, tactile senses, and tactical mind were with the infantry. What an incredible perceptive expansion.

WAH-DOOMP!

XAH-CRUMP!

YAH-BLAMAH!

ZAH-APTUMPF!

The first flight of F4s expended their bombs. I called for napalm; they left half the village smoldering. After working a second flight around the village, the other half of it lay in smoking nothingness. The aircraft took some automatic weapons fire, as did we, but the F4s and the platoon's gunners wrapped up the hostile fire quickly. Endo that village.

Chapter 16

Divert

The battalion CO meandered through his COC bunker one night, just after a Magic Dragon reversed a NVA concocted plan to terminate a Delta Company patrol. I still had a "Basketball" (a GV from the VMGR squadron at Da Nang) on station dropping flares. No one in the bunker was willing to relax yet.

"So when do you want to go back to the wing for a few days," the colonel stated.

That sounded like a question didn't it? Well, battalion commanders really don't ask questions. They phrase things in the declarative with the inflection backed off, allowing opportunity to provide them information. It's a command thing that increases in complexity as the size of the command increases. If one doesn't understand the mechanism, meaningful conversation with commanders can be difficult.

"Beg your pardon, Colonel?"

It is cool to ask commanders questions, just not many. Did I hear that correctly? Was he referring to pleasurable activity in the future? The future had become fantasy-like visions of unlikely possibilities, rather than progression toward probability, and was attained by adroitly working the next few seconds of right now situations. The ambush of the Delta unit, along with considerations of what might happen next, definitely had my attention. The thought of getting an A4 into the sky, however, nearly completely displaced my attention.

"You must maintain your proficiency."

"Absolutely, Sir," I replied in a daze, "I'll have details tomorrow."

Things turned out fine for the Delta patrol, they found equipment and five dead enemy, ran their planned route, and got back sans anything farther.

"We have a bird that needs to go to the PAR facility at Atsugi," a squadron opso at Chu Lai told me on the phone the next morning. Atsugi was a Naval Air Station located not all that far from Tokyo. Hmm.

"I'm not able to cut anyone loose right now," he said, "and it's overdue up there. You could take it if you want, then wait a couple of days and return one coming out of PAR."

If I want? The major had no idea.

On second thought, perhaps he did. Three days or so between deli of an aircraft and pickup of another couldn't have been mere coincidence, any more time would have caused rattle from somebody. Passing the task to an aviator gone FAC was truly a princely thing to do. Had battalion and the group coordinated this deal? Sometimes I had the wonderful feeling unknown allies were covering me.

Next day, after an amazing series of transportive devices and helpful people getting me to Chu Lai, I flew a bashed up A4E, a veteran of many sorties, to NAS Cubie Point in the Philippines. Cubie Point was the NAS at Subic Bay, a nice harbor on the southwest coast of Luzon. I ran into a couple of FAC friends who somehow managed to get to Cubie Point for something or other. The three of us contributed to the Corps' sterling reputation for sober, intelligent behavior that evening in the nearby city of Olongapo. I was so glad to be where hostile fire wasn't imminent, that over-relaxation occurred, you might say.

The following morning I woke with not one clue as to my whereabouts. There was this rack—you know, soft, warm, thick mattress, linen. I was in it and it was inside a normal room with normal fixtures and plain old windows with views of trees and flowers. Was I dreaming? No enemy outside the perimeter, not even a noticeable perimeter. The sweet fresh air didn't smell like cordite, smokeless powder, death; I had not the foggiest idea of how to behave. Thank goodness for friends, they're likely the only reason I was at the BOQ at all. One of them was stretched across two racks, looking about like I felt. The other wasn't available for comment. Articles of his clothing were sprinkled indiscriminately about the room. I didn't have the heart to wake the one or interrupt the other. I wish I had at least thanked them for covering me. One was killed shortly after returning to the combat zone; I haven't seen the other since.

I wandered about the base, listing a bit to starboard, over to port, then back to starboard. This listing continued while getting a weather briefing, filing the flight plan, and checking out the aircraft. I don't think the Navy particularly cared about one Marine or his shot up aircraft. After all, a Marine is just a Marine. A listing, mumbling combat Marine is probably even worse.

Now I know you know we breathe oxygen, and I know you know oxygen is a smaller portion of a breath. Okay, but the A4 fed pure oxygen from a LOX (liquid oxygen) converter, which meant each breath contained only oxygen. I mention this because of the amazing effect the pure stuff has on a less than completely alert state of being. Two deep breaths—bink! Head cleared. Two more—zampopple! Eyes, which had been squinted against light, opened to rediscover that light was for seeing.

After taking in a few sights, the queasiness evaporated, brain re-fired, normal awareness returned. Forty footer and I accomplished acceptable separation from the planet's surface, flew the SID reasonably precisely, and managed to turn out of the SID in the proper direction. Machine noises from the Scoot were strong and balanced as we climbed northward. I realized, rather suddenly, that I was alive, and wouldn't have to kill anything here to remain that way. We leveled at cruise altitude, passed Clark Air Force Base, and cleared the island. There was nothing but gaseous blue around us, liquid blue below. In a machine I loved, working the medium I dug, everything else dropped away. Life was good.

Cubie Point to Naha, Okinawa, is a zink or two over eleven hundred nautical miles, with just a pinch of the leg over land. For about six hundred miles of it, you're out of contact with anyone by physical means in a Marine Corps combat version Alpha four echo. Chu Lai to the Philippines was the same sort of thing, but due to ecstasy, octoflugerons and whifferdoozies (nonspecific aerobatics done just for joy) the whole flight out of country, I really didn't notice. I checked my position once and lo, the destination lay directly off the forty footer's prow.

On the Naha leg I felt detached from the things of men in the magnificent blue, though I sat in a manmade machine and spent some time thinking about friends that were no longer. It was comfortable up there alone.

My form of navigation was old as compasses, dead reckoning (DR). You know, take into account everything you can, fly this heading for this length of time at this speed, look around for checkpoints or your destination. It's not possible to accomplish serious positioning using this method on long legs over the ocean. You have to believe in yourself.

Population on this planet may be a little cold, but the planet is nonetheless beautiful. The ocean and sky take on new meaning when afforded time to view them completely. Colors, shapes, and textures calmed, leaving me with a sense of awe. Getting lost in the blue high over the Pacific for a few hours was definitely in order.

Not in the least intimidated by all that space, the forty-foot weapons platform rushed along making noises to itself while I looked at the ocean, clouds, and atmosphere from our position quite some distance above white puffy clouds scurrying across the ocean. I couldn't sit up there amid all that wonder as just an observer, and so, I played a few games with the sky and ocean. What magnificent views of this Earth. What a fabulous time.

Okinawa popped onto the horizon as expected. Naha Air Force Base was CAVU to the moon and I had the runway in sight from forever. Good old DR with an accurate compass can take one a long way in this world.

Naha AFB was soft, warm, at ease. And there was something about the sea and the way the sun illuminated things on the west end. I had the aircraft refueled, went to the officers club to eat about three lunches, which caused interesting looks from a few Air Force pilots. Their eyes seemed to ask if all Marines were like that. I just nodded, smiled, shoveled in more food. It was unlikely any of them were in Olongapo clubs the previous evening, and likely they all managed decent breakfasts that morning.

Scoot and I encountered a horde of returning F102s on departure, say about six thousand of them, seeming to come from everywhere as we crossed the island's coast. The weapons platform had two full drops, too much fuel to maneuver well against the

Delta Darts, not enough to allow time for flailing about. I was on my way to Atsugi and so declined obvious but unspoken offers of F102 versus A4 maneuvering contests.

NAS Atsugi was obscured by a storm front. Forty footer and I executed an actual Tacan penetration in heavy wind and rain. Yokohama approach handed us to Atsugi for a precision approach. I finally saw runway lighting, right at the two hundred fifty feet, quarter mile, single-piloted aircraft minimum. Despite gusty crosswind conditions, the precision approach crew did a beautiful job of lining us up, and the weapons platform and I landed straight ahead in the rain, right on the runway centerline. We taxied to the Overhaul and Refurbish (O&R) flight line through crashing sheets that brought Iwakuni to mind.

A plane captain with an umbrella met us, his eyes wandering to the patched bullet holes and banged up areas of the flown-nearly-to-death A4E. You probably know the Marine Corps manages to use tactical equipment in tactical situations, but that particular Alpha four was about used up. The plane captain held the huge umbrella over us while I accomplished a post flight walk-around. I patted the delta-winged amigo on its wet little radar nose cone. Though obviously ridden hard in combat and some rather serious play with the planet, that Scooter unfalteringly flew us across an appreciable chunk of it.

"What's it like in the combat zone Sir?" a Chief Petty Officer asked after I handed him the aircraft's yellowsheet on which I had griped everything as either inoperative or marginally operative (everything but the Tacan and radio, that is). Good pieces remained at Chu Lai.

"Oh. It's - umm, ah," I stared out a few clicks for a moment, "agh, I can't remember, Chief."

I didn't mean to be unfriendly, but I just didn't want to think about it. People here were accustomed to carrier-based aviators with Yankee Station tales of glory, not of infantry horror. They could still smile and laugh easily. The chief nodded in an understanding way. I asked if they had coffee (have you ever heard of a NAS that didn't?). They also had many questions combined with a lot of good treatment. We all know Marines don't need to be treated anything like human beings, even so, those few days at Atsugi were pleasant.

Before aircraft could be released to fleet service, an acceptance flight test was required. The PAR maintenance officer had A4s in hold status for these test flights and was looking for a designated test pilot. My return aircraft wouldn't be ready for a couple of days. No doubt Yankee Station squadrons could use the aircraft, so I flew several acceptance check flights. Disconnection of hydraulically assisted flight control systems, to measure aircraft mechanical state of trim, was part of an A4 acceptance check. Of course with just a mechanical flight control system, the aircraft flew like a slug. Well, Nihon (Nippon, Japan) also has beautiful sky and striking scenery; there is nothing like a little ride around glistening Fujiyama with the aircraft's hydraulics unplugged.

One morning the aircraft I was to return sat on the flight line. The bullet holes were gone and so was the black residue around the cannon mounts. It wore a fresh coat of new paint, with compressor blades that shined from inside the intake ducting, a canopy with no scratches, and tires that were black instead of dark olive-gray. What a pretty thing. You see, PAR didn't just masking tape an aircraft and paint the thing with spray cans. It was disassembled, cleaned, and reassembled with anything out of spec returned to spec or replaced. The new-looking aircraft contained a large number of new pieces. I took the magnificence on a test hop, signed it off, and headed back to Chu Lai. It was considerably crisper than the shot up collection of metal and heart I left at Atsugi, although its fresh engine needed a few hours of serious spinning to properly loosen. The engine was within spec, exactly what PAR was supposed to do, but the A4E's Pratt and Whitney engine wasn't really combat aviator responsive that way. Within reason, looser was better where combat aviators and A4 power plants were concerned.

Return was reverse of the course up. Out of Cubie Point an A3 bound for Yankee station escorted us into combat zone airspace. Single-piloted tactical aircraft required an escort into combat zone airspace, which was fine as interceptor scrambles and possible missile shoots weren't on my just-gotta-do-it list anyway. As Our Lady of the Luck would have it, the country was still there, the coast was familiar, first-encounter mystique long gone. I thought about the battalion, wondering what I would find at the hill as I broke off from the A3 and set up a cruise descent toward Chu Lai. On the east field, ground crews were loading ordnance, repairing things, doing the usual. I taxied into the chocks and shut down the shiny aircraft.

"Nice looking bird, Sir," the staff sergeant behind the squadron yellowsheet desk said as I signed the aircraft in with everything fully operational. He smiled, "A few missions will fix that."

I smiled, interfacing with him okay, but empty again. Check-in with the battalion via telephone was a real experience in telephone circuit management practices, also an amazing show of cable stringing and equipment planting. It seemed there was actually a means of connecting hundreds of segments of EE8 wire pairs between Hill 10 and Chu Lai. Incredible. Some brave men covered by capable infantry strung a large portion of those segments through something over sixty miles of not at all friendly country. Patching various segments, after the enemy cut them somewhere every fifteen minutes, had to be a real task. After about a million circuit connections, and less than one hundred minutes, I got the battalion, then went to the rigger shop where I picked up my gear, flak jacket, M-16, and a collection of full magazines. I caught a hop to Da Nang with an old squadron mate in MAG 13's Hummer.

"How have you been?" he asked.

"Well," long pause, "I'm still here. How are you?"

"I'm okay. Man you've changed. Your body and face are real hard now. You look killer mean. That grunt stuff isn't much fun, is it?"

I should look mean; I am a killer. Not by complete free choice, not even in my wildest dreams, but I am. Now I knew I had killing blood. I didn't want to know that. I'd probably do it again in a few hours, him too, in the service of our beloved country. I covered a sigh with a long noisy breath.

"Oh," not as long a pause, "Oh—it's um -"

That was an introduction to the tremendous gulf separating combat infantry from people who haven't been out there. It's like the gulf between combat aviators and other aviators, but somehow much more dense. I really couldn't talk about it with him because there existed no frame of reference. If you've been to a place, you've been there; if you haven't, you haven't. All the words in the world can't paint a reasonable picture for a non-participant, nor do they fool a participant. Never did give him an answer.

A battalion jeep met us at Da Nang, a considerate move on the part of the battalion. About halfway back to the hill we took a few rounds of sniper fire. The driver looked about fourteen, like he'd been in country for two minutes. He turned an even lighter shade of pale, looked at me with a most imploring oh-please-Sir-get-us-the-fuck-out-of-this expression. I swung my M-16 toward the fire and gave him a real Joe Combat set of instructions.

"Drive fast. Stay in the middle of the road," I barked.

Pretty good, huh? I didn't mention snipers were sometimes diversions for mines. I didn't have the sniper's location, so I cranked a few rounds into the most suspicious places and quit waiting for the mine about a click down the road.

Artillery was running a fire mission when we arrived at the hill, which seemed to increase the driver's nervousness. I dropped off the jeep, waving him on toward Motor T.

"Glad you're back," the battalion XO greeted between howitzer blasts. He found me fast.

"Oh yes Sir, me too." Yes indeed, max titillation.

"We need you to plan air for an op."

"Aye Sir, let me check on the TAC party, I'll be right along."

"Your people are fine, let's get over to the COC bunker."

The hill's battery of 105s was firing on something out in hostile country to the west, on Hill 502. Familiar gray-black eruptions, small things hurtling through the atmosphere where rounds impacted, brought me completely back to the hill, the war. Is life not a grand gas? Combat framework, in-country odors—a real cold reworked thoroughly into me. The Atsugi trip diminished to another of those some other life, almost recallable memories. I checked the M-16's magazine and made the weapon cold. Looking around again, I took a breath and followed the major.

Chapter 17
Shuffle

There was a little area northwest of the hill near a turn in the river in Alpha's TAOR that was continuously worrisome. Alpha Six actual had modified patrols to accommodate checks of the place but our uneasiness remained. I went to talk with Bravo Six Actual about a reconnaissance patrol across the river to the south where a portion of his TAOR offered an excellent view of the area.

"Okay, take the second platoon out overnight and set up a 'bush," the company commander said with a smile. "I can move everything in my universe around for you one night, and a little overnight will help snap in some new guys. But I won't let you cross the river and I won't let you go with less than a platoon. That's not my TAOR over there. The area you want to look at could get hot in about a heartbeat. Charles sneaks down the river and camps out in the damned caves they built under those flats."

He took a breath, speaking more or less to himself, "We need another company," pause, "Alpha needs a couple more platoons, I need two more here."

"Then maybe I'm right about rockets staged there."

"Maybe," he nodded, "I think so." His voice diminished considerably, "You'll hear in a few days. We're setting up to go in there soon with two companies. You'll run air first." His smile implied a lot of air.

"Okay." Something active at last. "What about my patrol?"

"Do it. Shuffle on out there. I can find a lot of reasons for it." He thought a minute. "It'll be a new nugget and a few new guys, you take care of them. The brown bar runs it unless he's dangerous. If you cross that river, don't come back. I'll finish anything the NVA leave of you." As the wicked smile slowly disappeared from his face, he turned to a battered map and pointed at a hill across the river from the suspect area. "See this hill?" he asked.

"Sure," I smiled. He had worked out the whole thing before I even asked.

"Might work okay if you set up there. You could get a look at the area to know what kind of air you want. The new guys can set up a 'bush with something behind their backs. It won't spring, there won't be anything to spring it, but it'll be a good snap in. See this area here?"

He placed his finger on a draw between small ridges, about halfway to the river. "Go through there on your way out and look around. Bravo three heard something in there last night. I've got eleven alpha looking at that area today, but it won't hurt for you to check it out."

He walked me out of his tent. "I'll set it up for tomorrow night and let Alpha know you're out there."

As we stepped into the company street, he spied the company gunny herding two Marines about thirty meters away. He grabbed my arm and hurried us back into his tent.

"You sorry-assed maggots!" he snarled.

"What's up?" I asked.

He shrugged his shoulders. "I don't want to know yet. I don't want us to be seen and put the gunny in the position of having to do something official. He'll involve me if necessary."

"What do you think?" I asked.

"Weed."

In a hot area? "You're kidding." Maybe ignorance was why extranjero officers were avoided. After registering my disconcerted look, he shook his head.

"Hel-LO-oh. Awake now? In a way I can't blame them," he said.

He lit a standard Marine Corps Marlboro cigarette with his camouflaged Zippo lighter. So did I, with a flat black one. Incidentally, unlike the commercial version, Marine Corps

Marlboro cigarettes are cured in bulldog urine, to assist in maintaining our bearing.

He casually blew at least three thousand cubic feet of smoke upward. "They've seen *tacsan* shit. We all get our share when we go out, I know, but these people get it every day. It gets to them after a while. Smashed up buddies and the rest of the shit they see so often makes them weird. They want to forget things. A little marijuana reshapes them to numb, which I think they take as comfortable. It doesn't solve anything." He deftly flicked ashes about seven feet, into his trash 105 casing. "As far as I'm concerned it makes things worse because they don't deal with anything well. But they're numb for the moment. I think that's what they want; they don't have to deal with pain or that confusion about what's right. That's probably nice, but it also fucks with their selective mechanism. Looking at a piece of dirt can have more priority then getting rounds into the NVA about to kill them. It makes people miss things and it puts us all at more risk." He checked the company street. "I don't like it, but will not article fifteen or court martial any of my troops unless they fuck up royally. I need them. I need the salts cuz new guys can't cut this shit for a while."

I knew what he meant, shared his feelings about things seen and combat people. I didn't know drugs were a problem. "Didn't know it was a deal."

He peeked out at the company street again. "It isn't really. Not here. Not yet. I hope we can keep the shit out of here. We definitely don't have the problem some other organizations have with it. Remember the sweep with that outside outfit?"

Outside meant other than Marine Corps.

"Yeah." I recalled how loud and disorganized the unit was on the hill, during the op we heard them from over two clicks away. They took most of the op casualties.

He turned back toward me. "Gunny and the Top handle things unless they're huge. I'm not there until they pass an issue to me. The arrangement works fine, everybody seems happy with it." He walked me out of his tent a second time. "Come see me when you get back."

Saddle up. Those eternal, infernal, diurnal, sometimes nocturnal words. The set up for a hump, maybe worse, one never knew. Through the wire in time to achieve the objective hill before dark, the platoon trudged rice paddies, into high-grass country with its myriad of tree lines and good ambush sites. New guys ceaselessly looked around, missed things; combat vets confined themselves to using as little energy as possible, missed nothing. New guys showed interest in everything. Old timers' interests lay in potentially threatening things. One group was completely responsive, the other limited concern to protecting or destroying life. New gents wanted to talk about things they saw; salts just tilted a head or briefly inclined a weapon's muzzle toward points of interest. No doubt you know how we looked from the mass of photographs, TV feed, and video footage. Anyone perceive the incredible group dynamic? The camaraderie, professionalism, dedication, precision, and concern for each other I experienced in the bush were powerful.

Good Marines are many things to many people to be sure. When the lies have ceased, the startling truth is right in front of you: they are pros. When the bullets are real and the stakes are body parts and lives, good Marines are my pick for the people I want around for flat out unit combat.

AK rounds cracked over the serpentine column of Marines when the point was a little way into thick trees. New guys dropped like something jerked their feet from under them, as nearly everyone did the first time. The Salts simultaneously moved weapons to their individual shoot right now positions; turned alternately outward while settling on one knee; scanned the underbrush for trip wires, booby traps, enemy, etc.; set up to cover the machine gun, radio ops, officers; ensured new guys remained well-positioned and ready; checked grenades, knives, ammo; communicated with looks, gestures, quiet sounds; and arranged themselves to handle about anything, from any direction.

That all occurred in perhaps two seconds. A Thumper coughed its sudden chug near the front of the column, most likely the point's as this one favored the M-79. A single M-16 fired a short burst as the M-79 round detonated, probably the slack in support of the point. I couldn't see the front of the column, but it was an easy picture to paint. Then silence. Everybody alert and set. Weapons ready. Silence.

Talk to the company on the radio, quietly, set up support fire, and let what was going to happen come on in. Silence. This time nothing happened. Soon we were on the road again. We all got a look at the sniper's mangled body as we passed. Bullets tear up and push around bodies; thumpers definitely do not leave neatly arranged pieces.

We swept the draw, finding only crushed grass where the overheard people apparently stopped for awhile. This set of new guys was good. They showed a lot of spirit, heading into the draw like it was Tarawa, thoroughly covered by the old timers. There just wasn't anything around.

Darkness vacuumed up the last little areas of light as we got to the objective hill. "No fires!" echoed around the position as new guys made sure they did the right thing. I suspect people on the west coast of the U.S. could have heard them. The position afforded a great view of the suspect area. I broke out some beans and franks, which were a lot better when cheese could be melted into the beans, and turned to observing the place through binoculars.

Pop!

An 81 mm mortar flare blossomed overhead. Unbelievable. The new lieutenant registered our position with mortars on Hill 10 to confirm preset fire mission coordinates should we require that support. But he also registered our position with many sets of eyes along the river and out in jungle hills to the west. It was a textbook response not fitting the live environment. We all had to learn of course, but damn, not only would there be nothing worthwhile to observe across the river, we would have to worry about getting hit all night.

In the morning I managed a decent look at the target area while we saddled up for return. Fortunately we didn't see beanso on the trip back. Setting in an ambush all night, even one that didn't spring, precluded sleep for the involved gents. New guys normally were so hyped their first few 'bushes that they exhausted about three months of energy in a few hours.

"So," Bravo Six said when I found him, "I heard about the Quantico move."

"So, now he knows," I replied. "I think the lesson was inexpensive, we'll know fairly soon. They need to learn of course, but looked fine to me. They worked together, have spirit, paid attention to the old timers, and forgetting the night patrols' 101 move, the lieutenant seems promising. He's appropriately cautious, looks after his troops, exhibits good tactical sense. He did a nice job of setting up that little rush."

"That's good," he nodded, showing satisfaction. "A confirmed kill and no one hit is a good way to bust cherries. Do you know how you're going to cover us?"

"Yeah, thanks for the patrol. I'll prep the place with delay fused ordnance to dig things up, then proximity fusing to clear the surface, paying special attention to that little wiggle at the bend." He nodded again. The uneven riverside area bothered all of us. "We'll keep a couple of flights on station with delta twos, nape, and guns for awhile, presuming wing has the assets."

He looked at me quizzically, "What's a delta two?"

"Oops, sorry. Five hundred pound Snake-eye. Want arty prep?"

He smiled, "Hell, I want everything, but not without air."

"Okay. How's that scheme?"

"Good, but you're air, you tell me. I'll take anything you get us. You're welcome for the patrol."

As fate would have it, Tet of 1968 interrupted our scheme. The cease-fire caused the operation to be postponed, and the Tet Offensive occurred before we got to the place. NVA fired rockets at Hill 10 from the jungle past Hill 502 to keep heads down while they launched at Da Nang from the area observed on the patrol. The hill's howitzers were too short-ranged to hit the rocket site firing at the battery, and the artillery CP was principal recipient of the rockets. Remember the accurate sketches of the battalion's positions? Eighty-one crews got rounds off that prematurely ended the rocket fire into Da Nang, but not before a couple of the damned things hit the airfield. Hill 10 took many hits, including a direct on the artillery CP. Many Marines became casualties that night. Patrols from every company were in contact. At one time it seemed the entire world was a firefight.

Next day came the sun. NVA lost several thousand troops and the demise of the VC was assured. I've heard 55,000 VC died that night. I don't know about the figures, but I do know that was the end of southern control of the war effort. There weren't enough VC left to mount anything. Hanoi picked up undisputed military and political control of the invasion effort, losing thousands more troops along with the couple of objectives they took within a short time. More destruction, more war, more death; probably even the Reap needed a little R&R.

MACV, or somebody, insisted upon counter-insurgency tactics while NVA steadily increased its invasion efforts, escalating the war. Didn't any high-level people read Clausewitz, Mushashi, Sun Tzu, study tactics anymore, or just listen to troops in the field in the situations? Remote leadership, boorah.

The Tet Offensive was set up by a thirty-six hour cease-fire, which of course meant we ceased while they fired. This was essentially the same type of situation as the Christmas cease fire of 1967, during which many good combat people, forced by administrative leaders to just stand there and take it, were killed. Not initiating conflict is one thing, but can you believe combat people in an active combat zone were ordered to not return fire? You know, watch your compadres die while you whistle, or something like that. One of those distant administrative egomaniacal leaders should have come to the hill, gotten involved in the show for a day or so. Think they would have stood in place with useless weapons, flashing their preposterous false smile while the NVA shot them to pieces? Think their I-know-everything-in-the-universe ego would have repelled the bullets?

I wasn't aware there were people who considered Tet 1968 a hostile victory until I returned to the USA. Damn the effect of delusory words. No one ever asked us, the gents out there in the situations, about anything, or came to learn anything. I guess they thought they knew everything. Is it ever thus?

An Apache saying: "It is better to have less thunder in the mouth, more lightning in the hand."

Chapter 18

Matter of Time

In country, the Marine combat infantry version of the bush was a collection of different places at different times. More importantly, it was a state of being. People related to the bush from individual shaping and viewpoints, with little regard for specific location. Mountains, jungle, rice paddies, plains, sand hills, or beaches. All could be the bush, the place just a means of expression, important in that comprehension of the medium being worked was essential. A moderate venture through the 'bush could easily get through a variety of places. I should imagine conversation with combat veterans would result in that number of different pictures of the bush, even if the people served concurrently in the same unit. I believe the conversations also would reveal a shared basic mental framework.

A remote command post might be the bush, a position within the DMZ, places north, sometimes just ten meters outside a perimeter. At all events the bush was away from known routines and expected occurrences, questionable concepts at best in combat. Nothing was on time and often not at the anticipated location, which probably didn't matter as activities rarely occurred as one thought, anyway.

Running across "friendly" locals was always thrilling; we upset them, walking around out there with weapons and death around us. They didn't know who the good guys were either. We all wanted the right thing, but right was difficult to view at times. Cultural differences, years of oppression, and a deep suspicion of outsiders, added to our incomplete knowledge of their situation and attitudinal presets, all helped keep right well veiled. The right thing normally gave way to expediency of the moment. It was prudent to keep it simple and continue to live, which demanded most of one's attention in the bush anyway. Local population was uneasiness added to a much too long list of uneasiness.

The NVA carried the antithetical responsibility of destroying us so it could accomplish its purposes, charged to it by the government. It's possible that numbers of NVA did the required job while also wondering what it was all about. I don't know, never had an opportunity to talk with one who wasn't trying to kill me. The NVA was a dangerous enemy: ruthless, singular of purpose, tenacious, and deceitful. Training taught NVA soldiers that only dead Marines weren't bothersome, and that it was less horrible to die than to be taken alive by Marines. I didn't see Marines decapitate and dismember anyone, much less set up the separated body parts just so in an obvious location. I did see the results of NVA doing such things—I suppose just another little uneasiness of the bush.

One Seven sat in a defensive posture to assist Da Nang in remaining in place and friendly, obliging us to take whatever NVA cared to hand out. The battalion didn't have the privilege of running down the enemy on its turf, or taking the fight to it, which is what we really knew how to do. The Marine Corps is assault, not occupy, those are different mentalities requiring diverse tactics and mechanisms. The battalion was required to be set for anything; I was obliged to expand my idea of anything.

The bush was an isolation requiring individuals to do everything for themselves. Support was far away regardless of distance, likely nonexistent if your radio had bullet holes in it. If you were out of water, you were out, that was that. The same went for food and ammo. A re-supply may or may not occur, and it was never advisable to bet on one. People who got immersion foot, the trots, rashes, that damned fluttery high fever peculiar to the area, or whatever, just got it. Anywhere but the bush those things were cause for attention. But in the bush, in combat, people had to do the best they could with what was immediately available. Bones always did what he could to assist, but he was on his own also. After a firefight or two it was likely a couple of hits or dings required attention because a simple little nick could become a festering monstrosity in short order. Nicks and dings hurt, throbbed, and sometimes caused poor weapons movement when precise movement was necessary. They oozed, bled, and generally drove people nutso.

One encountered various defoliant agents in the bush, disbursed by the Ranch Hand gents, the most notorious of which was Agent Orange (though Agents White, Purple, and a few others also were used). No one with whom I worked could tell the difference. None of us knew which agent was where, or even what the stuff might be. I remember weed-killer chemical odor in some areas and a little shortness of breath, slight tingling, or bristling sensations on exposed skin. In one area, I remember fairly intense feelings of nausea that caused us to break the patrol for perhaps twenty minutes to regain ourselves. No one advised us of sprayings or potential danger, and of course we didn't question activities that seemed in support of us. No one on our side would do anything to damage us, right?

Sleep in the bush meant becoming unconscious for short periods, or perhaps nodding off from time to time, but definitely not sleeping as in rest. One continued to grind along until one dropped, which with a little regard from Our Lady of the Luck, wouldn't occur until one was out of the bush.

No doubt you've heard about C rations. These are, theoretically, a sort of food. Some meals were okay, most were acceptable only because people were so hungry that what was consumed didn't matter much. Usually remfs "liberated" popular C meals, leaving things for bush people I'm not sure a hungry non-Marine animal would eat. I've heard the meals were nutritionally complete. I don't know if I believe that. It is true I'm still here with a healthy body, but some of that stuff, particularly the egg slime in wolverine vomit, was too horrible for words. And ham and butter beans, affectedly known as ham and motherfuckers for good reason, could rearrange your system, precluding eating anything for a while. Not all the weight lost in the bush was due to the stresses and strains of the job.

Cold prevailed, not icy hostile intent, just absence of warmth with no attempt at friendly, hostile, or anything. Groups went out cold, usually came in colder, sans at least one starting member. Even without contact people were dropped to booby traps, snipers, sometimes to the "just had enough" thing that caved people in on themselves. People-to-people combat is hard on everyone involved.

It wasn't really possible to fault a gent who had been in the bush most of his time for finally arriving at a point where he just couldn't do it for an interval. Going through one thing encountered out there once in your life was a big deal. When sudden traumatic events came in series of multiple, near-daily occurrences, they got weighty and involved—people got weird. Though some lasted longer than others, everyone in the bush in combat knows that weirdness. Slowly or quickly, the bush moved individuals to a state where nothing meant anything, and the only important thing was enduring. The bush was a stark, ruthless place, having not much to do with being human, only with being at all.

Understand something, for all who participated, combat clearly displayed its results to everyone involved. We knew our individual endos lay ahead; it was a matter of time, that was all. How many seconds, minutes, hours did you have before the Reap executed a pick-up? Would you get home before it happened?

Consider the change in your working mental posture that would likely occur if you lived with a group of people trying to kill you daily. Imagine if you had no idea where or who they would be, that you couldn't put anything between them and yourself, that either they got you or you got them, and that there were considerably more of them than you. Say they killed your work partner, the family across the street, or the people in the car at the corner. What if you could hear them killing somebody every night? You really wouldn't be able to consider much outside the conflict, would you? Give some thought to the monumental effects that would likely have on your life and you'll begin to get an idea of what I mean by weird. The longer you're in the situation, the more incidents you get through, the more of them you get, the more of your compadres they get, the weirder it—and you—become. And should you depart the situation before resolution, whether or not you had a choice in the departure, you have to live with an internal feeling of having quit on people.

Most people I was with aimed everything at keeping them, their compadres there the next few seconds. If you could be there a few seconds at a time and you could do that enough times, you might get through it. Throughout all this there was a mission, a reason for being out there that had to be considered as well as survival. Hostile fire or not, the question of what must we do, what must I do to remain alive, prevailed in the bush. Another approach was complete fixation upon each little detail of whatever one was doing. Or one could think about nothing, just not be present until response to something became necessary. People who spent too much time in the bush, saw too much combat, lost too many combat partners, could frame such that it didn't matter if they endured or not. It was only important they were moving well when the Reap showed up for them.

The kind of combat where opponents see each other clearly enough to completely grasp what really happens to individuals and groups during the combat requires considerable recovery time once out of the environment; to return from the place I mentioned above takes a much longer, continuously dedicated effort. All SEA combat veterans have had to find at least one reason to rejoin the civilization that put them there and then seemed to abandon and curse them for their service—not always such an easy task. The latter, more serious condition requires finding a reason satisfactorily explaining still being alive, and a reason for remaining on the Earth, before the issues of returning from a combat posture to rejoin or reject a civilization may be addressed. As I said, return is difficult; it requires continuous effort and years.

The time-tube blur was worse still in the bush; one's past was gone, the next time-unit was questionable at best. Some people talked about getting back to the world and what they would do. To me, that seemed a desperate attempt to construct something warm amid the destructive, noticeably insane environment. People died in the bush, and not cleanly. Their dying under grotesque circumstances was something with which to deal that also generated effects. It was impossible for me to look at a ripped-apart carcass and figure I would get it like that. There were fewer weapons to offer cover, so everyone had to work harder. Who was next? What was next? When? The group diminished in number, chances diminished, and the world moved farther away.

NVA, along with a few leftover VC, wanted to ensure none of us saw the world again. Its soldiers were competent at destruction and death, requiring us to become the same to survive. You could try talking to them, but they didn't want to talk; they wanted to put a bayonet in your heart, blow your brains out, kill you any way they could. I don't know why. It was what they did. And it was what we did back to survive.

One could not work the bush in combat using logic from a normal life viewpoint and expect to live. The bush required bush combat logic, which required a reduction in normal human response to situations. This, in turn, reduced the state of being in my eyes, producing greater internal strife and anger, which had to be stuffed somewhere to be dealt with later. That is, if there was a later.

All this was playing on one's tube, yet one had to remain alert, fast, accurate, and fierce to keep one's compadres—and one's self— alive. We were tired, hungry, sore, hurt, and heartbroken. We felt less than human and written off as we dealt with tremendous loss and suffered from stupid little things like dysentery or war wounds. A lot of staff-level leadership had never seen combat or been near the bush, leading to demands for inappropriate or risky activities.

If you learned five million things in combat, you knew unequivocally that the five-million-and-first thing would show up within a short time, as every trip out opened a new world of possibilities. One had to be strong and functional, or it was likely that he, and probably a few immediate compadres, wouldn't come out of the bush under his own power. There were no decent options available. Everything had to be handled and I consciously and subconsciously invented means of dealing with everything. Though probably not the most healthy issue-resolving mechanisms, they supported continuance.

The reward for surviving the bush was the opportunity to go out again. Each situation survived bought us a little time and meant that the chance of getting back to the world with our pieces normally attached was perhaps a little brighter.

Chapter 19
Sheathed

The battalion XO primed me for a two-company sweep with tanks, through a section of Alpha Company's TAOR. "I want you out there," he said. "We're looking for a regiment, we'll need air if we get into something good."

Oh yeah, good. The XO needed to hit the bush a little more often. If we must have air support, it was anything but good. At zero dark thirty on op day one, a long line of combat Marines threaded through the hill's perimeter, zigzagging across dark rice paddies to the west. About ten meters off the hill I was dizzy, my eyes wouldn't remain focused.

"It'll be okay," I mumbled as I stumbled.

Bad call, right? I mean to participate in an op knowing you're not fully functional. Well you're right. It's a bad thing to do to your compadres. They expect and deserve your best, especially when their lives could depend on your state of function. But I heard prodigious grousing about officers in general avoiding the responsibilities of their positions, particularly in the field, and I was determined to be of service. So, I locked on the dilemma's horns: Can't manage the job at one hundred per cent of your capability if you go, which is what your compadres expect and deserve, but regardless of circumstance, you're just another wimp motherfucking leaky-dick officer if you don't. Your call?

After crossing the paddies, Bravo and Charley units linked with Marines from Alpha Company while Delta Company covered the south. The full op infantry machine proceeded toward the tanks that were to meet us to the north on firmer ground. By afternoon there was no indication of enemy activity and I was unable to stand. Either I had to move or I would fall down. So I staggered and stumbled, sauntering in little unsteady circles when we halted. Things progressively became stranger; my focus flicked back and forth between embellished memory and reality. Zap. Suddenly I was talking with a dead friend when he was alive. Zip. Was humping along on the op. Zap. Was talking with friends back at Chu Lai. Bip. Was with the column again. Bap. Was in the middle of a mission I flew north. Wap. Was back to the op. Each scenario was real; banging back and forth was especially good. Where the hell … what good was I?

Day receded, the sun settled behind mountains as the tanks set up in good-looking night defensive positions. The companies set in for the night as daylight diminished. I dropped, legs folded. I think I spoke to my corporal as I fell past him. I remember the pain when my chin collided with my rifle barrel. My sweat smelled a slightly saline scent as it hit the cool dirt.

Four days later I woke soaking wet in a rack with real sheets at the medical battalion facility near Hill 327. The bay was full of Marines from various field units, but I was the only officer, also one of few with no obvious physical damage. There were quiet comments, like "Fucking pussy officer medevaced himself." I presume I wasn't supposed to hear them, but one can never tell. I didn't react to them. I didn't care about much at the time; explanations to ignorant ridicule least of all. After several attempts at standing resulted in corpsmen scooping me off the deck, assisting me back to the rack, the comments ceased.

"Your fever got to a 106," a Bones told me. "You're lucky, Skipper."

I guess. Our Lady of the Luck again. It took a few more days to begin to feel even partly alive.

"What did you do to yourself?" the case surgeon wanted to know.

"Ah, well. I think forty four or so days without any real sleep may have something to do with it," I replied. "I've hardly slept since Tet, can't get my system to settle down enough to take the five minutes to eat right. I may have to kill some hostile in the middle of dinner. The fever had me off in la-la land. Anyhow, it just sort of came on, not the best timing."

"I don't know," he looked at me, "another few hours and you may not have been sitting there. You're not in any shape for combat or anything else right now. You've been taking your malaria pills every day, haven't you?"

I nodded, "They turn your feces into little green balls."

"Yes," he smiled, "well, they're important, they work. You looked malarial when you got here."

"Oh." I thought of fading into this semi-alive state a couple of times a year for the rest of my life, if I had a life.

"But I think you just ran all the way down. Antibiotics will take care of the malarial symptoms and fever, supplements and food will take care of the malnutrition. You need rest." He looked right at me, "I mean it. Your body looks strong, but it doesn't test strong. Rest. You hear me?"

"Yes. Okay. Thanks for fixing me up."

"You're welcome. Take the vitamin-mineral tablets and the electrolytes twice every day, and not multiple doses at once. Spread them out."

I guess the surgeon had seen a Marine before.

"Eat a lot while you're here. Rest. I thought about sending you home, but you've responded well to treatment. We need to watch you for a while, that was a high fever. Probably in ten or twelve days you can go back to the field so you can come back with bullet holes or shrapnel wounds in your Marine ass." He paused, "When you get home it's important to continue those malaria pills for a full year. I'm concerned about those symptoms."

I nodded. He said when you get home; I would have said if you get out of the combat zone.

The com-bat zone, fry-die zone, red zone, dead zone, kill it zone. I thought about cube gleamers in the combat arena: those high-order gents whose deaths hopefully entitled them to something completely wonderful wherever they might be. The max-do, sans-bullshit, buck-stops-right-here zone. The here-it-is-handle-it-or-die-right-now zone. The reality zone, the highest order zone, the alpha-omega zone. The first-and-the-last, best-and-the-worst, mashed-together zone. Yeah? Well. I wanted to sleep about ten years.

I couldn't stand for more than a couple of minutes. This meant considerable rack time, which brought on a bad thing—thought. Shit, I did not want to think, but there was nothing I could use to intervene, nothing to occupy the think monster.

If something didn't change, I'd exit in a plastic bag. I survived air missions by being quick and fortunate. I'd survived ground activities by being quick and fortunate. The difference between some dead people and me was the physical position in the universe at the time of the gun work, and that's all. A smile from Our Lady of the Luck, a few inches of space, perhaps mental framework and posture, or my own postulates concerning myself had something to do with it, I don't know.

Combat and the Reap have an arrangement: the former sets up individuals for the latter. Combatants who are still here are skilled or fortunate, usually both. But they weren't picked up by the Reap only because they didn't do combat long enough. I'm fairly sure most combatants consider every minute after combat as a gift.

Don't think so?

Ask one.

At the rear I was reacquainted with people not saddled with killing people to stay alive, who did not look at everything in the environment seven hundred times to see if it was safe to take another step. Some of them worked on keeping people alive. Some demeaned everything as best they could. None had people waiting in the bush to end them, because people like those on Hill 10 existed. Many rear people actually ran down combat people. Now why were we dispensing blood and energy to keep things off those chumps? What did they think kept enemy off them so they could freely walk around verbally carving up their cover instead of worrying about staying alive? I'm sorry I heard that garbage.

Something inside me clicked. Everything changed again. Life view number four. The first change was osmotic, the second noticeable immediately afterwards. This one was a participatory process.

⊙

"How do you feel?" the XO asked when I got back to the hill.

"Tired, Sir." Yeah. Tired, abandoned, used purposelessly, in a universe by myself, mean as a Sidewinder, dangerous as det cord about to go.

"How was the op?" I guess I had to say something.

He smiled, "No contact, a three day walk. You know the bastards won't engage when we're sharp. They have to catch us asleep."

I stared into space for a while. I guess that was good. I mean nobody died because I dropped. Nothing was the same, not me, not Hill 10, not the major, the ground, nothing.

"Major?" I couldn't leave now. "What about my extension?"

I requested an extension of my tour to go back to Chu Lai to fly more missions.

"You've got orders to CONUS, Captain. I don't know anything about an extension. You have a week left."

Didn't I ask for an extension? I gave the paperwork to the administrative officer, had I dreamed that? And a week? Was the world ending next week?

The major handed over a torn piece of paper. "Here. Know him?"

Oh well, the extension didn't matter, the hill didn't matter, going home didn't matter, memory didn't matter, one week didn't matter. A4s mattered. M-16s, my Kabar and Fairburn mattered. I could touch those things. They could keep me, and others, alive. I really didn't much care about anything else. I looked at the scrap of paper attempting to make the unfamiliar name into something I knew.

"No, Sir."

"He'll be here this afternoon. Give him a tour, snap him in, go home."

"Aye, Sir."

What a change. All the while I lay in that warm sheet-covered rack the think monster crunched away, working on ordering the last year or so of chaos. Perspective had gone south. Even the word home had revised meaning. Home was a place with a lot of fire support immediately available where you could eat without a ready-to-fire rifle across your leg, right?

Life before combat was a vague movie I thought I remembered seeing. I couldn't recall coming into country, it seemed as though I had always been there. There was no future to view, it didn't matter until I got into an environment where something would be there next time I looked, or somebody would be there next time I turned to speak with them.

I couldn't get a damned thing out of my sensors. They all worked, I heard fine, saw great, smelled, tasted, had full tactile senses, and received paraphysical environmental shapes okay. But with all the perceivers working, only perceptions equating to intent to harm or kill compadres or me had any meaning. The rest of the stuff was just inchoate data.

Aimless wandering around the hill eventually led to Bravo Company's area where I went to see the six actual. "Do you feel like this?" I asked him.

I wanted to know if he had the same dullness with which to deal.

"I don't think so." He was reassembling his M-16. "But I haven't been where you've been. I don't know why you're still alive."

Wonderful to hear, sounded like still being around was a gross error. One of the internal switches clicked and he converted from a friend to just another person. These little switches I talk about are sudden.

"Yeah?"

"Yeah." He looked at me. "A sniper targets you, caps off two rounds and what happens?" He snapped his rifle back together, looked back at me. "An angel pulls you back so the rounds crease your arm instead of killing you."

The distance to reality opened again. Normally I wasn't clumsy, but that day I stumbled. The incident caused a lot of thought, but an angel?

He continued, "The damned commanding general of the division comes to the hill to pin a medal on you."

"That was a battalion formation."

"Yeah, I know. Have you ever seen or heard of that before or since?" He absently clacked home a full magazine, chambered a round as he sat on his howitzer ammo box table. "I saw you run through the Tet rockets. You looked like a damned apparition."

An apparition? Thank you. "I figured we'd get a human wave after the rockets." I didn't know I appeared weird to other people. I was really by myself, wasn't I?

"So did I. Are you okay?" he asked.

I must have been staring at nothing. "I don't know. Yeah. Fine. I just wanted us all to get through everything okay."

Why couldn't I feel something, anything? He must have read my thoughts.

"Too much blood, man. Too much death. Too much horror. You've seen too much. Go home. Forget this shit."

Yeah sure. Just hat on out. Leave everyone, don't finish a thing. My body shook his hand, my voice wished him the best, but I was far away. I hadn't seen anywhere near that which some had. Did he think I was worried about horror done to us? *Tout au contraire.* I learned I was capable of dealing a little horror all of my own. I had done some damage. How many structures, how much equipment had I smashed up? How many widows and fatherless children had I manufactured? I had run endo processing on how many fathers, sons, and brothers? For what?

Life.

◉

The major and Bravo's skipper both said "home," where was an abundance of fire support immediately available and I could eat without a ready-to-fire rifle across my leg. I must be home. I thought about the world but couldn't remember much. I didn't want family and friends to see me like I was.

Heya Mater, Pater. Have I damaged you? Killed you? Did I tear down the house yet? Blow up the cars? Machinegun the neighbors? Napalm the next block? Rocket the downtown area? Bomb the airport?

No? Oh. Whew. That's good.

Let me tell you about it. We killed a lot of people. They killed a lot of us. I got to watch a civilization of decent people vanish. And I learned a few things:

SAMs can be dodged.

Heavy flak synchronously rings all my bells.

Explosively removed human pieces don't go back on, that includes mental ones.

Dropping ordnance on moving targets is great, trains and boats are particularly good. What the ordnance does when it hits them isn't.

Better always have trips (trip wires) out at night.

When you shoot off a person's screamer, the scream is still audible.

Other people's blood smells funny.

Fear and courage have unique, clearly discernible aromas.

You'd be amazed at how far away you can drop a person with a rifle.

Not many people care much really.

I didn't have enough to keep everybody I wanted alive.

Medals are a lot heavier than the stuff of which they're made.

There are angels; sometimes they assist you.

I had enough waiting. How about invading the north, end the damned thing or end me? But there wasn't support available for a single captain invading a country. There wasn't a place I wanted to be.

Was I, was I not? The last petal lazily floated to the ground, drifting this way then that as it rode down high strung air. I couldn't remember which.

I wandered to the LZ, my response to a distinct whupping growing louder as it came across the paddies. What was my replacement like? Probably didn't matter. Everything was of consequence, but nothing mattered.

Chapter 20

Little Sister

"Oh, God!" My replacement's breath caught as a family passed en route to their little home. He turned toward me, horror dripping off his face while his exclamation dissipated into the environment.

I saw the family, we all did, then immediately went to the next thing. Perhaps I exhibited a similar reaction first time I saw people in that condition, I couldn't remember the first time. How easy it would be to cry at the tragedy, rage at the injustice and violation; but here it was cold, any of that just interfered with actions required to keep one's heart beating.

Some less published results of governmental armed controversy were in clear view as the family passed, manifest four part harmony, probably no voice of which had ever considered political power struggle. More likely each simply wanted to live versions of normal decent lives. But as fate would have it, the family lived in a certain area at a certain time. It was helpless, hopelessly involved.

The man dragged along on a leg and a stick, doing his best to show dignity. The woman had a completely usable arm and an intact eye. She was also working on dignity as she stumbled along a step behind her husband. The boy, limping purposefully along behind his mother, head down, good hand on his younger sister's shoulder, had most of his face and an untwisted leg.

Weapons have no capability without human intervention. Even ready-to-fire weapons, undisturbed, will sit idle for eternity. The members of this family presented lucid illustration of utilized weapons that, without hesitation, would accomplish their designed function at the hands of humans, irrespective of who was or was not around.

Little sister, the fourth family member, seemed healthy and complete until her face could be seen. It was a pretty, wide-eyed, frightened face, an unintentional placard projecting the terror she had know in her short life, the horror of her most likely future.

Considering what might have happened to the family, the heartbreak and tragedy, only added to my rage. I understand there were people in the USA who supported the NVA. They needed to see that family, and the thousands of others, to clearly perceive that to those not present, words can completely obscure intentions and actions.

Turning onto the little path leading to home, the family went deliberately unnoticed by the platoon of Marines and group of ARVN soldiers standing in the street of Phouc Nhien village, a few miles from Da Nang. On that early morning in April of 1968, the Marines and ARVN were looking for things unusual or threatening; disfigured family members were neither.

My replacement looked at the Marines with backs turned to the family, then at me as his horror phased through pain and guilt, to anger. "Don't those people deserve attention?" he shouted, asserting that idiotic accusative edge to his voice untested people so willingly employ. "Are all you people cold-assed animals?"

I heard the same at the rear when called back there. Perhaps he'd figure out things, if he lived.

"Don't you care about those people?" He moved toward the dwelling, two nearby Marines stepped into his path. "Get out of my way!"

But of course, they didn't. Instead, they stood silently in place, turning eyes to me with faces saying, "Captain, do something with this asshole before he kills us."

Care about those people? He cared enough to get them brutally murdered with his U. S. of A., corporate mentality, oh-help-the-poor-things bullshit. They weren't poor things; they were distressed human beings, in distress because a group of people farther north, not even from the damned country, decided they weren't living in the right way. Then another group of people from much farther away, who knew even less about how they lived, decided it was essential to become involved. Maybe that was the right thing, I don't know. I lived in this panorama of waste and heartbreak long enough to realize people who hadn't really been here knew not one damned thing about it.

I turned to him, "Come on. You've been here two days, there's more."

He looked at me with fire in his eyes, started to speak.

"Hey!" Not even slightly interested in hearing a swarm of normal emotional clatter, I interrupted. Normal U.S. culture based thought here was about as useful as a small piece of tissue paper in a hailstorm. "If you knock down respect in the beginning, you'll have a difficult ride."

He glared at the two Marines blocking his path while I continued, "Any, I mean the smallest direct assistance we give these people only makes life worse for them. We can destroy their version of dignity, their honor, arrange it so VC or NVA torture or obliterate them, just by doing what may possibly be a customary thing in the world."

"Aren't you capable of normal human feeling?" He made use of that unbelievably stupid, never-been-anywhere-or-done-anything accusative tone again, placing his ignorance and narrowness in view of everyone.

Fuck. What do we do with this guy? Would it be better if a little normal metallic feeling were positioned so as to pass through his heart?

The blocking Marines moved their eyes upward, I dropped my head, took a breath, looked at the shrapnel scars on my arms. At that moment I do believe all would have been much happier if he just vaporized. The weight of more guilt piled on as I realized I was leaving a critical job to a person starting out with a poor attitude.

Exhale, look out across the paddies, "Answer for yourself when you've been here a while. You'll see more of this, and worse. There were Marines here that look like those people now, it could happen to any of us."

After a couple of minutes scanning the area I returned attention to him, "Look. Get this. Those agents in the bushes will kill you and everybody in sight if you let them, they won't just kill you either. They aren't fucking around." Another look around. "This is not a field deal somewhere in the U.S. of A., it is the heartbreaker, a compound study in the nuances of horror, the destruction of human life and anything else nearby." I repeated words the FAC I replaced used, they seemed appropriate, "It's going to hurt you, it will change you; you need to learn or you'll kill Marines other than yourself."

No response.

"Extinguish yourself if you like, that's your privilege. But cause the deaths of other Marines through ignorance, internal pettiness, incompetence, or anything like that, and you will burn a long time."

He stared at me like I'd punched him, then began to look around. Our excellent aviator vision wasn't required to see more banged up local citizens, Marines and ARVN with covered wounds and ten-click stares. His face changed as he hooked up to a little combat zone personal peril reality. He looked away, the emotional slump obvious. The two silent Marines looked at me, knowing what just happened to him. It happened to each of us when the nearness of our own maiming or death, the horror and insanity visible everywhere finally got in there. He could let that show, a good sign. Combat also places people in position to mutually understand many things without need for words. The two Marines moved away with little nods toward me.

New guy was quiet, observant; it seemed he was at last really seeing the place. Things pointed out were acknowledged with a head nod or a thoughtful question, rather than previous expressions of disbelief, disdain. Back inside the wire his eyes asked if he would live through this. Though he didn't say anything, I answered anyway.

"Pay attention to the salts. They know what to do, will give you many assists if you let them. You can save lives out here if you stay together."

I didn't mention preserving Marines and locals meant killing enemy, the quantity of death was probably greater. I exhaled, "Don't know what else to tell you about this," meaning it's the most sorry piece of shit about which you've ever heard. "Good luck to you."

He nodded and walked away in a familiar disconnected state. I took a deep breath. He would work out all right. I wasn't in need of additional guilt or worry, looking for a way to go back to the world and be okay when I knew being okay in the U. S. of A. was listed under "Chances: exactly not any."

✺

The job wasn't finished, my tour ended, I was thrown away. Into the jeep, for the famous last ride to Da Nang, though it didn't matter where it was going, I didn't know what I was doing anyway. Reasons to do or not do anything were gone, and, after months of bloodshed, destruction, the witness of the suppression, terrorization, violation of a people, I was to return to a land of ridiculously fortunate people and immediately resume a normal life.

Perfect.

The jeep whined, pinged, rattled, and bounced along the familiar road to Da Nang. We eventually rounded the south of Hill 327 and started down the little incline to the airfield. I shifted the M-16, now an unconscious extension of my arm, and watched tanks headed the opposite way. Tanks. I'd seen them and their crews torn to shreds by RPGs. Faces of people who wouldn't see Da Nang, or anything else in the world, streamed through my mind.

"What is it, Sir?" the driver asked.

Perceptive driver.

"Oh—ghosts," I exhaled. Slumping back in the seat, I stared into space. "The coming nightmare."

He seemed to consider a question, then returned attention to the jeep. Just as well. Think he would have understood I felt like a man without a world in which to live?

"Okay Sir," the jeep lurched to a stop in the departure area, "you're here."

Yep. Dragging my gear off the jeep, I suddenly noticed I was thoroughly banged up. I handed over my flak jacket and helmet, then hesitantly, with deep trepidation in my heart, gave him the M-16 and magazines.

"Okay. These go to the armorer, the rifle's hot. Watch yourself, good luck to you."

He positioned the rifle next to his for immediate use and set the magazines in the space between the front seats so he could get at them quickly and so they would line up with the rifle correctly. He'd been out there too. Normally one wouldn't pass a hot rifle, but combat Marines baptized under fire can pass anything among themselves; there's mutual trust, respect, understanding going along with that.

"I will Sir," he smiled. "Good luck to you, Skipper."

"Know how to get up to division?" I asked. He had a couple more things to do and two people to take back to the hill.

"Yessir. Thanks." The jeep departed. I stood in the hot sun with my Kabar and the Fairburn, sensing the busy rush for threats and hostile intent.

No firearms.

Blades only.

Oh shit.

The Da Nang temperature was 100 degrees. I was freezing.

Chapter 21

Reinsert

Little sister's face came to mind as I exited country stage right, her image quietly looking straight ahead showing terror and uncertainty. I sat staring out the airliner's small view port showing cold and uncertainty. The trip to Okinawa was a trip, is all, I mean, we got there.

I sat and stared, sometimes would sit and stare, occasionally for variance I sat, stared. Things crashed around inside as an internal glacier assembled, but I was calm from an external viewpoint. I couldn't sleep. Would a weapon settle me down? I went to the armory.

"It's not authorized, Skipper. Sorry," the armorer said.

"I don't want ammo, just the damned rifle."

"What for, Sir?"

"So I can sleep."

He looked at me, obviously crunching away on my mental state, then gave my sanity the benefit of the doubt. "Sir, I can talk to the major and see what we can do."

Imagine the major's response. He wants what? To sleep with? Doesn't that sound somewhat strange, Staff Sergeant?

Well, I imagine most non-combat people have no idea how comfortable an assemblage of cool steel able to reach out some distance and smack the shit out of those intending to cause one harm can be. I was in and out of various states of alarm with no rifle immediately available, as though I had lost an integral element.

◎

"Do you want to talk?" a well-intentioned American Indian captain staying in an adjacent BOQ compartment asked one afternoon.

"About what?" I really didn't know what he meant.

"Oh, come on." He looked exasperated.

"Oh." Oh that. "Well. Um –" my speaking trailed off.

"It was bad wasn't it?"

"Oh. Um –" Ah, combat. I didn't know if it was bad, good, hyperbolic, purple, permeated with top quarks, or what; I only knew I had been there, probably should still be there. "You know, you were there."

"I was with division logistics on 327," he looked a little embarrassed, "I didn't get to the field."

So he wasn't directly involved in combat, which didn't bother me at all. *Au contraire*, he was probably the sane one. I remember looking up and down the passageway, finally responding to his sentence, "Oh."

We stood quietly for some time.

"You know you're abnormally silent, don't you?"

I exhaled again as I stared at nothing. "I'm still here, everything is still attached."

"Yeah," he nodded, "I guess it's like that."

"It's over for me," I exhaled. Sure it is. (Insert off-stage group laughter.)

"I don't know," his face reflected sadness. "It isn't over 'til the Spirit Horse comes."

◎

Presently I boarded a transport. Ages later, liquid blue below gave way to an indistinct large land mass to the east, some people cheered when the coast of the United States came into view. Everyone held his breath as the transport landed. Reverently silent people began to move as the machine taxied to its arrival area. Heads twisted, eyeballs jumped toward sights outside the transport, the world was right out there, a travel agency promotional about someplace.

Things went well until reaching the exit gates in the fence surrounding the facility, where hurled names greeted me, along with an assortment of material things thrown from a group of people generally touting poor breeding, lack of individual intellect, shouting, "go back and die." Those people had no idea to what I had been exposed or what I may have done. They had no frame of reference from which to speak, much less judge. Apparently they weren't interested in real data anyway, only some excuse to splatter servicemen with their sorry emotional garbage.

Combat people don't cease sensing hostile intent just because they're home, and they're never unarmed, even when nude. Most everyone on the planet in a body received a decent working set of weapons, whether they know that or not. Perhaps you don't need to know, I hope that is the case. The yelling citizens throwing disgusting objects charged combat circuits in spite of the fact they were my people, purportedly the ones to whom I pledged to be of service. It was the same old hostile intent faced many times, with an extra attraction—these were my kind, a concept to which I held tightly. Appearances were they didn't think that way at all.

See idiots with no individual mentalities hurl rejection at their combat people. See the combat people's faces go cold, watch as they duck heads and look straight ahead, to refrain from damaging the idiots.

I wanted my rifle and no talk. I scanned the environment for threats, attacks; it was horrible, getting out of there was horrible. The drive from Sacramento to San Francisco International was a series of thrills. I had forgotten about driving in traffic, or about any kind of driving managed by external electromechanical control devices deemed superior to human intellect. Traffic lights? Lane markers and shit? Concrete surfaced roads and curbs?

I made it through the maze of machines, traffic devices, weird paint on the street, and several drivers exhibiting particularly uncivil behavior. I parked at the airport, sat a few minutes to get my bearings and settle down, trying to catch up with civilization a little. Unaccustomed to the number of people and machines in close proximity, the lack of open space, the amount of perceived hostility with no consequent action, settling down required time. I got out to walk a minute before returning the car to the rental desk, still wearing the Okinawa-donned tropical uniform with its new array of ribbons. A man about my age with a young looking girl draped around him walked by, I nodded a greeting.

"Are those ribbons for the women and children you killed?" he asked.

An assault move, verbal bullets from the passerby, then he spit at my decorations. The icy beast danced up to the surface. I had to freeze to halt the reptile-brained monster. I had just run into similar half-witted hostility from vacuum-brained people; this guy was in the open with toneless muscles, standing back on his heels.

"They're for the young I ate, dorqueface."

Pump and the pulsing ice beast were rattling away. I squeezed fists, held my breath, stood there looking at him. I can still picture his pale sweaty face, thin neck, glazed eyes. He was soft, didn't know it, obviously had never been in any kind of combat. The girl tugged at his arm, causing him to back off a bit. Her mouth dropped open when he asked, "Why don't you eat me, asshole?"

I had him but he didn't know it. I couldn't believe it. Here was this guy, about two quick moves from joining his ancestors, and he cranked off another insult. Amazing.

"Don't do that again," I said quietly. "Doubt you'll live through it."

I wasn't kidding. Nice frame of mind, huh? The guy's hostile intent felt like enemy shooting at me, which was simultaneously interesting and frightening. I was thinking of him as a threat to existence, he could have been the diversion for a sniper or machine gunner on a nearby building. That's the sort of thing combat had me set up to expect. I got hold of a good picture before things progressed. I would have to evaluate everything around, anything happening to me, carefully for quite some time. So I would do nothing here. I stepped back, concentrated on relaxing my shoulders, but his expression had already turned to terror. He grabbed the girl, ran around the corner of the building.

Yippee-kie-yay, yippee-kie-yoh, yippee-kie-yow-kie-fuck.

I didn't feel all that wonderful or particularly friendly as I stood shaking off the pump, cutting iciness carving away, hoping the beast would settle down quickly. Welcome home.

I might have been just a teensy bit less than perfectly social on the airliner to Dallas. It seemed everybody, including flight attendants, normally professional people soothers, did their best to convince themselves I wasn't there, while staring in saturnine fascination. The transport landed. I had to hang around for another crowd-hauler to finish the trip to Dulles. I found a coffee shop, was informed by a cashier with a soft, completely engaging Texas accent she didn't want to serve anyone involved in that atrocity over there.

Atrocity over there? How about the little one right here, Darlin'? I didn't protest or even answer, quietly set down the coffee with extreme delicacy, left. Dulles wasn't any different, neither was Alexandria. I was sort of expecting plain old normal human treatment. Reckon I shouldn't have expected anything. But, hadn't I just returned from a task the government, that is to say the people of the United States of America deemed necessary, a responsibility of the congressional commission I accepted? What was the tab I seemed to be picking up?

There was no fire support available nor did I have a rifle. Marines with whom I worked tedious situations, people I trusted and believed in, were nowhere around. They may not have addressed much conversation my way, but they covered me in sticky situations, didn't call me names, insinuate I was some kind of criminal, or hurl insults and run. I knew in country I shouldn't come home yet there I was with a completely redone values framework, feeling more alone than ever.

The little amble through the combat arena revealed multiple holes in systems of values, ethics, and conduct I had been taking in since birth. It also opened a view to areas of question concerning ruling structure, governments, motives, conduct of affairs, the general scheme of governing people. The foundation given by the civilization all those years worked only in a specific arena, the implanted framework was too inflexible to allow survival in combat, or re-adaptation to the environment that taught it. Incongruities in a civilization formed to real shapes are a nightmare with which to deal, yet there is no alternative. It was a real problem, another hump through contravening structures.

◎

The family had no frame of reference from which to work and neither did I. They did their best. The versions of the war they reflected were strange to me, I have no doubt I was strange to them. A happy, enthusiastic, rather alive, fairly refined young man left them. An ageless stone returned. Just being with them was difficult, to say nothing of trying to communicate. I barely managed minimal response to normal conversa tion, certainly no explanation or decent discussion. I'm sorry to say I was a social disaster, decidedly different from me before combat. Superimposed visions of dead and destroyed people over the frames of relatives and family friends would not desist. I couldn't begin to talk about combat, couldn't think of anything else. The body smiled, shook hands, kissed cheeks, laughed stupid forced laughter, nodded its head appropriately, while I was running an erratic mish-mash thought stream, jumping between the before combat, combat, and current frames of existence.

"I'll bet flying fighters is good, isn't it?" an uncle queried.

"Attack, actually. The aircraft are wonderful."

"Awfully complex, I'll bet," he replied.

I recalled a time flying back to Beaufort from NAS Olathe, Kansas. After the sun set close to seven nautical miles above the Earth, the aircraft cut a silver-white ribbon of engine contrail between deep purple vastness aft, black vastness pinpricked by stars above, deep blue vastness fore and directly below the aircraft. The view in the rearward mirrors was spectacular, the occurrence moving.

"Flight is fabulous. Accomplishment with the aircraft as a weapons platform gets a little complex," I told him.

"Oh you poor thing," one of my aunts said.

Pictures of gents missing pieces flashed through my mind as I turned away. No Ma'am, none of us are poor things. Auntie didn't understand fortunate, and though I wanted to tell her, shocking a lady with something horrible from outside her working parameters didn't seem as though it would accomplish anything constructive. I imagine turning away without comment was enough shock for her.

Drop everything, immediately return to normal was my desire (again, insert abundant off-stage group laughter). Normal people were difficult, not because of anything wrong with them, they were normal, hadn't seen much outside their regional existences. I may never have been normal anyway, certainly not now. It was wonderful that normal people didn't know about things I was attempting to handle, but that essentially left me adrift on a sea of my own.

How to deal with that which was invisible to those around me? How to mention the fear somebody would do or say something that flipped the beast's switch, causing it to attempt destruction of everything within a click or two?

"Oh you poor thing, we understand, we don't want to upset you, we know all about it." Yeah, all about it, sure. People clucking over me like they would a cigarette burn on a gaudy couch became taxing. If we could just get past the false sympathy or hostile posturing, one as cruel as the other as far as I was concerned as neither allowed interface in a present unit of time. From sources somewhere seriously bogus information regarding SEA was publicly placed, so no one needed any real story. They thought they knew.

I was outside the scope of normal people, pure and simple, and outside of my scope, which wasn't so simple. I needed time, space, double-cheeseburgers, crisp french-fries, thick chocolate shakes, tactical flight.

How was the battalion, how was the tactical air control party, how were the deathwalkers? What was going on, what was the enemy doing? What were the squadrons doing, was Chu Lai still there? What was happening across the DMZ?

Rambling around the area, no doubt with the intent of locating myself, I could not escape a tactical framework. The area had hundreds of good ambush sites, a half-dozen excellent lanes of approach, great cover for an assault group. The place could be had in about three hours.

It was spring, as you would expect, women and men cavorted as they do, unaware of anything but themselves. I wondered if they had any inkling of their privileged state of existence, and simultaneously was ever so thankful there was a place on the planet that allowed joyful unconcern. Pictures not worth mentioning ran right across the attractive, clean, healthy, inviolate, relatively free people in view. Maybe we were of an age, but I was considerably older than the few years I'd been away would indicate.

My eyes, the things they've seen. The spring-loaded continuous seek of something threatening grew tedious.

I soon received orders to the Third Marine Aircraft Wing at MCAS El Toro. I drove across the country nonstop, arriving in Tustin, California, nearly exhausted, but close to tactical aircraft I could actually fly. At a coffee shop not far from El Toro I cleaned up, changed into a uniform in which to report, had about three gallons of coffee. An attractive couple approached the coffee shop as I exited.

"Beast," the woman hissed. "Murderer."

At me! Damn! Beast? Okay. Killer? Under certain extreme conditions, okay. Murderer? Absolutely not.

"How did you like burning babies, asshole?" came from her friendly companion.

I was about to tell him I didn't burn any babies' assholes when he pursed his lips, giving the impression he was going to spit. Not that again. I moved my hand up to block the stuff right at his face, replied using my most friendly voice, "If you spit on me, I'll crush your fucking skull."

A friendly officer and a gentleman quality remark for the attractive couple; a wonderfully intelligent, sensitive, well thought out solution to the situation. Again, I wasn't kidding. The icy beast unleashed in combat is truly a beast, and once it's been out, any little old potential survival thing seems to rattle it. Sometimes you just have to hold on to that monster with everything you have. I latched on to the thing, pretty boy turned away without spitting, both of them appeared to have had two by fours suddenly inserted into their aft passages as they hastened away. I walked to the car shaking out the pump, working on getting Beastie settled, wondering about the women, children, and burning babies bit with which I was being hit.

The slashing tactics certainly weren't new, though my countrymen used different weapons. Heat internalized, cold external cover came up, warm southern California late spring afternoon sun streamed into the car. I didn't feel it, sat frozen, staring into the space of the parking lot through tears, waiting for the damned ambush to go ahead and spring. The nightmare briefly foreseen on the way to the Da Nang airfield unfolded into a journey from a world of active destruction to a world in various states of decay. The twisted hump was underway.

Chapter 22

Say You Are

Checking in to the Third Marine Aircraft Wing, I was greeted
with stares, whispers after I passed by, some head nods, a few
approving looks, some waves, not many words. Only a few people
talked to me, but it seemed many people spoke about me, or the
ribbons, or the scars, or—I don't know, maybe I should have worn
long-sleeved trops. The curious glances and hushed conversations
weren't hostile, just people discussing an object. An administrative
clerk directed me to the major assigning aviators to positions in the
wing. In the few minutes since initial check-in, my paperwork had
passed to the major.

He looked up from my OQR as I entered his office, closed the
dossier, smiled. The major had an impeccable uniform and
appearance, a paucity of ribbons, but none from combat.

"What about that tour as FAC?" he asked.

Well. What? What was he after? I shrugged, briefly looked out
the window at nothing, then back at him, "Heya, Major."

"Yeah, I know." Sure he did. "One of my students in the training
command was a FAC with the ninth Marines." He paused, said his
name, I didn't know the gent. "He's dead now," the major's face
reflected anticipation of emotional response from me, perhaps
shock, alarm, disbelief, horror ... something.

But death was an ever-present circumstance in my life, nothing new or shocking about it. I had dead friends from the east coast of the United States to points in North Vietnam, had been covered with dead people goo. He lost a favored friend, not exactly a new concept either. The isolating insulation that formed to protect against that particular pain caused loss of my whole peer group. It really wasn't anything about which to talk.

I looked out the window again. "Sorry that happened."

"Me too." The major came over, stood alongside as we looked out the window together for a while. He then turned to me, extended his hand, saying, "Welcome back to the air wing." It was a nice, warm, firm handshake. "In a few years people like you will be legends."

"Thank you, Major." I wanted to laugh, managed to return a smile. So what do you think, are we legends yet?

"Are you career?" he asked as he returned to his desk.

"I certainly was." I looked out the window again.

"Well, say you are," he said. "You know both sides of the combat picture. What about training combat replacement aviators?"

"Sure, Sir." Anything to fly. I didn't mention the profusion of sides to a combat picture.

I was reassigned to MCAS Yuma as an instructor with VMT-103. I drove along Interstate 10 to Indio, motored down the huge sandbox on the east side of the Salton Sea that runs to the southwest along the western edge of the Chocolate mountains. As I crossed white sand dunes to the south and turned onto the interstate highway toward Yuma, Pilot's Knob came into view. That unique pile of dirt is an excellent landmark that has warned many aviators of an inconvenient little corner of Mexican airspace. It also indicated proximity to tactical aircraft.

Yuma wasn't totally unfamiliar, after all, I deployed to the fascinating place about a hundred thousand years previously, even recalled the air station's location. The low desert surrounding Yuma presented ten or so miles of visibility in any direction while lying on the ground, which may sound a little silly, but after the nervousness experienced in more densely vegetated areas, I found it relaxing. MCAS Yuma had tactical jet aircraft and a prodigality of space in which to fly them. Yes, yes!

Chapter 23

Every So Often

One can accomplish rather precise maneuvers in an A4; I worked all of them. Little trips down the Colorado River low enough in places to leave its surface shimmering. Sixteen-point rolls with no altitude loss or gain. Zero airspeed hammerheads with compressor stalls banging the entire airframe as the aircraft slid backward perfectly straight to a ninety degree falloff. It was wonderful to get my hands on an Alpha four again. It was sanity, life, a reason.

VMT-103 flew TA4s, training aircraft delivered to the Marine Corps while I was in the combat zone. Training aircraft? It didn't matter, they flew well, had guns, carried ordnance. There were differences between TA4s and A4s, the most notable being the second seat in the T of course, and though the TA4 was a bit less than the combat A4s in many respects, it did have some strong points. My primo don single-seatitis, however, was far overshadowed by tingles of flying again. I flew at night, on weekends, as much as allowed, completing the instructor-under-training course quickly to pick up a share of student training. There wasn't much warmth on the ground and I smiled frequently when disconnected from it.

The squadron, a melting pot of capable aviators, was charged with polishing new arrivals to fleet readiness, training combat replacement aviators, providing instrument and weapons training, and accomplishing a few odd jobs as designated. An instructor ran most of the tactical mission set regularly. Mission priority allowed normal flying while many tactical fleet outfits were juggling things to manage the four hours of flight time necessary each month to qualify aviators for flight pay.

One morning a small group of Marine officers with silver Air Force wings mystically appeared in the ready room, checked in hesitantly while the instructors scratched their heads. Turns out they were Marine officers out of the Air Force basic flight training command. They flew Tweets—I beg your pardon, T-37s—then Talons, and received Air Force wings. Their training placed them close to a Naval flight student near completion of basic flight training at NAAS Meridian. Positioning them in the normal fleet preparatory course would have seriously abbreviated training in several areas, so we designed a new program to accommodate them, a glorious program, one at least as much fun for instructors as it was instructional. Shared responsibility for development of the air combat maneuvering course and sole responsibility for field carrier landing qualifications were added to my duties as schedules officer, target coordinator, and flight instructor. I was devoted, you see, I knew this stuff. It was easy to attend to that which I knew while ignoring that which I didn't know. How to manage the myriad of things accompanying a normal life? Not a clue. Though I once may have been social, I wasn't now, couldn't seem to manage that either. Normal and I had parted company quite some time ago.

Sleep? Couldn't. So what do you think, maybe a rifle? A local firearms store had something suitable, along with a gun store sales person who immediately upon my entrance began exhaustive discourse, almost a lecture as to why he couldn't go to combat. That was new. I listened politely, though no doubt with a funny expression. Never did unravel the message beyond his literals, or calculate who he thought I might be. Post rifle selection, he slid boxes of ammunition across the counter. I slid them back.

"No, thanks."

"Don't you want to shoot it?"

"Not yet. Right now I just want the rifle and magazines."

He regarded me as if I was nutso, and perhaps I was. But, do you suppose he had dreams of completely solid sheets of incoming automatic weapons fire, or flak so intense it blew you to pieces without touching you, or of small children wandering around dazed and crying amid violent explosions, looking for their parents? You see? The reward for performance in combat? Visions of sugarplum widows and elfin, fatherless children created by your excellent capability.

The rifle was to settle me down, not shoot. I could hold it, perhaps get some sleep, maybe feel a little better, especially during thunderstorms.

Thunderstorms are incredible phenomena, are they not? They cool down things on hot summer afternoons and evenings. Aviators don't like to fly in them much, I suppose power companies aren't overly fond of them, but they are magnificent elemental displays. Even so, at the time they really weren't the best place for me, particularly at night. Lightning flashes were reminiscent of flak bursts, Claymore mines, explosives, incoming mortar rounds, many automatic weapons firing in concert, incoming rockets, grenades, artillery rounds, bomb detonations, probably a few other things that don't come to mind at the moment. The sound of close thunder with its accompanying concussion was entirely too reminiscent of 122 mm rockets, waiting for shrapnel was taxing even when I didn't feel like doing weird things to get out of its way.

My heart beat faster, and though the beast didn't come up, it let me know of its presence. With the rifle, I could get through those unbelievable Arizona thunderstorms without finishing in too much pump. I'd find the thing, get into a good position with it, and just sit there. I didn't want ammunition, there was no intent to use it, nor did I think NVA were crawling around waiting for the rockets to stop before they attacked. I knew it was a thunderstorm and was completely cognizant of my surroundings, the noise and feel just fired off a few things. The rifle was a comfortable, reliable thing to hold while dealing with ghosts, waiting for shrapnel that would never come, wondering if I'd live through the thing.

In a few weeks the Opso discontinued pressing for volunteers to fly utility hops, such as night air refueling tanker, Chocolate mountain impact area TACA, and evening or weekend test hops. Instead, he'd pencil in my name without hesitation. I would always drop the hops to somebody who wanted them, but most other aviators had families, ladies, something human to do. Other combat aviators didn't seem to be going through my kind of weirdness. I was the only combat FAC in the squadron. On weekends without utility hops, I flew instrument stage cross-country flights with a student. Complete absorption in tactical aviation precluded bother of anything else, naturally everything else in my life quickly deteriorated. Didn't notice, too busy.

◉

"The banner's hung," my escort said as I climbed away from the banner drop area east of the MCAS one afternoon after having attempted a normal banner release. If you've ever flown banner tow you know he really didn't need to tell me that, the high-drag thing at the other end of the thousand-foot cable made the aircraft feel like it was dragging through muck. I had been the tractor for a gunnery flight when the banner wouldn't release. Shame on me, I stayed on the range qualifying students a little longer than I should have, so we didn't have all the fuel in the world.

Tactical air is always thus. If one pushes on a facet, others loosen. Motion away from unchanging circumstances starts the demons dancing, they are easy to see coming. It's part of the fun. If one buys into that intimidation, nothing will ever be done. As long as one is competent and has things well covered, there isn't much to it. Even when things are fine, those things are out there making faces and pointing, watching everything, all the time. One becomes accustomed to it.

"Yeah. Let's go around, I'll drop the rack," I announced.

On an A4, the banner tow cable attaches to a rack that hangs on the centerline pylon. Drop the rack and it's off with the banner. Well, the rack wouldn't release either. Though Yuma had two runways, the short one wasn't available to military operations unless something horrible was in progress. I didn't want to shut down the active runway for an hour with a hung banner approach.

"Okay Escort, I'm going to drag the thing off."

The principal stress point on the cable was at the loop around the rack fitting. If I could set the banner in the sand and drag it correctly, the cable ought to break at the aircraft end. That seemed infinitely cooler than spreading garbage all over an active runway.

"Say again?" my escort asked with surprise in his voice.

"You know. Use caution when you check for the cable."

"Roger that," he exclaimed, not at all interested in being whipped out of the sky by flailing cable.

We ground around the prescribed route, again lining up on the banner drop area. I descended, oh so slowly the last few feet, until the banner bounced along in the sand. A little more descent; the bounce became a steady drag.

Klink! The aircraft popped free as the banner separated.

"Say, Tractor," the escort said, "the cable broke right at the pylon."

Aha. Once in awhile Our Lady of the Luck turns away the demon's faces for a moment.

An IP (Instructor Pilot) seat during BAW (instrument basic airwork) hops was definitely not one of aviation's most thrilling positions. The hops were punctilious ninety-minute endurance contests. Nevertheless, a Marine aviator must possess excellent BAW skills. In keeping with this necessity, I was about to fail a student's AJB-3A over the Imperial Valley one afternoon. The student was under the bag, grinding along eastbound accomplishing standard and half-standard rate turns combined with five-hundred-feet-per-minute climbs and descents. He was doing well, which is why I was going to complicate his life by failing the aircraft's principal attitude reference.

SooBOOP!

A Marine F4 picked that moment to magically de-cloak at our eight-thirty, executing a textbook gun run. It wasn't possible for me to sit there more or less straight and level while some F4 guy demonstrated to his RIO, the ease with which an A4 may be blasted out of the atmosphere. That was a Marine over there prancing and banging on our cage bars. Ignoring Air Force and Naval aircraft attempting to engage in a little waltzing was not easy, but could be done consistently. Ignoring another Marine out there jerking one's chain just wasn't doable. Marines are designed to confront, engage, handle—that is what the training is about. If a Marine presents a proper stimulus to another Marine, there is a far better than average chance a little waltz will occur.

"I have the aircraft," I told the student as I fed in a little left rudder. "Pop the bag, check eight-thirty, a little high."

The F4 had reversed, was setting up his lead.

"Is he making a run on us?" he asked.

Um -, duh. Well, after all, he was a student.

I added power, pulled into a climbing turn toward the attacker. The F4 didn't even yo-yo (do see the glossary). He put many gees on that F4 to stay inside the radius of our turn, but he overshot, allowing the great pleasure of setting up on his six with a couple of seconds of shoot time. All manner of flame appeared as the F4 went buster, departing at the speed of heat. He disappeared in the horizon haze.

"Hot damn, that's showing him," shouted my excited student. "We would have got him!?"

"Maybe," I told him." He was in range a couple of seconds." Having cloaked again, I looked for the F4 to re-engage, to materialize somewhere else in the universe. "For your information, these A4 cuties are nasty little old things in thick atmosphere. You can be a real bad boy with guns and Zunis."

"How about missiles?" he asked.

"We would never have known what hit us. If it were for real, it's doubtful he would have made a gun run if he had missiles. Of course, we wouldn't have been zickying around with the bag up, practicing these keen standard rate turns with zippy five-hundred-feet-per-minute climbs and descents, either. But they're important, so re-bag yourself now, my son."

My son. There was probably a year or two between us.

The Imperial Valley was that way. People from other stations, along with some from other services, pounced upon most things military in the work areas south of the Salton Sea. We were told to ignore them, which we largely did; upon occasion that was just too much to ask. I flapped with a particularly aggressive F8 one day that wasn't satisfied with three or four passes. It resulted in a draw and I had to incomplete the student's instrument hop. That didn't affect the student as I took responsibility for the show, however, it did get a squadron skipper a little unhappy with one of his instructors.

"Taxpayer's money, Captain," he said. Of course he was right.

"Yes, Sir. I know. And you know I'll cooperate, Colonel. But damn. Every so often..."

"I know, I know," he waved, "you're a combat aviator." He looked at me with an almost sad smile. "Fly the damned prescribed hop. If the FAA and everyone else get their way, it won't be long before an aviator will be unable to fly their own aircraft. It's that way, we have to adhere to those rules."

He looked out his window. "Real combat and excellence are about gone," he said. "They want paper now. Paper quals, paper ability and excellence, there's no room for men and women. You don't have to be good anymore. You just have to look that way on paper." He looked back at me.

"You probably got the last of individual man and machine aviation," he continued. "It's going to be computers and standoff weapons, and completely machine-driven crap soon. We'll be button-pushing drones driving delivery trucks, run by central brain colonies having no idea of the situation they're attempting to run. It's bad. It makes me sick. I think I'll puke now," he forced a laugh. "I don't want us contributing to non-aviators ideas of dangerous flight. Many want us out of the air," he said with a sad smile. I'm not sure how I set him off, but his disappointment with the manner in which aviation was developing was crystal clear.

"It was good once," he continued, "I mean really good. You got some of it, I'm glad you did." He looked back out the window. "Damn it, a man or woman in a situation is worth more to that situation than a host of remote leadership or any amount of paper. Or guidance systems. Or control devices."

He stood quietly a minute, turned back to me. "People like you are the last of a good breed, Buddy. Now don't come in here about this again. I'm not kidding. Got that?"

"Aye, Sir. I do."

"Okay. Get out of my office. Behave."

As you can see, the little soliloquy left an impression. He was an aviator when the Marine Corps flew Furies (FJs), Demons (F3s), and Skyrays (F4Ds or Fords), even had time in such things as Chance-Vought's F7U Cutlass. After having been involved only a little over six years, I was disturbed at a growing inability to practice aviation. I wonder what he really had seen in his long tactical aviation life?

The Naval Air Facility (NAF) El Centro, located in California's Imperial Valley near not much (no offense to El Centro residents), allowed us to conduct field carrier landing practice (FCLP). It was an agricultural community without much around but fields of various forms of plant life. Hopefully that meant all our turbojet racket at 500 feet AGL didn't bother anyone. I'd fly over to get the place set up, which meant accept the completely satisfactory setup offered by the gents there, go sit at the LSO cart, and await the birds. The little facility was not one of Naval aviation's busiest places. When my aircraft showed up, the tower gave me the field and I worked students on the Fresnel lens for a while without interruption.

Most of the time, the LSO cart sat abeam the landing area on the port side of the west runway, in approximation of the position of a ship's LSO platform. At the cart one had the privilege of seeing the effects of everything done to the aircraft by the aviators on approach, the total pleasure of having the cilia in one's ears knocked completely flat by screeching and roaring turbojet engines at full power.

The first few sessions went something like: "Nice pass, One, looked like a three wire." That meant he was on the glide slope, on speed with good lineup all the way down the groove, and that his hook likely would have caught the third arresting gear cable. One designated the instructor flight leader, from whom okay passes should be expected.

"Speed, Two. Work toward on speed all the time." In this case, Two was consistently a little fast, most people were in the beginning.

"Okay, Three, regard the ball until your landing gear touches the deck, that's why it's there." Three was gauging his approach by looking at the deck rather than the ball. Many aviators do that at first, it can be bad-bad aboard ship.

"Stay up on the ball, Four." Four was under the glide slope all the way. Obvious he didn't yet have the picture.

Next time around: "A little more power sooner will fix that low in the middle, Two. Anticipate. Work ahead of the aircraft." Two went low in the middle from a high start, waited until back on the glide slope to make a power correction. By then he was too late.

"Three, spotting your landing is no good. Watch the ball. Hold everything steady over the ramp. Yeah. Like that. See? You can stop that starboard drift by setting up your lineup sooner." Three was still spotting the deck as he approached the ramp instead of flying the ball.

"Well, Four? Where's the ball? Anybody seen a meatball around here?" Ol' Four was having a shitty day.

"Okay, Gents. The aircraft just go, they have no idea of what you want, you must put them precisely where and how you want them."

Next time around: "Attitude, Two." He was jiggling the nose in close, nothing serious.

"Three, that's a lot better. A little too much power in close is why the ball shot out the top. The closer you get, the smaller the corrections." Three was working the ball all the way now; he'd be fine soon.

"Wave off four. Take that thing around this time, you could kill us all from there." Four needed additional attention, review of carrier landing basics, perhaps a couple of hops with an instructor aboard. He flew the aircraft well, his head worked acceptably so it was probably something about the overall picture that didn't frame for him. Most likely it was fixable.

The gents learned fast, it took only a few hops to quiet me down, then about all I did was acknowledge ball calls, send them home at bingo fuel. Sometimes the instructors would full stop and come out to the LSO cart to watch their flights work, perhaps chat a little. The rest of my life may have been shattering but the aviation part was running well.

Light crept up on the El Centro area one morning. I had a chair propped against the LSO cart, was sitting there with breakfast balanced on my legs in an appreciative state of torpor as the sun peeked over the horizon.

Wah-SHWASH!

A low-flying, fast-moving A4 came from behind, passed immediately overhead, knocked breakfast and me out of the carefully propped chair. I was getting up from the dirt having decided there weren't NVA around, it really wasn't incoming rockets or artillery, when the radio sounded off.

"Good morning paddles," blared this jocose voice. "Sierra Delta one four, initial with four, overrr-rrr."

"Your pattern, Paddles, altimeter two niner niner seven," the tower crew seemed to have difficulty concealing amusement. They presented the altimeter setting for me to pass to my aircraft, so my students could use it to reset their altimeters and prevent landings under the surface of the Earth or above it due to erroneous altimeter information. I don't know how bad it is to collide with the Earth's surface before you get to a runway or land up in the sky. I haven't done either of those things. I imagine they're somewhat startling.

"Roger, altimeter niner niner seven. Thank you, Tower," I acknowledged, getting the picture. "Break, good morning Sierra Delta one four, we have your overrr-rrr hanging, report the break on the west runway, altimeter niner-niner-seven, kindly arrange to replace my breakfast."

Now even in fairly ridiculous atmospheric conditions the altimeter would hardly get to thirty-nine point nine seven or nineteen point nine seven, so I dumped the two. Tactical aviators can get weird no question, but generally our brains work.

"Roger the break," snicker, snicker, "altimeter niner niner seven," snicker, laugh, "whatever do you mean?" responded SD-14.

See? No problem with the altimeter.

"I mean you knocked it off me onto the ground there, Dippy. You know how bad it is to spill LSO coffee? What do you think happens when you position LSO breakfast in the dirt?"

"Say Paddles," laugh, snicker, laugh, "couldn't have been us, we just got here."

The tower crew sent a truck with chow and coffee, a nice thing to do. SD-14, piloted by a friend from Chu Lai, called on approach frequency, which I didn't monitor at the cart, to set up the thing. He knew I'd be less than totally alert and would be looking approachward, and so took his flight around way to the north, staying low so I wouldn't hear them. The explosive sound brought back a few things from Hill 10 days, leaving me a little weird for a few minutes.

Wise guy full stopped, came out to the cart laughing. "Sorry about your breakfast there, LSO Sir."

"Yeah, I know, sorry," we shook hands. "That was good, but henceforth you are obliged to cover your six at all times you know. By the way, your gents are doing well this morning."

I balanced conditions between us on an aerial refueling hop by squiggling the drogue so he couldn't hit it. An A4 configured as a tanker had a slug of a refueling tank mounted on the centerline pylon, which during refueling operations trailed a refueling line three or four inches aft of the aircraft. Maybe it was more than three or four inches; it could seem a terribly short distance. This refueling line had a conical basket, or drogue on the end that stabilized the line and aligned an aircraft's refueling probe with the hose fitting designed for the purpose. Aviators were obliged to position aircraft precisely during this operation, to avoid unnecessary bending and tearing of sheet metal. It wasn't the easiest thing to do, though there were certainly more difficult things in tactical aviation, and could be particularly exquisite at night in the vicinity of thunderstorms. Refueling operations were also especially difficult when the aviator in the tanker wasn't feeling all that hot for whatever reason, or if either aviator's airwork was a little rough. I was the tanker, danced away on the rudder pedals while oscillating the stick fore and aft as he closed on the basket.

"Sure is turbulent. Ain't it?" I said.

"Okay," he laughed. "Boorah, I'm got. Let me have some fuel."

Fun is fun, fuel is fuel. I gave him a smooth tanker, he hit the drogue first time, as one would expect of a pro.

We lost a student. He was under the bag heading for an initial approach fix to shoot a Tacan penetration (an instrument approach to an airfield) when the aircraft began unpredictably flailing about. The instructor ran through every procedure of which he and his NATOPS flip pad could conceive, but the aircraft didn't respond, becoming increasingly less controllable as it continued toward the Earth. Passing through fourteen thousand feet in a rather startling descent, the instructor called for ejection, the student confirmed the ejection, his last public words.

The TA4 ejection sequence blew the canopy, suspended to allow the canopy to clear the aircraft, fired the aft seat, suspended for seat-aircraft clearance, and then fired the fore seat. This sequence occurred regardless of whom initiated ejection. I don't know if anyone ever figured out what happened, it takes months to put all those little crash site pieces and details into comprehensible form. The students were shocked, curious, upset by the loss; the combat vets were quiet.

"Captain," a student asked, "doesn't it even bother you?"

Guess I looked cold, huh? Captain Iceface. I couldn't tell him my switches auto-offed at tragedy, or that dealing with one death meant dealing with all deaths. Neither did I mention another fresh bright life snuffed out for nothing immediately evident.

"Oh," I whispered as I turned away, "yes it does."

Chapter 24
Pools

One ordinary day, I missed her. She had gone off to her mother's some time ago, declaring she would not return. I believed her, drove her and our daughter to the commercial side of the airfield. As their F27 departed, I stood there for a long time, no doubt with a slack face and a ten-click stare. One of the most beautiful women and attractive, affectionate little girls I have ever seen flew east, away from me. Not knowing what else to do, I went back to my quarters, sat, and stared. Soon after, she called to ask for a divorce.

"Okay, good luck to you," I said.

It was all I could say, all I knew how to do. Like all humans, she was a sovereign being with the right to live as she saw fit, consideration given to others and surroundings. I hadn't paid much attention to her or my daughter for a while anyway. I just plain neglected them both, though it didn't start that way. Our daughter was born while I was in the combat zone. I may have been the girl's father, even the woman's husband, but it didn't seem to matter to anyone. I never felt part of the family regardless of what I did. Nothing made my wife or mother-in-law happy, I couldn't do anything that was even acknowledged. It wasn't long before I stopped trying. The thousands of dollars sent to her while I was in the combat zone vanished without accomplishing anything measurable. That was an additional fence in the way as was my state of cold. Not surprising that she left I guess; it nonetheless left more cold wind blowing over cold rocks. Well, since I couldn't do anything for or with them, I became immersed in tactical aviation, where I could do something.

Visions of my ex-darlings ran rather frequently. Would there ever again be warmth? If a beautiful woman and a completely breathtaking little girl couldn't warm my heart, then what could? Flying tactical aircraft excited it, but nothing chased away the ice.

Administrative collateral duties also began to fade in importance, as all my time and energy went into aviation, aircraft, and flying—my life. Everything else was just waiting around. I had professional acquaintances, a few respected compadres, but no life outside of aircraft. I was so single-pointed I don't think I even spoke normally. The close friends room was sealed off during combat, I didn't know how to reopen it.

Lord, wrap your hand around me and make a fist. Hold me there until warmth returns.

More aviation stuff. Orders to Landing Signal Officer school at last meant completion of a process begun the previous year. A commercial transport lifted me to Jacksonville, Florida, from where I was to go to NAS Cecil Field a few miles farther inland, join Miramar squadrons, and board the USS *Independence*, upon which I would become shipboard LSO qualified. I telephoned the NAS for transportation.

"How about some wheels?" I asked the MOD at Cecil field.

"Your name and grade, Sir," came back through the phone.

In time the wheels showed up. A salty master chief petty officer disembarked, looked around a while, and then asked if I had seen a captain looking for a ride to NAS Cecil. I told him I called for wheels. He looked at my captain's bars, became annoyed, blustering about Marines all the way back to Cecil. It finally registered that when I said captain, they set up on a Navy captain, which ranks equivalently with a full colonel in the Marine Corps.

Oops.

The Carrier Air Group commander looked at my ribbons as I entered the officer's mess that evening, nodded, and then in a good-natured way blasted me for using the Navy. I explained I didn't think, just automatically gave my rank.

"You must think, young, highly decorated captain of Marines," he said to a table full of catcalling Naval aviators. "You must consider these things, and deal with them properly."

Dinner was served, as was fairly continuous good-natured haranguing of the only Marine aviator.

"You may become afterburner toast," an F4 aviator cautioned.

"An arresting wire," a lieutenant looked around with a mischievous grin on his face. "Do you suppose a hook in his body would hold an aircraft?"

An F8 aviator mentioned scooping me up the aircraft's intake. "Marine aviator molecules evenly distributed throughout the stratosphere to provide lift and thrust for Naval aircraft."

There was a lot of laughter and good feeling. Even a pinch of that boisterous camaraderie is intoxicating.

The Independence was huge, with six arresting cables strung ninety feet apart in the landing area. The centerline seemed off in the next county from the roomy LSO platform, a considerable distance from the Lexington. "Wave" or "to wave" is an expression from the days when paddles in each hand were used to convey information to approaching aircraft. The plan was for me to "wave" A4s (Skyhawks), F4s (Phantoms), A6s (Intruders), and F8s (Crusaders). The Navy was also working A7s (Corsair IIs), a few A3s (Skywarriors), and an A5 (Vigilante). An S2F (Tracker or Stoof) or two managed to show up, as did an E1 (Tracer). I was on the platform as much as allowed, day or night, taking in everything. The aviators and LSOs were well prepared. Day qualifications proceeded quickly, night quals went well despite a little skittishness.

The A5, spectacular enough during the day, was awesome at night. It was a fast, big, incredible looking aircraft that gave the impression of being alive. It flew fast, flat approaches, and seemed to tug the ship along when it arrested. The approach had to look pretty good far out, as the near side of middle was getting late for even small corrections in an A5.

A4s and A7s bounced around in the groove, and were able to make reasonable corrections right up to the last minute. As long as speed was good and they weren't too low, they could get into a wire from about anywhere. F4s jiggled about as they moaned, groaned, and smoked down the groove, hyper-responsive to power calls.

F8s were feral looking things, with aerodynamic design issues causing an aviator to work fairly hard to get the aircraft nicely set up for a pass. An LSO had to busy himself with something when an F8 turned in, to avoid nervousness. Normally F8s came out of the approach turn fast, went high, occasionally accomplishing rather spectacular moves to get back on glide slope. The aircraft was designed to haul along smartly, it did not like slow at all, and fast and weird at the start was definitely better than an aircraft in the drink from a skidded turn stall. Once set up they flew nice passes, but an F8 setting up could be exquisite viewing.

A3s were stable everywhere, all the time. One just acknowledged their ball calls, watched them trap. If their approach didn't look good, they self-waveoffed before the LSO would call for anything. A6s were also stable. I think the worst A6 pass I saw was something my FCLP students could shoot for.

VMT-103 had no access to a ship. Arrested landing training requirements were satisfied on a SATS (Short Airfield for Tactical Suppor) equipped with MOREST E2 gear for arrested landings and a Fresnel lens for glide slope information. It wasn't shipboard ops, though many of the same skills were exercised.

A ship moves up and down, pitches and yaws about the center of its mass, rolls side to side while moving forward to maintain thirty knots of wind over the flight deck during flight operations. The motions can be irregular and extreme. With any luck at all the ground holds relatively still, although California's ground was perhaps a little less relatively still than other locations, and wind over a SATS depends entirely on nature's show of the moment.

The port runway of the northerly set of parallel runways at MCAS El Toro had a SATS on the approach end that VMT-103 was able to use for qualifications. We ran a Charley pattern (ship's landing pattern) inside the normal traffic pattern, which probably drove the tower crew nutso. They had ultimate control of the aircraft, could override me at any time with remotely reasonable cause, but like tower people at El Centro, took pains to assist everyone in qualifying. Operating conditions were more stringent then at El Centro. The base was home to several tactical squadrons operating daily, and the third MAW commanding general lived there.

I would fly over from Yuma, park on the HAMS flight line, coordinate with base ops, and then a station vehicle would deliver me to the SATS. Of course the first bird absolutely always called the ball precisely at the prescribed ramp time. From there, off we went, merrily SATS qualifying, turning downwind over various station buildings at five hundred feet AGL.

On one completely fine southern California afternoon I was working four birds.

"What's the deal, Two?" I asked in my most gentle LSO voice after dash Two remained in the arresting gear much too long. Dash One had trapped, exited the gear, and was nearly at the HAMS flight line across the field. I had two more birds approaching the gear Two occupied. Even simulated carrier ops run closely timed event streams.

"Um -, I -, I was slow coming off the power, Sir," Two answered.

That wasn't new, horrible, or even mildly embarrassing on a first trap. It did mean the deck crew waited until power was reduced before pushing back the aircraft to clear the hook from the arresting cable. I had the pattern carrying more interval than normal to cover these little things, but nothing stops for fixed wing in the air.

"Okay, proceed no delay when clear of the gear, Two. Hold between the duals (parallel runways), contact ground," I told him.

"Roger," he paused a second, "moving now."

I acknowledged and turned my attention to the gents in the air. "Say state, Three." By state I meant fuel state, fuel remaining expressed in thousands of pounds.

"Three, one point four, ball, hook," Three answered immediately, at last getting to make a nice ball call after Two and I had cluttered the frequency.

"Roger, ball Three, calldown, break. Four, say state."

One point four translated as fourteen hundred pounds of fuel remaining. Calldown in this case meant land, go to the HAMS flight line to refuel.

"Four, one point three, ball, hook."

Another nice concise ball call.

"Roger, ball Four, break, Three continue, check your lineup, break. Four continue, calldown."

The word break in the world of radio chatter s eparates subjects and addressees, obviating requirement to execute transmission termination and initialization procedures.

"Three, roger calldown."

"Four, roger calldown."

I was about to initiate a foul deck waveoff for Three, when the MOREST crew gave me a clear deck call, right on time.

"Hold what you've got, Three." He had a nice pass working, was messing around with attitude a little at the ramp, like everyone does sometime. He responded, stabilized, and I turned back to Four.

The MOREST crew called. "Foul deck, Sir. Two folded his gear rounding the turn. It looks like a dirty deck for a while."

Shit. In the two seconds since I returned attention to Three and Four? Do things happen fast or what?

"Damn," escaped, "aviator okay?"

"Looks like it. He's out waving at us. There's no fire, Sir."

So Two was already out of the aircraft, a five second exit drill, good for him. There really shouldn't have been fire, but it was nonetheless nice to hear. Four wasn't going to get aboard this session. I flashed the wave-off lights, he responded immediately.

"Foul deck, Four, break. Tower, do you copy, Paddles?"

"Affirmative, Paddles, tower has you five by."

Unlike us aviators, tower people used prescribed radio language. Five by meant five-by-five, or a strong signal and clear vocals.

"Request that Four remain in the Charley pattern, turn over the cross runway (the east-west) for a full stop on three four right. Four is minimum fuel. I have a long foul deck. Also request Four remain this frequency."

Minimum fuel in Naval aviation interprets as special handling, land without delay. It's not the pronouncement of an emergency situation; however, it does imply an emergency isn't too far away. The tower knew about the long foul deck, but I said it anyway, habit I guess. I wanted to turn Four immediately, but he would have over flown the wing commander's offices, and generals, or at least their staff members, seem to get upset when things fly directly over their buildings, particularly at a third of normal pattern altitude.

"Approved as requested, Paddles," the tower answered after a long pause, during which they checked all their VFR traffic, all their IFR inbounds and departures, the surface vehicle traffic around the field, the winds, and anything they thought pertinent to Four safely doing as requested. Sometimes tower people also have a lot to think about quickly. "Crash crew reports the port main gear collapsed on dash Two. The aviator's okay, the situation's in hand."

The situation's in hand. Part of that lifted off a number of things. Little phrases like that, stated with conviction by the right people at appropriate times, can simplify one's life. Two hit the starboard turn onto the taxiway between runways a little fast, attempting to clear the deck for Three, causing the aircraft's port strut to collapse. He was doing his best to assist a compadre, but pushed on his aircraft a little too hard. Tactical aviators must sometimes work along fine lines.

"Roger, Tower, thank you, break, Four did you copy all of that?" I asked.

"Four affirm, Paddles. All of it."

It was always good to work with alert people.

"Okay, Four, full stop on three four right, avoid station buildings, contact tower this frequency when wings level downwind."

There was just no reason to have him change to tower primary frequency at five hundred feet in a turn.

"Roger, Paddles."

A trail of sparks during his full stop on the right runway probably wouldn't have aided anyone in settling down, I looked and saw that his hook was retracted. Good wave-off technique, good radio technique, good flight skills. These gents made my heart rattle. Dash Four executed a full stop landing on the starboard runway without further ado.

It was an incident for Two, the investigation board called for a statement, I could only confirm he was a promising aviator with nice skills and a healthy attitude. With two other aircraft in the pattern I really didn't see anything useable by the board. Still, a famous old LSO line came to mind though I didn't vocalize it, "Well damn! He looked great as he went past me."

Chapter 25

Unwrap

On a windy evening, as the sun packed into the desert again, I realized I had become hermit-like. How the hell had that happened? When did it happen? Did it mean anything?

On leaving the squadron area I went to quarters, staying there until time to go back. Most meals came from the little sandwich joint adjacent to the squadron administrative area. When away from aviation I sat around staring at nothing. No thinking, absolutely no thinking.

A compadre with whom I flew several interesting combat missions, who left the Corps with hard feelings towards it, sold me his motorcycle, a BSA Rocket. Once familiarized with the machine, I took to riding miles out into the desert. There was something wonderful about banging along on the rhythmically noisy thing out in the middle of nowhere. The Sonoran Desert around and to the east of Yuma was stark yet enchanting, accented with various cacti and sparse patches of colorful plants, sandstone hills, and jagged rocky ridgelines rising sharply from the granular surface. I could stare through silicate sheen forever out there, jump gullies, run up slopes, go ridiculously fast; reasons to think about anything specific did not make themselves at all evident. It wasn't long before the motorcycle caused problems with a few key old line officers regarding officer image. I sold it under duress. It was a nice thing for a little while.

I then invested a respectable sum of money into what seemed a going little firm; however, the business director directed the business of fleecing the firm. I went to check on things one day, and found no one around. The place was closed forever. A non-aviation thing. Bad boy.

A county attorney politely, almost apologetically, informed me the few thousand dollars was unrecoverable. I didn't get mad or even feel anything as the attorney haltingly explained how a criminal could fraudulently take people's money via certain loopholes in state laws, leaving them with no recourse. Now I knew of a few recourses I'm relatively sure could have persuaded those particular lying sacks of shit to part with any sum of money. VC and NVA had introduced a whole world of seriously motivating mechanisms, any of which could have been applied here. Then I remembered I was in a society, a culture, a civilization. You know, where plain old civilized people are manipulated, controlled, and victimized by civilized power structure and criminals, without recourse. The law takes care of these things, right?

Yeah. Does it ever.

So, more betrayal, further isolation, more inclination toward distrust of the old "system." I logged it in the lessons learned section, stuffed the heat and betrayal bashing around internally, and ensured my switches were off.

The squadron lost another student, this time in the desert north of Blythe. Again, clear cause was difficult to discern. Everyone in the squadron flew over the charred gash he and his aircraft left on the windblown surface; no one asked if it bothered me that time.

"Why didn't you deck the jerk?" a fellow instructor asked one evening as we walked back to our cars from the motel club we left to avoid further confrontation with mindless suit-clad individuals. "He had it coming."

I had been the recipient of verbal lashing and ridicule that grew louder, more personal, and insulting as the individual's audience spurred him on. The quivering chunk of loose flesh pointed out that blonde hair and blue eyes weren't what you wanted in a dark-eyed, dark-haired environment. It made you a freak he said, along with less repeatable things. Beastie and I stood quietly, looking coldly at the idiot until the thing took a swing at us. The beast made some faces as I avoided the swing but remained restrained, we didn't engage.

"I can't do that," I responded to my friend's questioning eyes.

He put an arm around his wife. "You could have just knocked him down."

"Nah, not anymore. Violence isn't for fun; it's for survival. I didn't care for the comments, but that was hardly a survival threat." I wiggled out the last of the pump.

"What about the punch?" he asked.

"Show only. He's untrained, was unarmed, and too drunk to understand anything. Disgusting conduct from a complete boor certainly, but nothing requiring violence."

"What if it hadn't been show?" he asked.

"That would have been bad."

"I don't understand, buddy."

Yeah. Maybe I didn't either. He hadn't been to combat, was one of those incredibly fortunate people with a cruise life. How could he understand human-to-human violence?

Violence is everywhere. It's part of our existence. Tremendous violence was most likely involved in the creation of this universe. The universe continues to violently form and destroy items and solar systems. Our planet and ecological system are studies in violence, with tectonic plate movement, volcanoes, hurricanes, typhoons, cyclones, floods, tsunamis, earthquakes, thunderstorms, natural fires, tornadoes, gusting winds, and celestial bric-a-brac moving haphazardly through our solar system. We possess a food system requiring life to take other life of some form for purpose of continuance. We amuse ourselves with violence, willingly hurtling off of hills, out of aircraft, using powered and un-powered machines of various types to position in postures of violent motion with the most damaging consequences. And we actually enjoy it

But the use of violence for purposes of control, suppression, manipulation, damage, or death to another human being is quite a different thing. Internally weak, uninformed, or suppressive people use that nature of violence as a means of asserting themselves, and of course when one's life, which may include family and group, is in imminent danger and reasonable communication is not available, violence is a mechanism naturally available to all human beings.

However, human-on-human violence is a dangerous special-use tool, to be employed only during life-state emergencies. When one acquires good grasp of that, one's violent responses seem to reset to no engagement or complete engagement, neither of which work well in more or less normal situations thrust upon one by the unknowing.

The end product of human-to-human violence is death for somebody; it heads there every time. That the mechanism can be interrupted, that it doesn't complete its little old cycle every time, is fortunate for thousands of people, particularly women, children, and those who don't know anything.

I would have thought people would respect and protect a precious peaceful environment, but many don't seem to know it's precious, or that individual moral principles, practice, and some effort now and then, are required. Manners, dignity, respect for individuals, and general good conduct offer a workable solution to this problem, but it seems a lot of people also lack those concepts. Although we live in a civilization, I'm not of the opinion we can call ourselves civilized.

"A Marine Corps Hymn to that jerk, he's got his own ride to take," I said to my friend. Certainly you know a Marine Corps Hymn. Himmmm, himmmm—brief pause—fuck himmmm. It's chanted at the source of your displeasure and may be applied equally to her, them, it, and those.

The Opso and I, who had a sort of continuum of little chats concerning ACM and altitudes of less than ten thousand feet AGL, conducted the final conversation relevant to the issue. I knew that maneuvering close to the deck was unsafe, but even so, I couldn't see why I should break off a maneuver bottoming out at around 9,000 feet. A lot of valuable lessons could be learned in those thousand feet was my argument to the Opso.

"This is the last time we're going through this, buddy," he stated. "You might be right, but rules don't allow for it, that's the end of the issue. The wing is sending somebody down to check on us because they've heard things." His facial expression let me know the wing SG (super guy) was coming to look at me, I'd best behave. "We will run by their book, their book calls for termination of ALL air combat maneuvering at ten thousand feet above ground level. YOU WILL break off at ten thousand feet."

When an Opso shows that particular face and tonality, the point isn't at all negotiable. "Aye-aye, Sir."

What would wing paper pushers do in a combat environment? Did non-participants understand combat was dangerous, and that training for it required some simulation of that danger in order to acquaint individuals with a little reality toward that into which they were setting up to be dipped?

The wing SG arrived to check out the four ACM instructors in Yuma. He seemed, however, to be more interested in demonstrating his magnificence and aeronautic prowess. Well, after having his doors reattached and then confirming the four of us, meaning we remained certified ACM instructors, he went home shaking his head.

He knew theory and from that standpoint could maneuver the aircraft well—the end of his thrust was position for a shot. But just position for a shot is not a kill, and there are several varieties of the next few actions past a hostile aircraft kill, as well as techniques for handling multiple targets along with their sets of next actions.

A combat aviator's maneuvering thrust was emphatically toward accomplishing a mission. That meant a hostile aircraft kill was a necessity, a requisite checkpoint along the way, a part of the deal. I do not intend minimization of concentration and skill required, or the importance of dealing with a hostile aircraft intensely; if not done, things end right there. But relative to a sortie, it's only one situation, one event in a stream of events.

ACM for fun is a rewarding, exceptionally beautiful, complex study. ACM to stay alive, eliminate threats, complete assigned missions is another thing. Some of the wonderful form and spirit-soaring jollies are lost when transitioned from the former to the latter, but there is considerable gain in fast moves, timing, accuracy, and overall capability. A tactical aviator ought to be well versed in both.

Wing directed the teaching of toss and overhead deliveries, which resulted in scheduling several training deli flights for instructors. Could any of us still fly a decent overhead deli profile? Early one enchanting morning, I was zickying along the desert surface from an initial point toward one of the local manned targets with little space between the aircraft and the planet's surface. I hammered along in ground effect, pulled up into the deli, knew the profile was good, released the Mark 76 practice bomblet, and headed for home while the pseudo-bomb zoomed upward a few thousand feet before gravity overcame imparted energy. The hit turned out to be fine, the profile was decent, and target people reported my kicking up a rooster tail of dust during run-in.

"Why don't you just move in here?" the Opso said looking pained when I appeared at his hatch, one more time. "Low! Damn it, those aircraft cost money!"

I knew the aircraft cost money, so did I. Taxpayers had much more money in me than in an aircraft. Tactical aviators are expensive, the training process is complex, and can't be abbreviated if there are to be competent aviators out there. After thorough training at great expense, the flying of expensive-to-fly aircraft, deli of an abundance of expensive ordnance all over that Asian peninsula, and another mint spent training others, I was easily worth a few tactical aircraft. In any event, I was happy with a precise deli. But things had changed and training was to now satisfy paper requirements, not prepare aviators for anything real. I hadn't noticed that occurring, only that it was that way.

Paper training doesn't pass the little things combat people have had to figure out on their own. The differences between a 450-knot deli and one at 550 or 600 knots, for example; or dropping ordnance well within its deli envelope or working nearer the edge of the deli envelope; or a straight-on deli and a deli with an angle of offset; or drifting one way or the other and dumping at the last minute to help keep the guns off. It's all these kinds of little things that provide tiny bits of a better chance. The "system" doesn't seem to embrace people who have been out there by themselves contributing all their valid information. Instead, a staff has to have seen an item to get it into a paper program. Most administrative staff didn't have a wingman shot off their wing at Xepone, nor had they experienced the excellent gun work at many locations that made meat out of book deliveries. Ergo, they looked at things from a comfortable environment, or limited specific experience viewpoint.

A big smile as I apologized to the Opso, promised I wouldn't do it again. He returned a wicked grimace.

I worked the aircraft just to work it, to really understand. An Immelmann on take off with two full drop tanks, 280 knot loops at low altitude, unloading (approach zero gee) to get maximum acceleration in considerably more circumstances than previously envisioned, working flaps and slats in combination to aid radius of turn in gnarly situations, aerobatics with the hydraulics disconnected; anything, everything toward the edge of the aircraft's flight envelope.

"You're nuts," said an untested cohort.

Perhaps he was right. I was doing things just to see if they could be done, by me. There was a wealth of knowledge to be had about the A4 (likely most aircraft) far outside the scope of good old NATOPS (Naval Aviation Training and Operational Procedures Standardization, a program detailing various standard procedures for Naval Air equipment). There is no question NATOPS was excellent, necessary sets of works providing means of getting through many situations well, and in at least a marginally predictable manner. There was just more to an aircraft, and a tactical aviator needed to know those things in really on, full court press, right in one's face situations.

Most tactical aircraft documentation splendidly portrays the operating envelope, but offers no clues whatsoever as to what working that envelope means or is like. People can blather away about potential aircraft capability, but it's all just talk that can be accomplished by anyone who can read. In order to comprehend an aircraft's performance envelope, flying the aircraft throughout that envelope is necessary. Normally there isn't a need to work operating envelope extremes, but should the need arise and an aviator has never been there, oh dear—the Reap hangs out at such places. Aircraft envelope exploration wasn't something about which to twaddle while sitting around the ready room; you did it until you achieved consistency. Then you knew and it became part of you—a working, subconsciously maintained, spontaneously useable internal structure. Had I been able to work the aircraft to the same extent before combat, I could have been more effective in several situations.

The Scoot really was a fabulous little device, a product brought forth from a man named Heinemann and his set of intangibles. It was tagged as "Heinemann's Hot Rod" during its development period, before the Douglas Aircraft Company was merged with McDonnell. Great tag.

○

Occasionally, tower would approve an unrestricted takeoff for a combat aviator. The aviator would then "unrestrict" himself, execute a spectacular half Cuban eight on takeoff, blow a little sand off the downwind end of the runway, and then accomplish an Immelmann. My, my, what beautiful work! Though certainly unexpected, the activity was legal. But the fiendish Opso would get him anyway.

"That was nice," I said after the Opso verbally blistered one such combat aviator. " Pretty."

"Tenqu," he laughed. "These aircraft are really fine, aren't they?"

"What's with you guys?" a peacetime-only aviator asked. "Why do you do those risky things?"

"They're not all that risky," I answered. "The idea is to know."

"What?" he asked.

"Just to know."

He shook his head.

"To know how, to do, to be able. To keep warm. You don't know how cold I get. It's cold on this planet." *Keep warm* fired sympathetic vibrations in the other combat aviator. He looked at me, looked away. Head nods from the combat vet, nothing from untested.

Everywhere there was noticeable motion away from things tactical, toward things administrative. The Corps, or certainly VMT-103, looked headed toward an 8:00 to 4:30 administrative posture that placed real training and readiness a good distance below administrative graphs and appearances. That Southeast Asian thing, as I once heard it called, slipped out of focus to become an unpleasant sideshow soon to be ended. Not privileged with a command overview, I had no idea of long-term strategy. I wondered why all those women and children had to grieve. For what had my friends died? Why had we killed all those people? We tossed our existences for what? What the hell was this anyway?

The officer corps seemed fraught with amateurism, mistrust, incompetence, faction building, and petty bickering. Excellent aviators I knew were gone or going, it looked like dark days coming. There were no prayers for me in an organization moving away from the reality of people and an operational framework, toward the easily manipulated, symbolic system of paper and an administrative posture. As flying tapered off, I had horrible visions of becoming another unhappy desk type sitting around wistfully babbling about those thrilling moments of yesteryear. New instructors had no combat time, they flew and taught by numbers and books, which is what they knew. That was a way to turn out aviators; it was not producing razor-edged, capable tactical aviators. Combat vets were in the way and the show was winding down. Talking about doing was in; actually doing was out.

So was I.

"Hey!" emanated from somewhere as I crossed the hangar deck. I stopped and saw about the only old friend I had in the squadron. A combat aviator I had known since the training command was standing near an A4 he was inspecting.

"Let's walk," he said. We walked and after an inordinately long time he looked at me. "You're getting out."

"Aye," I nodded.

"Your wrapping is loose or squeezing you, I can't tell which. Isn't fun is it?"

"Yes, it is not fun. I don't know what to do about it."

"There's nothing to do. It's like flak. You're fucked when you're in flak."

I felt the concussions, heard the rattle of little pieces of metal splattering against the aircraft and the canopy, recalled that sense-heightening wondering if I'd live through it. I shrugged my shoulders and exhaled, "Yeah, I remember."

"All you can do is haul on through," pause, "you don't want it to get you. I don't know what you're going to do about that infantry stuff. My brother-in-law was a platoon leader with the one hundred first Airborne, and he is fucking weird right now. Sis doesn't know what to do, right now they're thoroughly hosed."

"Ah. Sorry to hear that," I said. His sister and I had gone out a few times with him and his then fiancée, a brother-sister relationship developed between us. She was smart, pretty, and had picked her husband, wouldn't quit on him. But I guess they weren't having much fun.

We walked along a minute and he mentioned a couple of mutual friends who left the Marine Corps to seek their fortunes. They weren't having much fun either, complained of no one with equivalent experience with whom to relate or talk, that no one really took the time to see their capabilities. Both stated they felt out of place and diminished; neither of them wanted return to the Corps.

"You're combat, an attack aviator and a combat grunt. That's the big part of what you know, and it isn't worth a thing out there." He stopped, looked at me.

"Thank you." I spent a lot of time developing those skill sets.

"Man they can't even see you, and nobody cares," he resumed walking. "I care, I'll even think about you sometimes, but I won't do anything about it. You know how this is."

"Yep," I exhaled, "and it's okay, buddy. Me too." I stopped, faced the aircraft. "But at the moment, out there is better than in here for me."

He laughed, "No doubt about that for any of us. But I really don't think there are places for combat people anywhere."

"Except combat," I replied. "I agree, or should I say it certainly feels that way to me." Yes sir, step into ultra-normal for five minutes, turn back, and find the passageway has been blocked. There is no return. It's just that way.

"God I'm going to miss the aircraft," I told him. Tears came, I had to re-establish a grip. "I love them," sniffle, wipe my face. "I have always."

"I know man," he nodded sadly. We walked along for a few seconds. He stopped, stretched, looked at me. "Look. You can't return anything. You'll mangle somebody, or worse, you'll fuck yourself."

He was referring to one of our friends who stepped into deep doo-doo when a group of hecklers cruelly assaulted his wife and he attacked the hecklers. I know where he was: physical assault on your darling definitely qualifies as threat to state of being. It was a survival issue. It's doubtful the disgusting trash he thumped would ever do that again, but he and his darling were picking up the tab for other peoples' poor breeding and imbecility, nothing new there. What do you think of a group of people that allows boors to physically assault a well-behaved woman, then punishes her and her husband for defending her, in the land of the free, the home of the brave, with liberty and justice for all? In combat the dismal maggots would have been dead in about two heartbeats.

"I know," I replied with a sigh.

"The walking dead out there can hit us with anything, if we counter we're out forever," he looked out the hangar door. "Hell. I thought people would be decent."

I looked out the hangar door also. "Never gave it much thought. I certainly didn't expect to be abased."

"Yeah, well pizzonem. They don't know anything." After a few minutes of silence he asked, "How do you feel?"

My turn to laugh. "Like my parts are concurrently working multiple headings. What are you going to do?"

He continued to stare out the hangar door. "Duck, man. Dodge the whole thing. I'm out next month. I'll hide in my family and an airliner, try to forget everything."

"I'm glad you still have your family, man. Make it work."

We parted with a straight arm, chest high handclasp that sounded like a shot when our hands met. The sharp sound reverberated through the hangar to silence. With tears in our eyes we turned and walked away from each other.

The squadron gave a farewell party in my honor that I really don't remember. Seems the man inside who ran the man outside was off somewhere. Exiting the main gate at MCAS Yuma as a civilian, I was completely lost. I wasn't confused; there just wasn't any place to go or anything to do. Reasons to do or not do anything were gone again, as was tactical aviation.

Where does one find the sense of being, the stimulation a no-kidding firefight with the infantry provides? Where can that level of teamwork be located? What lights one's lights after single-place tactical aircraft? I mean an ultimate version, combat, then training people for combat. What fills a heart after that?

It's entirely possible the gate guards confused me with somebody who cared as I exited the main gate for the last time. The issue was clear to me. The car motored slowly toward the interstate highway on another 100-plus degree day in Yuma. Don't need to say it this time, do I?

As I turned east onto the highway toward Gila Bend, a division of A4s passed overhead, heading for the break. The break is where individual aircraft turn away from a flight over the runway to establish landing interval as they turn downwind. I had to pull off the road to watch. The flight of four broke beautifully. I watched them for a minute, then also broke. Tears for people, tears for aircraft, loss, Lord. I must have sat there a couple of hours.

Chapter 26

X Tahsee

No aircraft, no compadres, little about which to talk, nothing in which to get involved that made much sense. Time amaranthine. Trips through "B" tracks. Looking at everything fifty times a second, so important in combat and tactical aviation, seemed counter-productive in a "normal" environment. The lessons were too deeply etched to be dismissed.

I met people of course, attempted conversation using words based upon dictionary definitions, as I had been taught. I was startled to find that most people seemed to use word and expression meanings based upon expected conversational content as derived from every day experiences, and pronunciations based upon, well, I don't know. Connection and meaning were the issues, correct or incorrect language the means. What happened to my language constructs? Had I moved out-of-phase far enough to alter even the most basic communicative structure? A little review of dictionary definitions and grammar indicated the books and I were fairly close, but accomplished nothing in regard to a lot of speech I was encountering, which of course lead to more isolation. Was this a modern version of the tower of Babel? Not disparate languages so much as word meanings based upon whim, a language per person, nonstandard definitions within the same symbolic set.

People asked questions, filled in answers of their own before I could respond, and then argued with their own answers as if I had introduced that line of thought. I just stood quietly as people applied data constructed from within them to me. Then, regardless of my state of being, speech, or actions, they had me indelibly typed, cataloged, and symbolized using their internal data. Unknown reduced to subjective connotation, rather than examined. Talk about abstraction, I had the feeling the variant used to protect from dealing with emotion in combat introduced serious issues of restricted response and avoidance; the version applied by many normal people gave impression of protecting from necessity of accurately dealing with anything at all.

People connected in the current moment and to the current surroundings were only occasional in my life anyway. Even so, this apparent intentional general disregard exhibited by most was new to me, and frightening. One could be thrown into prison for something heinous, or be exalted for something beneficent, without ever having done or said a thing.

All that aside, most people didn't appear to be involved with much, seeming to be concerned about themselves, their paychecks, recreational pharmaceuticals and alcohol, their car or truck, and getting laid—but little else. Perhaps my outlook was tainted. I could discern minimal to no interest in other human beings, or direction toward other than personal gain at the expense of others. A general working posture seemed to be short-term gain and screw thee—a mien that under most circumstances could have killed people in tactical aviation or combat.

Working at becoming a normal citizen, I soon discovered there were no jobs in which one can merely be competent, get along well, do the job. One must line up with political silliness present in any job environment or one will be discharged, or perhaps demeaned in some way and then discharged. Pointless concocted dramatics. What fun.

After working about two months at an executive search firm, an idea of what things were about in that arena began to emerge. One of my client companies called.

"Why don't you interview for the regional manager position we gave you?" the voice on the phone asked.

The position involved considerable travel and a probability of reasonable money, so why not? After speaking with management to determine acceptability of such action, and a trip to the client company's corporate headquarters, I settled into the local offices as regional manager, with a territory to develop that included a couple of east-coast states. I found an excellent manager for the local area, journeyed east to locate another. The company refused to expense the trip. Why wouldn't a company pay for business expansion? Though unsettled, I continued expansion efforts, but the company refused to pay commissions as agreed. One day, the organization mysteriously disappeared, leaving the area manager scrambling to keep his family running along well, while I was stuck out east. Again, attorneys politely advised there was nothing to be done. Laws to protect people indeed.

Things didn't work anywhere. People wanted to know about the military, then combat. I was showing enough cold to cause nervousness in people, I couldn't get it under a mask. Though not volunteering information about military experience, I didn't misrepresent when asked. For about four years frequent interviewing went well until the combat experience came up.

"What did you do there?" an interviewer asked.

"Well, it was a war." Sometimes I'd ask what they thought I did, sometimes I'd shrug and be quiet. I wanted to mention I lived through it, have a complete body, and am here and willing, let's go. Think they would have understood?

"Were you in combat?" asked another.

Still am, I thought while answering, usually with a head nod.

"Did you kill anybody?" Often it was phrased as "shoot."

"Certainly," was really not what people were set up to hear. They'd squirm, look sideways. You know how difficult it is to interview us governmental killers.

War. Shoot or die. Shoot or watch compadres depending on you get blown apart. What did they think war was? Several times I attempted to explain combat, but no matter, the interviewers' presets moved into place and they stopped seeing what was present, started running their internally filtered versions. So I stopped explaining.

"Why did you go?" Bang! "Don't you feel guilty about it?" Blam! Verbal shots.

"It was the right thing to do. No." Pow! Pow! It would have been simpler if we had used rifles.

"Did you ever shoot women or children?" That was an eyes-upward question I really couldn't dignify with acknowledgement. Did they think war was just hose everybody and everything in sight? Is that what they would have done?

No one asked what I thought about it, what issues may have been prevalent, what the enemy was like or may have done, what it took to live through it, or what I may be able to offer their company. It didn't really matter what I said anyway, when the subject came up and it always did, the interview was over, the job possibility evaporated. Some interviewers ran righteousness and blame at me, some acted like I suddenly turned into an abhorrence. Most just got chilly, making clear there was no job for me. There were a few who aimed and fired emotional garbage, names, ranted and raved like nut cases. Nut cases yowling at a probable nut case; ought to have videotaped one of those. I'd sit with the beast wriggling away in there while some misinformed, frightened, narrowband, obfuscated citizen fired names at me, acted like the three square mile area in which they lived all their life was all there was to know.

At an interview with a particular freight company I was called some of the most sophisticated, intellectually cutting names ever. As I left, an escort of five out of shape, apparently rather dull people appeared. These delightful blobs pushed me around, shouting considerably less intellectually inclined names, making it clear that SEA combat vets ought to have their asses kicked and that they were the ones to do it. They rattled off obscenities while shoving me back and forth between them, generally exhibiting intellectual nothingness and seriously deficient breeding. I kept walking to the bus stop.

Most animals received better treatment and the stupidity and cruelty around me everyday wore me out. I had descended as far I was going. Those five people gave the impression of never having been anywhere or having done anything. They seemed to be hanging onto their lives by their fingernails, and, wanting more of my dignity, refused to cease. When one of them came abreast, kicking at my legs while shouting obscenities, Beastie made a noise from hell. I grabbed a fistful of tee shirt and belt, threw the mass of protoplasm into the trailing group. Cutting iciness volcanoed through me, Beastie nearly jumped out in the open. We faced them, I set my feet, and calculated a first couple of moves.

I clearly saw five startled humans standing unmoving in a state of astonishment. They didn't know tactics, did not set up at all. Reptilian-brained Beastie saw a small group of indistinct, threatening animal shapes gathered to destroy it. It didn't care about tactics or setup, wanting only to remove the threats and continue being. Both of us were ready to dance to their demise or ours.

Blob eyes opened to huge as I stepped toward them. Nada. They just stood there. I took another step.

One of them said, "Somebody's gonna get hurt."

I believe Beastie had something in mind there. I nodded toward the speaker, hoping I could work through them quickly. I wanted to take out a couple and see where we were. Beastie wanted all of them gone, right then.

An individual in a tie ran over from the warehouse. "Get back to work! Now! Go on!"

Having done nothing in my direction since the beast popped up, the disconcerted overweights grumbled and milled about, eventually sauntering to the warehouse. Beastie pranced and salivated, wanted to spring at all those still threatening unprotected bodies, but held for me. The primitive strength and vehemence that monster shows when one is pushed until civilized veneer finally collapses, is definitely startling. I didn't move or speak. Beastie growled and danced while I stood, shaking down the pump. The man in the tie looked like he wanted to say something, but didn't. I didn't have anything to say. He went back to the warehouse. When it seemed safe, and Beastie had settled down, I walked away.

I walked, arriving at my place a few miles later. It was another stare out a window night. No food or drink, nothing. Just sit and stare. I guess people couldn't see this verbal chopping and slashing was at least as damaging to the deliverer as it was to the subject of the remarks. Most combat people stayed away from that kind of thing, having realized how difficult it can be, particularly in clutch situations, to count on a person who has been the target of abject stupidity in the form of verbal abuse. The people around one are foundation, and mangling foundation doesn't help anyone. People who knock down people around them in any way also knock down themselves. It's really simple. Bolster those around you, rise with them.

Ask any actual combat veteran. Everything else kills you.

◉

No one would hire me. I went on a little job creation program, discovering there were plenty of fragmentary things people wanted done. The money was anything but spectacular, however, I could eat and was standing on my feet. I managed to acquire transportation in the form of another motorcycle, a Kawasaki F5, a great power line bike. My brother and I would swoop off into the bushes, riding for hours. The rest of the world worried about money, security, acquisition, and career development, while I went bashing through the brush worrying about balance, traction, power control, and form.

I became involved with a crisis intervention center; if I couldn't do much for myself perhaps I could do something for others. Definitely world class great thinking, wouldn't you say? The crisis intervention center was a small city's hopeful answer to a variety of social ills. Volunteers answered phones, matched available resources with people who could use them. Initial training was good, upon occasion intense. The number of calls each night was rather amazing.

A majority of calls were from lonely people who seemed to require a little direct attention, somebody to acknowledge it was okay for them to be out there as they were. Drug related calls were the second largest category of business. Many times we (we worked in pairs) would be on one phone with a client while using another phone to direct paramedics to the client's location.

Attention-needy, emotional, distraught callers usually seemed to be asking for help on their terms, which is what we attempted to give them. It's true they were ready to hurt themselves, and would if mishandled; there is no question they were in a bad way. But, if one listened closely and tracked with them, one could at least be of some service. Calm quiet voices on the phones stood my hair on end, those even voices seemed to be asking if there was any reason to continue hanging around, which caused harmonic resonance in me. I was easily one of the least valuable resources for that particular question. I spoke with a combat vet one morning around three o'clock.

"Hello, how are you tonight?" I asked.

"Okay," my hair stood up at his too-calm voice. "How are you?"

We talked about nothing much a couple of minutes. His phrasing and general attitude let me know he had been in combat.

He was even, collected, all of his switches were off. I asked if I could do anything for him.

"You already did man," pause, "you sound calm and strong, thanks for talking with me. Let me finish this fucker."

I asked what he was going to finish. He replied, "Good luck, man." Then a pistol shot crashed through the phone. Through tears I looked at the woman working with me.

"Have this traced, the other end is dead," I said.

Best boy, the Reap. If our light comes on when we're born and goes out at the Reap's pick-up, from a distance this planet must appear as a continuously flickering light show. This gent was a combat vet, knew how to self-cancel. He had lived through some bad stuff, came all the way back home, was nonetheless killed by the war. A reason to stay in the civilization eluded him. I have the feeling he just did what he thought people wanted as evidenced by actions and words toward him.

The next few hours were spent with abandonment. He abandoned me, I abandoned him, they abandoned us, and I abandoned them. I left before it was over; they got killed before it was over. Then guilt: What more could I have done? What did I miss that killed them? Why was I here? How come they weren't? Then anger: Who did they think they were, cutting out like that? Who did I think I was when I couldn't do something to keep more of them alive? The whole thing was too strange, much too intense to work with just then. I forced off all my switches and got cold, fast.

I was questioned and re-questioned. I don't think any of those academically oriented people got the mass of the incident. They were concerned with paper, abstract concepts, significance, cases, not with actual people in real situations involving real actions.

"He must have said something about suicide?" they asked. They had the call tape but I guess they just didn't want to believe it. Evaluation of something outside their experience could not be accomplished from within their experience. Those people couldn't grasp the nature of being switched off, nor did they understand defense against betrayal. Perception of betrayal can cause the holding of one's cards close to one's chest, even prevent one from showing they have cards. Anyone can say or not say anything, but intention along with accomplished action is the reality, and both can be obscured by words and preconceived notions.

After six months or so, the crisis intervention center became the new status thing for affluent men's wives and public servants wanting to appear concerned, neither of who demonstrated concern for the people they were engaged to service or the services to be rendered. They appeared as interested in only presenting the impression of doing something socially responsible, and the way they looked. Training became cursory and services began to suffer. Decadence in six months? Good grief. I went motorcycling off into something else.

I met a woman at the crisis center who had the best of intentions and who seemed genuinely interested. That was new. We worked a few shifts together, became friends, spent hours in coffee shops talking about this and that, nothing and everything. One evening she asked if I wanted to talk about it.

It. The it word. Oh shit.

"It'll help," she said, "getting it off your chest will help."

I didn't think the stuff suitable for public consumption, but she convinced me it was okay, that she could manage herself through anything, and that it would be a healthy thing. We went to her place, and sitting on her living room floor in front of a gas fire with unlimited availability of double espressos, I talked. The more I talked, the more distress showed in her face. I stopped several times in deference to her apparent state. She urged me to continue.

"Keep going," she said through her tears.

Yeah, keep going, oh certainly. I held her but couldn't cry with her; my switches were off, doo-dah. After she seemed okay, I left, feeling much lower than whale shit.

Trained counselors didn't get it either; they would just stare like you suddenly were some kind of horror, or like they were so sorry for you they could cry. Screw that. The startlingly redone mental framework of combat is for combat people who don't have to talk about anything or pursue morbid curiosity. They can just sit quietly, looking calm, maybe with churning insides, maybe not, but completely okay with each other, while everyone else jacks around with guessing games.

Walking down South Washington Street one morning, I ran across a small gathering waiting for an office to open. "Heya. What are you all doing?" I asked.

"Waiting," one of them said with a smile.

They were waiting for a Federal Aviation Administration (FAA) examiner, who would administer a series of qualification tests for air traffic controller positions. Hmm. I waited with them and took the tests. Notification of the results would come by mail in about three weeks, I was told, and the job waiting list was roughly two years long.

"Thank you," I said, promptly dropping it from my mental index.

◎

"Why aren't you flying?" various people asked frequently. "You could fly for the airlines."

The airlines, me, oh yes, certainly. What do you think you and everyone else would do if, while piloting your afternoon executive flight to Rome, I rolled our Boeing whatever into a run on one of the competition's aircraft? It's uncontrollable; it's what I know. Tactical weapons platforms.

"Because of my heart," I answered.

"What about your heart?" they wanted to know.

"It's filled with tactical aviation."

They looked at me funny. Well? How would they know?

The guitar crept back into my life. I played five or six hours a day, working Segovia's scales, Guiliani's arpeggios, Cordova's flamenco techniques. After stringing together a few arrangements I began playing a few spots, nothing serious, but there was enjoyment and a feeling of being a little more human.

One Saturday I went to purchase a new exhaust rig for the F5. The Kawasaki dealer persuaded me to ride an H1, the relatively new hot setup with a half-liter, three-cylinder, two-stroke engine, called the "Mach I." I took the thing out for a ride, and though it never got near mach one, the machine was remarkably fast in a straight line. It was small, fairly light, possessing interesting and perhaps dangerous traits in the handling and braking departments. A little right hand twist brought on a huge smile. I traded the F5 and rode the piece of lightning home via Virginia's northwestern hills.

An audition for a guitar and music theory teaching position resulted in a job. It was hard to believe. I taught elementary classical and popular guitar, and when forty students were enrolled it was almost possible to live on the money. I figured more students meant more money, so began a second teaching job at another music store. The first studio declared bankruptcy. The teaching staff went in for paychecks one Thursday to find we would have to sue for our money. I didn't bother speaking with an attorney.

Meanwhile, musical acquaintances started their own studio and I was invited to join them. Then a three-nights-a-week playing job magically appeared at a nice little specialty restaurant with a forty-one-page wine list. I played solo jazz on a sunburst Gibson L-5 and developed a small following. One night, between sets out in front of the place, I nearly obliterated a lady who came out with friendly intentions. She quietly approached from behind, a little too quietly I'm afraid. I didn't hurt her, but was on the way to it when I got the picture, halting everything before anything occurred. She was frightened, didn't know where that could have gone. I was terrified, knew exactly where it could have gone. Pretty dumb, standing there like a goon with no scan going. Now Beastie and I duly observe all things.

Notification from the FAA of a position in the Air Route Traffic Control Center at Palmdale, California, arrived one morning, referring me to the FAA facility at Washington National Airport for a physical and a tour. It also mentioned the move would be at my expense. It had been within a few days of two years since I took the exam. I passed the physical, toured the facility, which looked a lot like a Marine Air Control Squadron, and found the aviation jargon comfortable. A lot of thought, and considerable conversation with everyone I knew, finally prompted acceptance of the position.

As the airliner departed from Dulles International, I watched the surface drop away. It felt good to have atmosphere between the Earth and me again, even as a p-, pass-ah, this is hard to say, p-passenger in a -, um -, a transport.

Chapter 27

Owtov Mined

The packed airliner with teensy seats approached Los Angeles International through some of the most stifling brown smog I had ever seen, much worse than last I was there. Fleeting thoughts of landing among skeletal remains of a once bustling civilization ran as the airliner extended flaps, lowered landing gear for approach. After a myriad of turns for traffic sequencing to a busy airport, the transport vehicle landed; the airport was definitely full of life. The terminal had changed only in that it was larger and much more active.

Luggage and rental car bits weren't really more horrible at LAX than elsewhere, though they required a little more endurance. After escape from the airport complex, I headed north on the San Diego freeway to Interstate 5, the maze of concrete and people remaining fairly constant until reaching Sylmar. Turning onto the Antelope Valley Freeway placed Los Angeles tension behind rocks, the jangle dissipated. The drive up the Antelope Valley freeway was increasingly pleasant, though the surrounding country became less populated, less foliated, and less encouraging as I proceeded northward.

Palmdale hangs on to the edge of the Mojave Desert, nestled at its bordering southwestern foothills twenty five hundred feet above sea level. To the north is the city of Lancaster, to the northwest the little town of Quartz Hill, and stretching farther than one could see to the north and east lay the Mojave Desert. Though a genuine legal city to be sure, one would hardly mistake the place for oh, say Madrid. The Air Route Traffic Control Center was located just off Avenue P, northeast of town on the grounds of the Palmdale Airport with its huge aircraft industry hangars. After wandering around, feeling the high desert wind, becoming accustomed to the silicate mineral smell, I drove to the center.

Check-in. I was escorted about the place, met people, and received a little welcome aboard chat from the center chief, pleasant treatment that encouraged chances of doing well there. I settled into an apartment, began learning the air route traffic control trade, the new area, and another lifestyle.

Controllers were from a variety of backgrounds, everything from shoe sales to computer processor architecture and design. There were a couple of former tactical aviators, though most weren't aviators of any type. Nearly all were well versed in air traffic procedures and concerned with safe, efficient handling of aircraft. There were the expected few insecure know-it-alls, but the majority were good people, good at what they did.

A controller's collective bargaining organization, the Professional Air Traffic Controllers Organization, was campaigning unhappiness with pay and working conditions. It immediately started running "Are you or aren't you with us?" pressure on me, the new guy. The working environment seemed all right to me, and though the job could be extremely demanding, no one seemed unfairly overworked or particularly underpaid. It was just a tough job at times. But I was a boot, and so calculated that I didn't know anything. Even as a boot, problems within middle and high level management were obvious, but those people were no longer controllers. Besides, the issue of individuals working at questionable or cross-purposes in middle and high level management wasn't new. The FAA was a bureaucracy and it seemed reasonable to presume most management people were attracted out of purely selfish motives. I checked switches off, proceeded.

Manual aircraft control training commenced slowly, working quickly to a fair pitch. The final problem, a pass/fail exercise involving simulated aircraft traveling in all directions with individual airspeeds of up to 600 knots at every conceivable altitude below 24,000 feet, was a little much for a person writing on strips of paper and using only radio control procedures. Of course the thing was designed to present a certain shock to one's system, and, should one be doing well, of course the instructors took great pleasure introducing a guaranteed ringer amid most concentrated traffic. If the ringer got past one, a rather tongue-in-cheek simulated phone call from one of the instructors went something like, "Hello, Los Angeles Center? This is the Bakersfield Sheriff's department. Do you know anything about sheet metal falling near the intersection of Route 99 and Interstate 5?"

It was an intense exercise. You probably wouldn't believe how hard people worked to keep simulated aircraft safely apart during that thing. Perhaps the idea was to load us up and see what happened. I believe they learned we each could employ a form of coarse language.

From the manual aircraft control classroom one proceeded downstairs to the control floor, which contained the master computer console, radar sectors, and the Palmdale Flight Service Station. The center was broadly divided into low and high altitude portions at 24,000 feet, then into geographic areas, which were subdivided into sectors established by volume of traffic. Some sectors, Burbank for example, were small; others, such as Bryce Canyon, were huge. In theory, traffic load was more or less equally distributed across the sectors. That may have been, but people working the Burbank sector tilted their heads back and screamed considerably more loudly and more often than did people working the Bryce Canyon sector.

In the normal computer enhanced working environment a good deal of information about each aircraft was presented on the radar display screen at each sector. Data relative to a specific flight could be displayed in blocks attached to the aircraft marker, and presented and positioned at the controller's option. The screen additionally contained information concerning air route structure, facilities, approaches, fixes, navigational aids, restricted areas, most things needed to safely move aircraft about. Sector screens updated every few seconds, causing aircraft to appear as hopping along routes of flight.

Raw broadband radar, the old primary but now backup system, showed only aircraft transponder readout, and perhaps an aircraft's skin paint. One could hear groans from all over the center when the computer-enhanced system went down and the place shifted to broadband mode. It was essential to work well in the broadband environment, but it certainly wasn't fun with even just a moderate amount of traffic in a sector.

There was a printer in each area that generated the area's flight strips, little rectangular pieces of paper containing aircraft, flight, route, altitude, and special circumstances information pertinent to a specific flight. These were posted at each sector passed through by the flight. The strips were notice that the sector would be seeing another aircraft at about such and such a time, at such and so an altitude, on this or that route of flight. Manual and computer handoff procedures were usually executed between controllers to pass aircraft from sector to sector. The little strips were valuable for planning and auditing, and during abnormal conditions. Controller trainees were privileged to spend days on their feet tearing strips off the printer, stuffing them into styrene holders, and delivering them to sectors. Albeit tedious, it was a good way to learn particulars of an area.

Normally, two people manned each sector—a radar controller on the "R" position and a communication/coordination person on the "D" position. The "D" side was responsible for communication and coordination with adjacent sectors; the "R" side handled aircraft directly. One eventually moved from the printer to "D" positions within the area. Once qualified on at least two sectors, then qualified on those "R" positions, one would then become a journeyman controller.

Working a "D" side after having been there about two years, the radar screen objects began to blur. I shook my head, blinked, wiped my eyes, but couldn't read the data blocks. The sector "R" man watched me make funny faces for a few minutes and called for the hot relief. I went outside for a while. No use, visual acuity had seriously deteriorated. I was awarded a medical down status. My vision worsened so I went to a specialist.

"It really isn't good," the specialist said.

Well no shit.

"It will probably get worse."

Probably worse, the specialist didn't know? Great. After a few days, colors followed acuity. The world became amorphous sepia shapes and shadows.

If it was larger than a couple of inches across, I managed to stumble over it. I knocked things around, burned my hands, poured coffee all over everything. I didn't dare leave the house because I might never find it again. Night, day, indistinct shapes were easily discernable, but I was not having a real good time. Bashing into things was so frustrating that I limited moving around to the kitchen and a small area in the dining room just through the kitchen door. For a while it seemed that little thirty foot space would be all I would ever know.

The phone rang once after I almost forgot there were phones. Two billion collisions and eleven rings later I got there, no one was on the line. Damn. Was I really that weak? Was this my exit setup? It couldn't be. I listened carefully, worked my tactile senses, and attempted to acquire environmental information with alternate sensors. The vision thing was a dealt hand, another hump to be handled. Eventually I stopped crunching into things. I even managed to brew and pour coffee reasonably well. I really don't want you to ever have to know this, but there is a wealth of good information available without sight.

The FAA walked me, naturally. What else could they do? The lost job was followed by the car, motorcycle, and house. All the government agencies I spoke with, you know, the ones constantly yapping about their eagerness to help, seemed to feel the same way as the FAA—too bad, so sad, tough. California provided unemployment pay for a while, but that was the extent of assistance given by all those agencies touting their wonderful helpfulness. It didn't seem fair to me; I had done my part. While the "service to people" line justified existences and obtained funding, it had nothing to do with actual service or performance. Government tax legislation forces the contribution of a huge portion of income annually for nothing but hype and pocket lining. Disgusting.

With time, my vision began to improve. Perhaps life wasn't over. I started getting around and could soon almost pass for normal as far as vision was concerned. Driving was a strain, but if really careful, I could manage in the low traffic volume local area. Of course, if somebody had inverted traffic lights things would have been bad. There wasn't a prayer of employment, however, and potential jobs became history the instant an employer got wind of the medical dismissal from the FAA. I sold the majority of things not in the house when the bank locked me out, a process seeming to position the California Homestead Act—ostensibly designed to assist people in need maintain their home—as just another piece of misrepresentative crap.

At least the climate was warm. For a while I hung around various places during the day, slept at friends' places at night. I returned to the guitar; if one could find the thing, one didn't need vision to play it. I managed to land a few gigs, ruthlessly budgeted unemployment money, got into a place, and eventually acquired an automobile, which helped get me around a little more. Weapons, unused or not even thought of much except for regular cleaning, now remained near so I could move out in no time. It was important to be ready during this period of time, but ready for what I had no idea. I certainly wasn't expecting anything, still there was a feeling of urgency, a sense of impending something, so I made a few presumptions based upon the most extreme circumstances experienced in my life, set up that way.

There were long periods spent in the desert by myself, and though my eyes weren't normal by any means, I could get along. Seeing only sepia hues wasn't too horrible an inconvenience in the desert, though I know I missed many things that remained motionless. But an environment doesn't hide because of diminished vision.

When internally urged, I'd hat out to the least populated area reasonably locatable, park and booby trap the car, and walk until finding a good cache location to use as a sort of base camp while wandering around for hours, days, weeks, sometimes months. Can't tell you what that was about because I don't know, it just felt like the right thing. Direct, uninterrupted access to self and my relationship with the universe allowed a much better viewing of things. It also may have precluded public unleashing of pent-up anger. I certainly didn't want to hurt anyone, don't believe I would have, but one can never tell. At least more embarrassment or confinement was avoided.

Thought a lot while out, observed everything, wandered everywhere, shot a little, and stayed away from other humans. I suffered from headaches, caused by working my eyes too much. Some of them lasted for days. But my visual acuity continued to improve, so I held my head and kept working on my vision. When really hungry, which was considerably less frequently then I would have thought, I'd hunt or set traps. The high desert didn't yield fat, fur-bearing animals, or carcasses weighing hundreds of pounds. Rabbits and snakes were the normal food *du jour*. When supplemented with a little store bought whatever, available from the cache, dinner was fine.

Every place on Earth has its own sound, if the environment quiets enough so it can be heard. The magnificent sound of the high desert wasn't something I heard right away. After a few days out I'd cock my head this way and that, close my eyes, and try to make my ears larger or attempt to shape shift to a wolf or some other animal that could really hear, while sitting for hours just listening. I knew there was a sound there; it was just elusive. Then, one morning while standing by a small waterhole listening for the something I couldn't hear, the sound focused, a kitten soft wind-whisper rushing over the top of a faint low frequency rumbling suggestive of mountain-sized things moving. It seemed to be coming from everywhere, contained in everything. The sound was also felt in the presence of the high desert, a unique marker for that part of the world, an experience involving much more than sound.

The sun was present as was my heat. The wind was there, and my breath, the Earth, my body, water, and my blood. The desert made its sounds, my heartbeat, the universe rumbling rhythmically, my spirit flaring in concert. The components were all present, interlaced, balanced. What a majestic, fulfilling occurrence.

Once in a while I did run across people out enjoying the desert. As far as I could tell, none of them knew I was around. Most looked relaxed and happy as they walked along, but how quickly they would have expired in combat. They weren't in combat though, so there was no reason for them to be in that mode. People like me did that, precluding need for their participation.

Late one night while walking through a little arroyo located exactly nowhere, I heard a woman moan. With visions of results of torturous things I had seen elsewhere in the world, I made the rifle hot and prepared to run interdiction on her assailant. I checked around for guards, approached quietly. As I snake-headed around a rock to have a look, the woman moaned again. Well. She and her lover were completely nude on a blanket under the desert stars, and there was no doubt of her enthusiastic cooperation with the hard-working guy. A used pickup truck was parked a few feet away, their little campfire was out but I don't think it mattered as they were generating enough heat to warm most of the arroyo. I moved along, toasted by their display of unreserved passion, frosted by my solitary state of existence.

One afternoon I found somebody's cache booby-trapped in a most familiar manner. Approaching a small draw the get-out-of-here-right-fucking-now feeling fired off. I hauled up a little hill and settled into a judiciously located clump of firm ground affording an excellent view of the area. Eventually I saw motion where he was set in, waiting for me.

"Hey, down in that little draw! Stand up! Let's talk!"

"Who the fuck are you?" came back at me.

"No one. You?"

"Nobody," pause, "how do we get out of this?"

I didn't know. "Hold your weapon over your head and stand up?"

"You mean me?" He obviously thought I was nutso.

"I mean both of us. We can do the Chieu Hoi bit unless you can think of something better."

"Who were you with?" he asked after a short silence.

"First Battalion, Seventh Marines. You?"

"The One Seventy Third. Wouldn't you know, a damned Marine!"

Damned? Could be. After checking for flankers, I moved to the other side of the little hill where I had a clear shot at the gent who was looking up toward where I had been.

"All right, man!" He held his rifle up in such a way as to use it quickly. "Let me see you!"

I held my rifle up, also able to bring it into rapid use. "Here! I'm over here now."

His head turned, eyes widened, "You fucker," he shouted as he stood up.

"Come on." I was suddenly tired. "I don't want to keep this going."

"Yeah." He dropped his weapon to his side. "Me too. It'll just kill us."

He was from Lancaster, about twenty clicks away. He had been in the desert nearly six months. He told me of the triple-cross that obliterated his outfit in the Ia Drang valley and the terrible turn in his life since coming home. Tears ran profusely. He couldn't stop talking about lying on the ground while pieces of his buddies splattered all over him, under fire so intense that bodies couldn't fall after they were hit, jerking about above him as they were shot to pieces. He didn't know how he lived through it.

Me neither. I went back to my cache, feeling worse than I had for a long time, packed up, and moved about ten clicks.

Chapter 28

Fifth Figure

The desert was still, soft, and beautiful as I regained awareness of my surroundings, returning to the present moment. Memories and the present—often there was little difference between them for me.

There was a twist to this alone-in-the-desert business: a feeling of uselessness together with the isolation. We all know that one is supposed to be able to do things for oneself, especially when the perception is that no one wants anything to do with you and you're unable to define a particular purpose. I sincerely hope you have somebody around wanting something you have to offer so that you never have to consider this issue. Presumably you get up, go about your business, picking up acknowledgment from various people as your day progresses. But when operating without a drive involving other people, one also is privileged with inventing a reason to be each day. A decision must be made, action taken to be there, every day. There's no one to provide reasons, they aren't automatic; purpose isn't automatic.

We pick up drives and rough accomplishment shaping early, from many sources in several environments most of us probably never consider. They're part of the inheritance from early environment and people examples. I think they're in a state of continuous small modification as they tailor to specific circumstances. But when basic structure collapses due to inadequacy for whatever reasons, and there is desire to continue one's version of a productive life, the structure must be replaced, and that includes drives and accomplishment parameters. It's meticulous and time-consuming; a process that often smarts considerably.

The high desert afforded the opportunity to investigate loneliness. I don't mean being alone. Alone was part of the desert scenario all the time, no problem. I mean loneliness. An icy, paralyzing wind blowing through the jagged gash in the middle of your heart that grants access to your entire being. The emptiness sitting in your center, masking you from everything, making everything you do seem stupid and inhuman.

That kind of loneliness, absolute loneliness, that can expand from a small internal speck to outside your reach in an instant, anytime, anywhere, with no people or with any number of people around. It is bad stuff that can cause self-botching of attempts to communicate with others despite your intentions. It can give you the impression there's no point to anything. Make you do stupid things that lead to further isolation. Make you scream at the anguish in your heart. Cave you in on yourself. Make you kill yourself.

One evening after a couple of intense days spent with the Monster of the Frozen Heart, I decided a planet exit was in order. I couldn't locate another solution that seemed to have the most remote chance of success and nothing else made sense. I felt dangerous to everybody, everything, and was sure I would eventually damage something or somebody despite my intentions. Beastie had been asleep for a while, but was still in there. Only the Lord knew what would wake that thing. A drastic environmental alteration seemed to be a deal, knocking myself out of the physical ought to accomplish that. Perhaps I would encounter some of the beings I knocked off the planet.

I carefully crosscut two bullets so they would explode my head. I cleaned the pair of 5.56 mm rounds to a dazzling shine, all the while thinking of a bright-eyed alert little boy running through a magnificent field, completely enchanted with life on the planet Earth. What do you suppose happened to that youngster?

Living through the thing with even less capacity was out of the question, as was lying around on the desert while my body died slowly. I figured quick trigger work should get the second round off as the first impacted. I sat a long time after cleaning the rifle, mixing with the wind, seeing if I could ride along. But riding along with the wind without a machine while still in a body is also in the "chances exactly not any" category.

Carefully positioning myself among the twilight-darkened rocks overlooking Palmdale from some distance south, I jammed the butt of the rifle into the sand and knelt. As I placed the barrel of the rifle against my eye, the tears that had been flowing all day moistened the flash suppresser. I angled my head so the bullets would get the center of my brain, released the safety, touched the trigger with my thumb, and took up the trigger slack.

All the knowledge, all moments, actions, experiences, feelings, perceptions, and conclusions were about to die with me. Everything. The total viewpoint, the entire knowledge base evaporated. It seemed a shame; somebody ought to know all this.

I could almost feel a bullet exploding in my brain. Suddenly, my being separated into three components. Spirit jumped around in a frenzy and seemed supportive of departure. Mind wailed in protest. Body acknowledged the action in a matter-of-fact way as it charged with adrenaline. The three-part tear in my being, the display of the composites' different views on the matter, caused me to feel stretched to the point of breaking. I thought I might just blow apart without ever pulling the trigger.

"Hey!" The voice crashed, reverberating through my being like thunder in the mountains.

"HEY!" It was louder the second time. I knelt, not really present, not yet gone, focused on the voice.

"Look," the voice said, "you are responsible for everything you engineer, whether you know about it or not, whether you understand it or not, whether you see what you are doing or not. Everything. Creation, construction, destruction, counter creation. Everything. This wipe yourself act can be done anytime. Go farther."

I shook. My breath came in gasps. Moisture poured down my face and I began to sense molecular structure in each grain of sand around me, each atom of air. Spirit didn't communicate anything. Mind seemed relieved yet frightened. Body felt smug and strong.

After regaining control of my hands, I made the rifle cold, sat back shaking like I've never shaken. The composites rejoined after a protracted series of noisy deep breaths and long exhales that took my entire body to accomplish. Eventually, thought resumed. Of course I can go farther, I realized—it's only another hump. After more time, the sweat stopped and the pump shook down. Throughout, Beastie never stirred.

I sat in a state of suspended animation the whole night. The next thing of which I was consciously aware was the sun breaking over the horizon, its warm rays smacking the side of my face. The warmth slid down my arms as sunlight splattered the surface around me, percolating into things, bringing life. I stood, hoisted the rifle onto my hip, and waited for something to break loose, as I had done countless times before. I looked at the sky and the desert a long time, sensed the environment, felt internal changes, and watched as Palmdale reconstructed in the high desert morning.

Thoughts concerning people starting their days in the houses below caused me to wonder about what I would find there. How would I do? How does one rejoin a civilization anyway? What does one say? "Hey, how are you?" I've been away a while, please don't ask?

A boy was suddenly present, looking at me. It was me, as a boy! What the? Me as the shiny new boot jet pilot focused behind him. The aviator was no longer shiny-new; there was a professionalism about him, a knowing look in his eyes. Freckles was suddenly there with his M60, quietly looking at me. Then Slim To appeared.

Chills.

A fifth figure appeared, his face pale, expressionless, with hard eyes and a straight line for a mouth. He placed the butt of his M-16 on his hip, stood quietly, menacingly, authoritatively.

Serious, blood-freezing, thought-halting, motion-arresting CHILLS.

I could nearly hear destruction, feel the death around him. Was the Reap there too? A part of me I never looked at nodded at me, at the others. The first four stood calmly, waiting for me to do something; the fifth figure stood quietly, clearly ready for anything I would do.

The first four were incredibly beautiful, but the presence of me as a FAC nearly knocked me into orbit. Damn. Is that how I looked?

Freckles looked at the FAC, back at me. "Okay, Sir, here we go. Remember what I told you." They were words he spoke in the rice paddies just outside Hill 10's perimeter wire one morning as we were going out. He set his ammo belt.

The FAC shifted his M-16, nodded at me, looked at Freckles, then looked down toward Palmdale.

Slim To's face formed his funny little almost smile. "Okay, PH," he said quietly, "time to ride."

Chapter 29

Fashe On

How in the world could I visually acquire manifestations of myself at various points in my life, to say nothing of manifestations of two other people? The figures faded, the energy didn't dissipate for quite a while. Maybe they were there, maybe not, either is fine. Replay of that scenario still provides energy.

I slid the rifle over a shoulder, took a huge breath, stood awhile longer. Maybe I had really flipped. Nevertheless, the sun rose steadily. Illumination shifted across the face of the planet as it climbed into another day, providing the means for the daily reconstruction of the little town in the high desert. The sights, sounds, smells, and feel of a high desert morning were comfortable and reassuring, whether I had flipped or not. And the colors—soft, hard, accent, pastel—were beautiful, majestic. My vision was nearly back to normal and color had returned, the return of which was a most remarkable experience. What a day that was.

Palmdale stirred. Cars appeared, collecting in bunches as they moved from stoplight to stoplight. The desert's soft whisper-rumble was increasingly occluded by the irregular sounds of civilization—light, groping, nervous, out of balance—not at all like the harmonious solid sounds of the planet.

I would soon head into Palmdale, then back to large cities with their mind-numbing, sense-reducing endless cacophony. Cities, where men and women routinely injure, mentally cripple, and destroy other men and women for money. Cities where various companies' rules are laws for their employees and people slaves suffer as their souls are torn out. Cities where an individual has only the value of the occupied job slot, families don't count, and children, one of our most valuable resources, are cast about like so much jetsam.

I knew that cities were the centers of the civilization, the lucrative markets, the arenas for professional advancement, and the only places where I stood any chance of re-establishing my life. But to me they were also confused, reduced-ethics, disturbed, uncomfortable places. Would the clarity gained in the desert remain? Would the new internal structure work? How about the accomplishment structure? Did I have the drives right? Well, ready or not, re-entrance was underway.

I exhaled most of the air, pulled the jungle cover down to keep the sun out of my eyes, and started down a rocky slope leading to hills below. Would this little walk really take me back into the world? I slid down another sandy slope, thought about going to the car, but dismissed that as it seemed more appropriate to walk. I wondered what to say to people, what would they say to me? No doubt the rifle would cause comment, but I wasn't going to leave it in the desert. The rifle? Hell, I would cause comment.

The morning was beautiful, my senses were peaked. I felt alive as I worked down rolling hills to the road into town. Upon reaching the road I unloaded the rifle, slinging it muzzle down under my arm. I pulled the heads off of the rounds set up for myself, dumped the powder, and threw the two bullets across the road and the casings back toward the hill I just left. Those rounds would never be fired.

"Hey! What the fuck are you?" The words came loudly from the window of a passing car.

"Just a human, trying to figure out a few things," I answered as the car disappeared over a little hill

Just a human wearing dusty jeans, rattlesnake skin cowboy boots, an olive drab T-shirt with the sleeves cut off, dog tags, jungle cover, gloves with the fingers cut half off, carrying a rifle and canteen, with a space blanket, poncho liner, and denim drover rolled up and tightly tied to the belt at the small of the back. And don't forget the Kabar, the large black knife hanging off the belt on the right side. What would you have thought had you seen me in the desert that morning?

A car rushed by with two children's eyes open wide enough to obscure their little faces. A pickup truck passed, skidded to a stop a couple of hundred feet in front of me, paused, then rapidly pulled away.

Damn. Too much attention. Well, nothing to be done about the apparel, so I ensured the rifle was tucked in close, held in an unthreatening way. I didn't want anyone upset on my account. I just wanted to get to civilization and execute the restart of my life.

Tires scolded the pavement for its light cover of sand behind me. Uh-oh! I whipped around, unsnapping the strap of the Kabar as a silver-blue Mercedes stopped. The driver poked his head out the window.

"What the hell are you doing?" he wanted to know.

Whew! Just an affluent couple in a nice car. I took a breath, re-strapped the Kabar, relaxed.

"I'm going to Palmdale to get some breakfast."

"You look like you're going to blow up Palmdale."

"Sorry about the inimical appearance. I've been out here a couple of days."

Sure, a couple of days. I had to look like leather from weeks of sun, desert, and dust. The lady tilted her head out her window, looked a minute, then smiled. That was a warm thing to do so I smiled back. They were quiet, looked at each other, then he spoke.

"Get in. We'll give you a ride, before somebody shoots you."

A stranger indicating even the tiniest bit of concern was nearly overwhelming. I hoped it was a pointer toward how things might go. Though I kept clean on the desert with sand and not much water, which works well by the way, I wasn't sure I smelled all that wonderful. However, living on the high desert didn't leave me with the same order of body odors as when in the jungle. I dusted off, got in the car.

The soft tan leather interior was plush after the desert. The leather, his cologne, and her perfume were a dazzling array of thick preternatural smells. I doubt they could smell anything anyway, and neither could I now. The lady looked at me, at her husband, back at me, started to say something, held back. His motions were stiff. He carefully kept his face away from my view. They both seemed to want to say something, but couldn't get it out.

"Thanks for stopping."

Why in the world would a pleasant, prosperous looking couple stop for somebody of my appearance?

"Do you always dress like that?" she asked.

"No Ma'am. Just when I'm on the desert a couple of days." A couple of days again, huh? Couldn't they see I had been out there forever, didn't they sense my uneasiness about something as simple as talking to people? What did they want to say?

"Are you all right?"

Wow. What a question. Lord knows, ma'am, certainly I do not. She turned her head to the car's front as she trailed off the words. Her voice quality, and the peculiar expression on her face implying a much deeper question, solved the mystery.

"Oh. Who was he with?" I asked.

She looked surprised, relieved at the same instant. "How did you know?" Her eyes looked toward me; she was seeing her dead son. "You were there, weren't you?"

I nodded. She took a deep breath. "He was in the Army, a Ranger. It's been five years," she exhaled slowly, "we have pictures, he looked a lot like you look."

She didn't mean the jeans and cowboy boots. She saw weapons, the combatant shape, a representation of her dead combatant son, the one in the pictures he sent home. Once you do something, it's done and doesn't go away; the combat shape, a part of me, there for eternity. I stopped trying to hide, ceased my attempts to run over myself.

"I'm truly sorry, Ma'am."

Damn. War. Years later it still hurt people who weren't even there.

"Thank you," her eyes were moist.

The man spoke after clearing his throat, "You look like you've been in a war."

"I was with the Marine Corps in that war. I just needed some time." It was the answer to what I thought he was really asking. "But it's over now."

Oh, really?

Over. High order of function, intensity of emotion, feeling of belonging, being an essential part, contributing something clearly assessable, the satisfaction, precision, action, concentration—gone. No more skimming within a few feet of the planet's surface at 600 knots or so, then zooming to twenty thousand feet plus to pick the next stretch of surface to rush. No more close head-on ACM passes with a friend at closure rates of 1300 knots or faster, to turn and twist, carving the sky with beautiful three-dimensional curve traces, leaving wispy aerodynamic contrails from gee loading as each attempted to best the other. No more popping up the aircraft into sky packing with jagged bursts splattering particles against the aircraft, then pulling the nose through to a target, setting up a run, wondering if you were the quicker, or the gunners below. No more firefight intensity hammering in, pounding your senses until all you could do was shoot, perhaps scream. No more living as forcefully as you could manage. Exceptionally high function, super adrenaline rush—gone. No more the pump. No more ultra-high game conditions with ultimate stakes.

I sat in the back seat, running things through my head, while they sat in the front doing essentially the same: she reflecting on her son, he focusing on the well-being of his wife.

And me, thought streaming ...

An existence where life was the valued entity, with each person having distinct worth and making essential contributions, where death was an immediate reward for poor performance, misted into memory. The exceptional performance of then was occluded by the system-generated, shadow-society numbness of now—a society dominated by a colorless, odorless, tasteless system.

Remembrance of the courage people displayed in the face of the Reap, whether it left them there or took them. Only brave people look into the face of the Reaper and continue to work a situation. Did anyone other than those immediately concerned see that? Does it matter? Do individual moments or the remarkable situations people handle alone matter? Would fortunate people warmly holding each other against humankind's cold see the haze-figures standing outside, detect the hesitancy to come in because of what those figures know, what they've seen, the feeling they may somehow interfere with normal people's chances, or perhaps damage them in some way? Who can see the haze-figures? With whom can they be?

And there is life, there is death, in the main there seems to be only excitation, continuous descent, moral decay, spiritual bankruptcy. The civilization's deity turned to money, currency *oben alles*—a philosophy potentially containing the seeds of mankind's destruction. A handful of metals, minerals, a fistful of paper—emerging as more valuable than life, thought, dignity, or the press toward better?

So. Rejoin a civilization of purportedly free people ruled by a government that condones murder applied as a business tool. Sure. American freedom, touted above all, the freedom to be, look, understand, and behave as I think you should, rather than as you believe. Do anything you want as long as I don't mind, and be sure to pay all your taxes and stay out of my business, or you may disappear.

Become a taxpayer—another deceived, exploited source of governmental income? Control, manipulation, and suppression under the banner of individual freedom and rights? The right to be executed as President because you're not lining up well with the corporates, Old Boy? Nineteen hundred sixty-three, few are alive who can see, that without rather drastic changes, the year of the beginning of the end for the United States. Didn't we transition from democracy to police state with the perpetual myth, a myth well designed for the purpose of mesmerizing people in order to control large portions of their money?

Re-enter the civilization indeed. Oh fuck yes ...

So a smile—a charming smile—for the distinguished looking couple that lost a son in a faraway hopeless place for indiscernible reasons.

"We're going to Mojave. Is this okay?" the man asked. The car stopped at Palmdale's edge. Sure it's fine, I nodded as they turned to look at me.

"You're crying," the lady softly exclaimed at the moisture collecting in the corners of my eyes. She did that so gracefully, with such respect for state of being, it was beautiful.

A boot camp cadence ran through my head, "Good Marines they never die, when they're hit they never cry." Sure they don't. They don't cry about compadres who get hit, or about good Marines that did die, or about their civilization throwing itself away while corporate and government entities enhance the process either. Certainly not.

"It's that sort of thing, Ma'am. Thank you for the ride. Good luck to you."

Exiting the Mercedes, the door clunked solidly as I closed it, placing more than physical mass between us. I could actually feel emotional separation as the car pulled away.

A seemingly endless stream of emotions and thoughts trickled, ran, and then gushed like blood from a head wound. That was new, not really exciting. Placing people in the position of having to deal with an unusually dressed person carrying a rifle, hesitantly walking along with tears dripping, wasn't what I wanted at all. So screw breakfast anyway. I moved away from the road. I'd be back together some day. But for now, get my car and do something about the gear.

I was still outside the civilization, but with a new respect for life, love, and peace forged out of time spent with no one. Could I make it back in? Would the blood on the moon go away? No doubt circumstances would become difficult now and then. Certainly there would be pain from time to time. And it's doubtful anyone with whom to talk or be with deeply would show up. But things had been worse, and as Slim To had so frequently said, "It was time to ride."

Black Granite Registry

The Wall stood there, quietly waiting, a blood-beacon source emanating exclusive multi-colored ethereal flames, siren voice symphonies, and combat zone pheromones, all of which specifically pulled on certain violated hearts and perturbed spirits. Effusing tractor beams of tragedy and triumph interfused with subliminal images of restoration, resolution, absolution, perhaps peace, and possibly one's integral destruction. The black granite registry silently insisted, demanded, visit by anyone in combat with any of those represented, as soon as could be reasonably managed.

After several false starts, one morning around three o'clock I sat in heavy rain on the steps of the Lincoln Memorial, looking toward the Washington Monument. Without utilities or weapon, the sounds of straight down rain on concrete, granite marble, and a leather coat weren't the same, but it was good enough.

Had I cleansed enough to walk among the names of all those dead without tainting them? Did I really want to see the Wall? Did I really not want to see the Wall?

There are better ways to observe that shimmering incision in the Earth's surface for the first time than alone at three in the morning in energetic straight-down rain. But, well, I was there. The shadow-edge for heroes gently pulled my chain taut, held it an instant, let it loosen slowly, gracefully repeating the process with increasing frequency until I was back on the sharp edge of a blade.

Guess I may as well walk down there.

Overcoming anticipation of automatic weapons fire from the trees to the south took some time. Actually getting down onto the walkway took longer. All those names, symbols of people dead in ways no one should ever imagine, spiked in granite, hung for eternity on a wall in a park located within a city with one of the nation's highest murder rates.

What to expect? I approached like a point, moving slowly, nervously, sensing anything, trying to hear through the rain, looking at everything a septillion times. The sun's rising was obscured by overcast and rain, but it didn't matter a bit. Sitting in the grass off of the walkway with a ten click stare and tears, sort of sensing white letters disappear into the dark granite as rain permeated the cuts in the stone, it was obvious there would be another day. People began to show around dawn. Passersby were gracious about not noticing, the rain was nonetheless fortuitous.

Ghosts, flashes of combat, each friend's name firing something in my memory. For days afterwards, too.

I returned a few weeks later on a Sunday to close the laceration opened by the place. The grounds were inundated with yammering people who apparently knew everything about everything. I believe it could easily be said I was singularly unprepared for that. In short order I filled with enmity toward pompous sightseers with ridiculous remarks about something of which I thought they couldn't even imagine. A particular individual stood near the angle formed by the Wall's two segments, loudly declaring what he would have done had he been there. I envisioned cranking off a couple of rounds in his general direction. Think a little combat zone personal peril reality would have affected his ignorant braggadocio?

A ghastly visit. I saw two other combat vets, a few apparent family members of some of the gents on the wall, and a whole herd of people who hadn't earned the right to talk while in the presence of those names. At the time I didn't think they even had a right to be there. No survival threats, Beastie didn't wiggle at all, but Lord I was ANGRY.

In a terrible state, I moved off to the trees to the south. Another combat vet came over, obviously going through about the same thing. We acknowledged each other and sensing that close proximity was not the hot setup, he parked at exactly the right distance, close enough to link, far enough away to obviate engagement. Deep, fiery, undirected, unfocused, monumental, inexplicable rage. We rode the bizarre anger together. I can't imagine how things remained intact with that much furor rushing outward from the two of us. We sat glaring at everything except each other, shaking, internally exploding for a few hours. Eventually we unwound, embraced, and went our ways without a word. I don't know his name or location; I do know of his internal stance and some of what he has done.

Subsequent visits brought out more items, none of which knocked me down too badly. Excursions to the Wall, along with a few other things cropping up now and then, served as evidence that I wouldn't make it all the way back to normal. It's just the way of it.

The black granite registry is beautiful, recondite, an appropriate memorial to the war I knew. Cuts in the dark stone darken when wet, bleed to light without assistance as they dry. The monument is in the ground rather than sitting contemptuously upon the surface, a constructed gash in the Earth with distinct polished surfaces that reflect everything in view including the viewer, focusing attention on other than the secrets beyond the names. The names, the points of the Wall's being, cannot be discerned from far away. They are individual entries neatly inscribed in many panels arranged in two linear segments that align with symbolic representations of concepts that have become tarnished and diminished. And in the end, people wanting to bring the memorial into physical existence were obliged to steam around teeming streams of acrimonious nulls emoted to serve narrow, selfish purposes or justify lame existences by people who could have easily arranged for the Wall.

Non-participant bureaucratic stamps in the forms of a statue and a flag were added by people who obviously had been nowhere near the SEA combat zone. Now, for what? I'm unable to recall support from the people and government of the United States of America during or after combat.

The statue is an excellent rendering, wonderful work with obvious pains taken. A participant could stand up with those three gents, squint a little, be there no problem. With all respects to the artist, his marvelous sense of aesthetics, detail, craftsmanship, exquisite execution, the statue and the flag belong in front of a community constructed to provide for combat veterans from any war still wandering about in attempt to locate means of acceptably returning to a more balanced state.

On a Memorial Day, I came to the place to pay respects, perhaps see a couple of people. The area was packed with pretenders strutting around bristling with the facade of having been part of what went on in SEA. It was clear they had not been. They seemed intent upon locating somebody with whom to quarrel over nothing, rather than paying compliments to dead friends, or attempting to spot misplaced pieces of themselves. There were speeches, long orations, disingenuous words without meaning, positioned for show only by prominent people, the net of whose existences equated to little of benefit—nothing new there.

People emitted brash noises about POWs, MIAs, war; other people were genuinely concerned with those issues. Many wanted to observe the tradition of Memorial Day but couldn't because of all the hoopla and Park Police preventing anyone from approaching the panels while the hoopla was active. Other combat veterans were there, in portions of their old uniforms, jeans and tee shirts, biker black leather basic, suits, and casual clothing. One wore tails. Some wore their decorations. Most looked fairly normal. I was happy to see them.

Pretenders coarsely moved along after dark, gravitating to their next things I guess. The environment returned to pleasant as people talked in soft voices and whispers. The combat vets fell silent. An unedited collection of strobe light instants streamed through my mind as I slowly walked the Wall, past the names in stone, symbolism for human beings now part of the color guarded organized so long ago, guardians for the dead of this nation. Halting at the panel upon which Slim To is registered, the PH line came to mind. I bowed, wished him—all of them—well. May each be of his/her own sovereignty, evermore.

A floral arrangement lay at the base of the panel. Red, yellow, white roses and babies breath emerged from a wreath of leaves and thorns in a display of sensitive, thoughtful expression. I added a 5.56 mm casing in the center, fired in a firefight near Hill 10. The metallic sparkle of a weapon's fired casing educed a calm, iridescent, almost mystical splendor in the flowers, something I had never seen.

A photographer, who had been around most of the day capturing this and that with his 6 x 7 camera, stepped into the grass aft. He ensured via looks, noises, and calm chatter that I was aware of his intentions and actions. He then took pictures of the little flowers and casing memorial, and my back. I stood there a little like a thoroughbred, nervous, breathing funny, tossing my head, prancing at the camera flash. He continuously ran a calming stream of soft chatter while moving around, getting various shots. There was no threat. The bristling iciness didn't, Beastie remained undisturbed, and I remained collected. Things worked out fine.

Flower arrangements and discharged 5.56 mm brass don't exactly come to mind at the same moment. That evening, in subdued lighting against polished black granite and the names, they were astonishingly beautiful together.

Glossary

0300 - MOS representing the parent class of infantry-related specialties in the Marine Corps. (see MOS, oh-threes)

1/7 – designation for First Battalion, Seventh Marine Regiment; the battalion's call sign was "Hanworth" while I was aboard; also One Seven.

3.5 - rather ancient rocket launcher with a bore of three and one-half inches. Rounds for this cutie were gingerly peeled (unpacked, armed) and loaded manually. Anyone trained could do this, but with caution, or the peeler/loader, gunner, and probably anyone else standing nearby might be explosively converted to many more but considerably smaller chunks. The rocket firing charge was initiated electronically, the round then hatted out one end of the tube, burning gases out the other. One would be well advised to have insurance paid up if electing to stand behind one of these things during firing.

12.7 - any of various 51- or 52-caliber, (12.7 mm) Russian- and Chinese-built automatic weapons. The slight difference in size wasn't of momentous significance to a tactical aircraft picking up a few of the 500 to 600 plus grain chunks of metal launched by the things.

81 - 81 mm mortar; a weapons company weapon. (see mortar)

82 - Russian 82 mm mortar produced by Chinese, used by NVA. (see mortar)

105 - 105 mm howitzer; a battery of these (six guns) on Hill 10 is likely a reason many of us are still around. (see howitzer)

106 - 106 mm recoilless rifle; the weapon had a vented breech, hence recoilless; the barrel was rifled, the round's trajectory relatively flat. (see recoilless)

A4 - Alpha four; Douglas A4 Skyhawk; Scoot(er).

abaft - toward the stern.

abeam - at right angles to the keel.

ACM - Air Combat Maneuvering; air-to-air combat, at one time "dog fighting." A world of relative motion, timing, precision, calculation, intelligence, knowledge, spatial relationships, four-dimensional plot, physical and mental conditioning, concentration, speed, nerve, confidence, courage, things to which many humans aspire, in a package. Despite compadres in nearby aircraft, much of what an individual aviator deals with and accomplishes will never be known by others.

ACT - Advanced Combat Training.

actual - 1. The real version. Actual combat for example is the killing variety, in which people may perish quickly if they aren't attuned to it, a much smaller subset of the "in the combat zone drawing hazardous duty pay" version of combat. 2. Designator for the person occupying a position or post as opposed to the position or post. For example, Alpha Six heard on the radio isn't the Alpha command unit, but somebody in the CO's shop, normally the radio op. Alpha Six Actual is the Alpha CO in person.

acute - position forward of a specific aircraft formation's ascribed bearing line. For example, should a parade formation call for position relative to the lead along a forty-five degree bearing line and you're sitting out there at forty-three degrees, you're a little acute. If by some chance you must look aft to see your lead, you are *way the fuck acute*. Position aft of a specific formation's bearing line is referred to as sucked.

AFGDL - Absofuckinggahdamlutely; exactly; precisely; perfectly horrible; perfectly wonderful; also afgdl.

aft - behind, to the rear, the back part, the stern. (see forward)

AGL - Above Ground Level; the distance between the aircraft and the terrain. (see ASL)

a-gunner - assistant machine gunner.

Air - a Marine Corps infantry term for any variety of aviation support.

Airedale - a Marine Corps Infantry term for Marine Corps Air Wing personnel.

AJB-3A - primary attitude reference instrument in an A4; the largest instrument, located in the approximate center of the instrument panel.

AK - Avtomat Kalashnikova (automatic Kalashnikov); though AK is a prefix designator for any of the Russian automatic assault rifles designed by Mikhail Timofeyevich Kalashnikov, in SEA the expression generally referenced Model 47 (Kalashnikov model 1947), a gas-operated, magazine-fed, automatic rifle also produced by the Chinese, distributed to VC/NVA. Not necessarily studies in precision manufacturing, the weapons were tough and generally reliable, though they jammed; the 7.62 x 39 mm (30 cal.) rounds did punch through brush. (see SKS)

ALO - Air Liaison Officer; a Marine Corps infantry battalion at tactical operating (TO) strength had two aviators in the TACP, the senior of which was the ALO. When I was with 1/7 and there were two aviators present, both were called FAC. Infrequently, and nearly always by a senior organization, the ALO was referred as "Big FAC."

ammo - ammunition.

APC - 1. Area of Positive Control; also known as positive control airspace (PCA); various areas of atmosphere controlled by the FAA and other organizations throughout the world, and any altitude above and including twenty-four thousand feet over the U.S. Positive control in that one may not spontaneously do as one may please there. Flight in the APC required specific equipment and a certain aircraft certification, an aviator with appropriate IFR rating, an IFR flight plan, radio contact, FAA approval for everything. Likely it still does, only worse. 2. Armored Personnel Carrier.

Article 15 - a Uniform Code of Military Justice; non-judicial punishment mechanism affording a six actual means of reconciliation in regard to certain breaches of conduct within his/her realm without requirement to convene investigative boards or to invoke court-martial procedures. None of "my" gents ever required that sort of thing.

arty - artillery.

ARVN - Army of the Republic of Vietnam. South Vietnam established as a republic; the republic's army.

ASL - Above Sea Level; the distance between the aircraft and the sea. (see AGL)

au contraire - on the contrary (French).

balanced - flight in which an aircraft maintains equipoise of yaw, pitch, flight roll, velocity, acceleration; plain old one-gravity flight. Operation of aircraft control surfaces purposefully unbalances forces acting on the aircraft to maneuver it; once desired positioning is attained (actually a little before), controls are neutralized, the aircraft returns to a steady, or balanced, flight state. Acceleration in this sense refers to force of more than one gravity acting on an aircraft. Remember, an aircraft's flight attitude may or may not have a thing to do with positioning relative to the surface of the Earth.

ball - 1. General purpose ammunition; bullets; usually consisting of a steel or lead-alloy core encased in a jacket of copper alloy, or of mild steel coated with a copper alloy. 2. Relative to aircraft carrier landing operations, the ball, or meatball, is specifically directed light visible to approaching aircraft to provide glide slope information. The term derived from the orange-colored blob of light reflected up the glide slope off a mirror on the ship. Decades ago the mirror arrangement was replaced with a Fresnel lens, a compound lens with much better optics and clarity at distance; the ball became more amber in color and changed to oblate in shape. Imagine an LSO acknowledging one's ball call with "Roger oblate."

ball call - mandatory radio call given as one acquired the glide slope indicator (ball) at the beginning of a landing approach to a ship; its format was call sign, ball or perhaps no ball, fuel state, touch and go, or hook if one was to trap. For example, "Snake One, ball, one point four, hook" lets the ship know Snake One has the ball in sight, 1400 pounds of fuel remain, which depending on type of aircraft could determine normal, special, or emergency handling, and the hook is down for an arrested landing. An LSO was required to respond to a ball call; presuming conditions were normal, response to this call likely would be something like, "Roger ball, Snake One."

banner - huge mesh rectangle with a bull's-eye on it, towed at the end of a thousand feet of cable by an aircraft known as a Tractor, to provide a target for air-to-air gunnery practice. Gunnery aircraft flew precise patterns while consistently dispensing all their cannon fire into the banner's bull's-eye. Shooters were differentiated by colored paint on their rounds. Takeoff with one of these things was always a thrill, banners not being the most predictable things when suddenly jerked into the troposphere by an aircraft on the other end of a thousand feet of cable.

Basketball - call sign of the VMGR squadron (C-130s) based at Da Nang in 1967.

BAW - Basic Air Work; fundamental aircraft and power control; slow, often agonizing, primitive, totally essential stuff; the basis of all aircraft maneuvering activity. One who after concentrated effort cannot accomplish decent BAW would be well advised to discontinue flying, before somebody is killed.

BDA - Battle Damage Assessment.

beeper - small locator-beacon/transceiver; the *beeper* (locator-beacon) portion of a rig emits an intermittent high-pitched sound on Guard channel, which via triangulation could provide location information. (see Guard)

Big Daddy C - Commandant of the Marine Corps (CMC); though certainly not to the CMC's face. Pops-oh and the boys indicated the Commandant and the Headquarters Marine Corps (HQMC) staff; also Daddy-oh, Pops-oh.

bingo - a state calculated around specific parameters; bingo fuel when attained normally calls for rather abrupt discontinuance of that which is in process and execution of the particular bingo scheme. Bingo fuel usually involves a flight path to a destination, calculated such that at the bingo state there will be enough fuel to make the destination, presuming minimal delay. A nicely calculated bingo is normally a slightly negotiable minimum, that if ignored can result in disastrous posture.

bird(s) - aircraft.

bogey - an unidentified flying aircraft, also referred to as a stranger, that when identified usually will become a friendly, normally calling for minimal attention. A bogey may also identify as a bandit, or enemy, which may educe a little full-tilt atmospheric waltzing. These things do not necessarily occur singly.

Bones - sobriquet for a Navy medical corpsman assigned to a Marine unit; "Doc" was also in common use. I have no clues as to why sane Navy people would do anything so rash, but I'm glad they showed up. As a rule combat Marines considered combat corpsmen as Marines, did all they could to cover them. A Bones saved lives, patched bullet holes, gave us all manner of weird shit for whatever was ailing us, got chopped up with and sometimes died with us. Unarmed, they fully participated in the gnarled situations we continuously encountered, attempted to keep us on the planet when we took hits, some accomplished unbelievable things along that line. I have tremendous appreciation, only good things to say relevant to any combat Bones.

boot - a Marine or Navy recruit in basic training; extended to mean a person who doesn't yet know the new job, operating arena and conditions, or the people involved. For most it's a transitory state in a new environment, lasting until one knows enough, presumes responsibility for the new post. There are people who use this term contemptuously, which is a little silly really; everyone starts as a boot.

Boys, the - command staff at Headquarters Marine Corps.

brain bucket - aviator's protective helmet.

bulkhead - any upright partition dividing a ship into compartments; also adds structural rigidity and prevents spread of fumes, liquid, or fire; extended to mean pretty much any wall.

burners – afterburners; devices that substantially augment thrust of turbojet engines, usually by introducing fuel into the exhaust gas stream aft of the turbine section where spontaneous burning occurs in the residual uncombined oxygen of hot exhaust gases. That's a simple view. Afterburner sections are sophisticated, can apportion fuel, open, close, set exhaust outlet sections, change the shape of the exhaust outlet; usually linked to an engine system as a subsystem, use amazing amounts of fuel, can get one from here to there, right now. "Hard" burners are on or off arrangements that dump the full fuel flow and open the turkey feathers (exhaust outlet sections) upon activation, and slam one's butt firmly into the seat. "Soft" burners dump fuel and open turkey feathers in stages, firmly positioning one's empennage aft in the seat also, but much more gracefully. (see turbojet)

bush - 1. The weeds, field, sticks, boonies, hostile country, out there, etc. 2. An ambush (only then it's 'bush).

buster - referring to afterburner engagement, one is buster when one's burners are active. (see burners)

camo - camouflage.

cannon - large, mounted weapon that fires heavy projectiles; includes guns, howitzers, mortars.

CAS - Close Air Support; sorties involving direct support of troops. I haven't heard anything definitive for "close," but as a rule in my combat universe, supported forces were obliged to duck.

CAVU - Ceiling and Visibility Unlimited.

centerline - imaginary vertical plane longitudinally bisecting an aircraft's fuselage.

CEP - Circular Error of Probability; a calculation using the mean impact point of missiles or bombs to derive the radius of a circle encompassing half the impact points. A bias calculation can be applied to measure deviation between the mean impact point and the aim point. The lower the CEP and bias, the more accurate the weapon, or in the case of uncontrolled free-fall weapons, the more accurate the aviator.

Charles - originally a slightly more formal form of "Charley," from "Victor Charley" (Viet Cong, VC); the South Vietnamese stemming from the Viet Minh; the term came to apply to any VC or NVA. (see NVA)

chocks - blocks or wedges usually placed fore and aft of main gear tires to ensure an aircraft does not roll about, or run over to an adjacent squadron to visit with its buddies, etc.

CIC - Combat Information Center.

clag - atmospheric conditions resulting in low visibility, as in one may not be able to discern one's own wingtips; often storm conditions with no visibility. (see IFR)

clean - relative to A4 aircraft configuration, nothing on the pylons, gear, flaps, or hook up; a medium-to-low drag coefficient configuration. (see dirty, slick)

click – 1000 meters; a kilometer; approx. 3,280.833 feet (1,093.611 yards); also klick, K.

CMC - Commandant of the Marine Corps; the six actual of the Marine Corps, also referred to as Big Daddy C, Daddy-oh, or Pops-oh, though I wouldn't think officially.

CMH - Congressional Medal of Honor; highest U.S. military decoration, awarded in the name of Congress to members of the armed forces for gallantry and bravery beyond the call of duty in action against an enemy.

CO - 1. Commanding Officer. 2. Covert Operations.

COC - 1.Command Operations and Communications. 2. Combat Operations Center.

comm - communication(s). 1. The act of communicating. 2. The exchange of thoughts, messages, information. 3. That which is communicated. 4. The means of communicating. 5. The technology employed in communicating.

compadre - close friend (Spanish).

con - with (Spanish; preposition).

concertina - barbed wire in loose springy coils, normally but certainly not necessarily about three to four feet in diameter, used as obstruction. 1/7 used layers of concertina over tanglefoot and loose barbed wire around Hill 10's perimeter; the wire was not breached while I was with the battalion. (see tanglefoot)

CONUS - Continental United States; occasionally Contiguous United States.

Cordite - smokeless explosive powder consisting of nitrocellulose, nitroglycerin, and petrolatum that has been dissolved in acetone, dried, and extruded in cords.

cover - concealment; support; protection; also can refer to a specific uniform article designed to be worn on the head, which I do not recommend calling a "hat" within the hearing of a DI.

cruise - loose aircraft formation that varies somewhat between aircraft types depending upon performance capability, in which the wingman maintains position to cover the leader. Consider a cone of about sixty degrees oriented along the aircraft's keel with the vertex at the lead aircraft; the bulk of the time a wingman in cruise will be somewhere in the cone, and within a few hundred feet of the lead.

crunching - processing; working; active; thinking heavily about.

away - something; doing something exclusively.

CSD - Constant-Speed Drive; any of several rather involved and apparently rather fragile mechanisms used with turbojet engines to provide drive for various mechanical and electrical accessories, designed to maintain an unchanging rate of turn without regard to engine rpm.

dash - used as a separator in a flight call, such as Snake dash two, the second member of the Snake flight. When working one flight for a while, the flight call was generally dropped for convenience; sometimes the dashes remained (dash two), sometimes not (two).

December - call sign of VMA-121 while I was with the squadron.

deck - platform extending horizontally from one side of a ship to the other; extended to mean the surface supporting one; the floor, platform, parade ground, surface of the Earth, etc.

det cord - detonation cord; a cord with a core of Pentaerythritol Tetranitrate (PETN, a seriously explosive organic compound of the family of nitroglycerin or nitric acid esters of polyalcohols) covered with various combinations of textiles, plastics, waterproofing materials, that explodes at a velocity of approx. 6,400 meters (21,000 feet) per second.

DFC - Distinguished Flying Cross; U.S. military decoration awarded for heroism or extraordinary achievement in aerial combat.

DI - Drill Instructor; noncommissioned officer who instructs recruits in close order drill, discipline, and various areas of military life. Often tough and sometimes amazing. Consider another side of the story: A DI essentially relinquishes any semblance of normal life during training for and duty as a DI, training that makes boot camp seem rather mild. From beginning to end, the DI tour is harsh on family life, extremely demanding of the DIs. Perhaps that's why they appear agitated a lot of the time. When preceded with an "S" (SDI), Senior DI; with a "J" (JDI), Junior DI—both designators having to do with experience on the job as opposed to rank.

dirty - relative to A4 aircraft configuration, things on the pylons (bombs, rockets, missiles, gun pods, nape, drop tanks, etc.) or gear/flaps/hook down, or holes punched in the aircraft from flak/hostile fire; a high drag coefficient configuration. (see clean, slick)

division - 1. Typical basic Marine Corps organizational structure from individual to the Commandant (i.e., fire team, squad, platoon, company, battalion, regiment, division, headquarters Marine Corps, Commandant of the Marine Corps). (see Mardiv) 2. A division of aircraft is two sections acting as a unit (four aircraft).

DOR - Drop On Request; a self-originated exit from the Naval Air Training Command.

DR - Dead Reckoning; point-to-point navigation without astronomical observations; usually involving course and distance calculations from/to determined positions.

dragon's teeth - wedge-shaped concrete masses generally arranged in offset rows to halt advancement of tanks, used post hostilities by children to construct all manner of fantastic situations.

drop tanks – aerodynamic (well let's say sort of aerodynamic) fuel containers carried on aircraft pylons that have fuel transfer capability and can be jettisoned. When carrying external fuel, A4Es normally were hung with 300-gallon drops on pylons two and four, or a 600-gallon drop on the centerline pylon.

du jour - of the day (French).

duty runway - the active runway; the one currently in use.

ECM - Electronic Countermeasures; electronic/mechanical devices that disrupt communications, fire control and surveillance radar, and infrared tracking devices; with some luck, some also prevent use of radio frequencies. A4Es at Chu Lai employed no ECM gear.

EE8 - an ancient field telephone with a hand crank, connected to another by a cable pair (a land line). Use of the hand crank rang a bell in the EE8 on the other end of the land line, although when in the COC bunker under heavy mortar or rocket fire, determining whether the ringing bell was the phone or the one in your head could be somewhat of a task. (see LL)

empennage - tail section of an aircraft; generally extended to apply to the aft portion of anything.

endo - pronounced *end-oh*; the end, fin, finished, done, over with, concluded, forever gone; not to be confused with the "end do" statement used by various computer languages to terminate a "do" loop.

extranjero - stranger, outsider, foreigner, alien (Spanish).

F4 - McDonnell F4 Phantom.

F8 - Chance-Vought F8 Crusader.

F27 - small high-winged, twin turboprop powered transport manufactured by Fairchild, commonly used by feeder airlines. (see turboprop.)

FAC - Forward Air Controller; in the USMC, a combat-qualified aviator assigned to an infantry battalion for the purpose of handling air support. Must be combat-qualified to know what kind of ordnance and tactics to use when; must be an aviator to effectively direct ordnance deli, select appropriate aircraft, and employ them well. If running medevac helicopters, gun birds, fixed wing air support, a flare ship or two at night, one had best know his aviation and tactical capability stuff. The numbers of people who have done this in actual combat remain small. I calculate about 120 in SEA and perhaps a fist full in Korea; have no idea about WWII.

FACA - Forward Air Controller Airborne; these people flew light, thin-skinned, slow, slick aircraft or helicopters, from which they coordinated air and artillery support. I don't imagine they had much fun at times either. (see TACA)

Fairburn - knife with a black, symmetrical, double-edged blade and brass hilt, designed during WWII by John Fairburn, with one purpose in mind.

far, far out - relative to carrier landing, the approximate first third of the groove, preceded by the start, followed by in the middle. (see groove, in the middle, in close, ramp, start)

faux pas - false step; a social blunder (French).

feet dry - one is *feet dry* when within an atmosphere over huge pieces of land.

feet wet - one is *feet wet* when within an atmosphere over lots of water.

field scarf - Marine Corps necktie.

'firm - contraction of "affirmative"; used by nearly every Marine tactical aviator with which I flew; "affirm" also was in common use.

flak - business end of AA (anti-aircraft) fire; from German *(Fl)ieger(a)bwehr(k)anone* (aircraft-defensegun). When I was running against this stuff, there were 23 mm rounds that burst little wimpy white puffs; 37 mm rounds that burst with less wimpy white puffs and added a little shrapnel for your consideration; 57 mm rounds that burst dark gray to black and added a lot of shrapnel for your amusement; 85 mm rounds that flamed when they exploded then turned to black, leaving many pieces of residual metal zinging through the atmosphere. There were several larger sizes available to heighten an aviator's interest, all of which only slightly more terrible than 85s. Often these things were radar controlled; once in awhile AA guns existed singly, normally they occurred in collections set up to cover one another. Single aircraft conducting straight-up waltzes against one or more gun clusters with unguided weapons required an aviator with rather developed nerve or suffering from a particular form of nutso; perhaps both.

flames - flame throwers; hand held or mounted.

flap - sharp, spontaneous, informal, usually brief conflict between aircraft. Frowned upon by command, aviators were often punished for participation. Most training environments provide work in unexpected operating conditions, but can't present completely unexpected events with a little mix of "nut-case human." A good flap offered that, taught a world of detail normal training didn't, particularly in the areas of timing, speed, and precision of execution; one's personal mental setup.

Fleet - short form of Fleet Marine Force. (see FMF)

FMF - Fleet Marine Force; the operating United States Marine Corps; responds should the president request Marine Corps presence in an area. The Marine Corps was, may still be, divided into FMFLant (Atlantic), which commanded Marine Corps affairs on the eastern side of a longitudinal line approx. bisecting the United States, and FMFPac (Pacific), which provided command services for the west.

FNG - F--- New Guy (do manage something suitable for the "F").

FO - Forward Observer; an infantry battalion-level position filled by an officer from artillery. An FO linked to artillery and naval guns, like a FAC, was a specialist, could accomplish nifty things at times to keep friendly people on the planet while dispatching unfriendly people. Marine Corps actual combat FOs are also a small group.

forward - to the front, the front part, fore. (see aft)

four - the logistics section, department, division. (see one, one four, two, three, six)

Fresnel lens - named for Jean Augustin Fresnel, a French physicist who in the early 1800's investigated polarized light and developed a compound lens for use in lighthouses. His lens technology was dilated to apply to mobile and stationary lens devices used during shipboard landing operations that provide glide slope information. A Fresnel lens of this nature uses five light panes, four of which emit amber-colored light, the fifth and lowest of which conveys red-colored light. The rectangular panes are oriented along axis horizontal and mounted in a vertical stack, with the middle pane marked on either side by horizontally oriented green lights called datum lights. The proper picture is an amber pane or "ball" in line with the datum lights. If one is high or low relative to the calculated glide slope the ball will appear respectively positioned in reference to the datum lights. Across the top of the uppermost pane or, and perhaps also on each side of the panes, are red wave-off lights, which when flashed call for immediate discontinuance of an approach. If one should gaze upon the lighted red Fresnel pane for more than a few seconds, it is highly likely one will experience these wave-off lights.

full metal - police and civilian designator for general purpose jacket ammunition, not used in the Marine Corps. Also the title of a terribly misleading movie that completely ignores standard recruit depot mechanisms such as Fat Man's Platoon, Custody Company, the general conduct of affairs at either of the MCRDs, and rather over dramatizes individual response to most situations, combat events in particular.

full stop - landing where an aircraft comes to a complete stop and usually turns off the runway; the normal end of a flight. Though an abnormal landing that halts flight activity might also be called a full stop, that event is more commonly referred to as a crash or prang.

gaggle - an ordered, rather relaxed collection of aircraft appearing unordered.

grenade - 1. Missile containing priming and bursting charges designed to be thrown by hand or deployed by a specially equipped launcher. 2. Glass container filled with a chemical dispersed when the container is thrown and smashed. From French (*pome*) grenate, pomegranate (from its shape).

groove - in respect to a carrier landing, the more or less straight approach beginning considerably aft of the ship with the start, ending either at the ramp or at the arresting gear, depending upon with whom one speaks. The groove is loosely broken into sections: *the start, far* or *far out, in the middle, in close, the ramp* or *at the ramp.* In rare combined conditions of perfect wind, weather, sea, aircraft, and aviator states, one can commence an approach on speed with a centered ball, fly the groove all the way to the arresting gear with no aircraft or power changes; however, this falls rather easily into the category of "almost never." (see far, far out, in close, in the middle, ramp, start)

ground effect - feeling as though the aircraft were shuttering along waves of liquid particles; more intense and regular, but rather like a Cigarette-class boat feels at about 65 knots with concentrated wave swell approaching moderate. About half a wingspan above the ground in an A4, noticeable ground effect was encountered, which transmitted a specific buffet through the airframe; the more velocity, the more pronounced the buffet. One was obliged to be ginger about everything other than away from the Earth's surface when in this buffet, lest one smartly bash the aircraft against the planet, and wreck a perfectly good self.

grunts - members of the infantry, that when in combat place their lives at extreme risk for the good of each other and their country; those who do as opposed to those who yammer about doing. I've heard the term used casually regarding infantry personnel, and heard people of various management levels using the term in derogatory contexts regarding employees. Disappointing to hear those who should know better openly demonstrate stupidity. Any Marine Corps grunt has earned use of the term however they may please; others ought to use a word or phrase about which they know something. A combat grunt has grasp of several significant things about life with which most people seem unacquainted, has worked things people shouldn't have to work, has seen inspiring things everyone should know about, knows the highest and lowest orders of human conduct, has been involved with that which a majority of people shouldn't try to imagine, and has had to internally reconcile all of it. Those living through multiple combat episodes know themselves in a crunch, and they know some tricks. Believe me. (see point, slack)

Guard - frequencies of 121.5 MHz in the VHF (high frequency) band, 243.0 MHz in the UHF (ultra-high frequency) band; reserved for emergency use by the aviation community. Use of these frequencies is limited to a real emergency situation or to benefit somebody in such a situation. All military aircraft of which I have ever heard had dedicated receivers tuned to Guard, enabling continuous monitoring of at least one of the frequencies. Monitoring Guard was a specifically charged obligation for any Marine Corps/Naval aviator. One had the privilege of hearing something horrible for somebody on Guard nearly every day in combat.

gun - weapon that fires projectiles, coherent light, particles, plasma, some form of cohesive energy (but not a rifle, pistol, revolver, carbine, shotgun, or automatic rifle, which are normally referred to as rifles, pistols, revolvers, carbines, shotguns, automatic rifles, small arms, weapons, pieces, and in the case of pistols and revolvers, side arms). In the world of weaponry to which I was introduced, a gun is at least a light machine gun, up to large artillery and naval guns that shoot automobile-weight projectiles, and laser guns having capability to project controlled streams of coherent light to the moon and beyond. There's a little rhyme heard at the MCRDs: "Touch your rifle and say, 'This is my rifle'; touch your package and say, 'this is my gun'; touch your rifle and say, 'this one's for killing'; touch your package and say, 'this one's for fun.'"

Gunner - 1. Warrant Officer; a commissioned officer ranking below an ensign in the Navy and below a second lieutenant in the Marine Corps, who derives authority from a warrant, usually in a particular area of expertise. 2. The gent directed to fire the gun, rocker launcher, mortar, recoilless rifle, etc.

Gunny - Gunnery Sergeant; a noncommissioned officer in the Marine Corps ranking above a staff sergeant and below a master sergeant or first sergeant.

GV - outdated designator for the Lockheed C-130 Hercules, one of the most worked aircraft ever to have flown.

H&I - Harassment and Interdiction; artillery fire missions and sorties against likely areas of enemy activity or storage. H&I and TPQ sorties often were referred to as "dum-dum" or "stupid squared" missions; dum-dum because they made one feel dumber than just dumb in the singular; stupid squared because two human brains, that of the planner/controller, and that of the aviator, could actually be duped into thinking there may be something significant at the coordinates given with the fragmentation order.

HAC - Helicopter Aircraft Commander.

hack – non-judicial, usually "unofficial" disciplinary action requiring one either to be functioning in official capacity or be in quarters; no exceptions, no excuses.

Half Cuban - an aerobatics maneuver one may commence in level flight at eight any old altitude by pulling into, for example, about a four-gravity loop. After about 225 degrees of loop the aircraft is rolled back to upright, then recovered at the starting altitude headed diametric to the original course. Two of these accomplished back-to-back are known as a Cuban eight. A certain vision and a little jockeying about of the aircraft likely will be required to execute these as proportionally correct parts of a horizontal figure eight.

HAMS - Headquarters and Maintenance Squadron.

hatch - a small door or opening; an opening in the deck of a ship or in the floor or roof of a building; the covering for such an opening; extended by use to mean pretty much any old door or doorway.

hat out - to depart, leave, go; when one makes one's hat, one exits not to return for a while; the same when one hats out.

HEAT - High Explosive Antitank; ammunition constructed using a shaped charge in a conical cavity to concentrate explosive energy into a high-velocity jet that can pierce thick armor; a normal load for the A4's 20 mm cannon used by VMA-121 at Chu Lai.

Helix - call sign of an Air Force TACA squadron.

highball - hand salute.

hipeg - gun pod, manufactured by the Hughes Pod Company, that could be mounted on pylons two through four of an A4, housing a 20 mm cannon that could manage rates of fire around 4000 rounds per minute. Consider the complex ducting in seriously restricted space required to feed sixty-some 20 mm rounds each second and also egress the casings. December normally hung these things in pairs, and though aircraft maneuverability was affected, the pods were nonetheless a gas with which to work.

hootch, hooch - dwelling, especially a thatch hut, constructed with bamboo and thatch in SEA; extended by use to include temporary plywood structures and strongback tents.

hot - loaded, safety off, ready to shoot right now; active; deadly; fast; good; extremely precise; exceptionally beautiful; spectacular; completely ready; firefight in progress; currently taking fire; currently firing. To un-hot or de-hot something, use the antonym.

Hummer - Douglas C-117; updated version of the venerable C- 47.

hump - difficult, trying, or critical phase; sustained exertion, such as *hump the hills, hump the bush, hump the equipment aboard the trucks, hump the bombs over to the aircraft*, etc. Humps consistently required more physical and mental exertion, determination, and time than initially projected; often reco was necessary afterwards, though time for that was generally not available in combat.

hyperspace - space having more than three dimensions.

IFR - Instrument Flight Rules; rules governing flight when the ceiling (vertical distance to obscuring cloud, smoke, dust, etc.) was less than 1000 feet and the visibility was less than three miles; usually necessitating flight by use of instruments only. The condition required an instrument flight rating to fly. (see minimums, VFR)

Immelmann - one half of a normal loop suffixed with a half roll; the points being altitude gain, course reversal, a normal flight posture. The maneuver is named after Max Immelmann, who invented or perhaps discovered it one fine day.

in - radio call made when commencing a run on a target; e.g., *One's in, Three's in*, etc. (see off)

in close - in regard to carrier landing, the section of the groove closest to the ship but not over it; approx. the last third of the groove, preceded by *in the middle,* followed by *the ramp.* (see far, far out, in the middle, groove, ramp, start)

in the garden - dead.

in the middle - concerning carrier landing, the approximate middle third of the groove; preceded by *far* or *far out*, followed by *in close.* (see far, far out, in close, groove, ramp, start)

IR - infrared; radiant energy situated outside the red end of the visible spectrum, at wavelength between about 700 nanometers and a millimeter.

ITR - Infantry Training Regiment.

Joyride - DASC (Direct Aircraft Support Center) operating in I Corps; the northernmost of the four sections into which South Vietnam was divided for tactical and strategic purposes.

Kabar - relatively large knife with a leather hilt and a blackened, single-edged blade with a blood groove; manufactured by Kabar for the USMC in WWII. The knives are still around, work fine.

KBA - Killed By Air.

KIA - Killed In Action.

Klondike - call sign of VMO-6, based at Ky Ha; though the "V" in the squadron designator indicates fixed-wing aircraft, the squadron had transitioned to UH1 series helicopters.

knot - measure of velocity using nautical miles (6000 linear feet); 600 knots is equivalent to approx. 682 statute mph. Incidentally, knot relates to speed and implies "per hour"; e.g., "airspeed of 600 knots per hour" would be redundant.

ladder - structure for climbing up or down; stairs.

LL - Land Line; referred to as "lima-lima"; term applied to the actual cable pair, but in general use referred to the phone at the end of the land line. (see EE8)

LP, lp - Landing Party; Listening Post. (see OP)

LSO - Landing Signal Officer.

MACV - Military Assistance Command Vietnam; decidedly not the most appropriately named organization that has existed. It appeared to be an organizational means by which some men played games veiled with a thin veneer of government activity, using other men's lives and energy without their agreement.

MAG - Marine Air Group.

magazine - container mounted in or upon a small arm or gun that feeds cartridges into the firing chamber; often referred to as a "clip."

Magic Dragon - C-47's fitted with mini guns; fire descending from these things looked like laser beams rather than streams of tracer rounds, the sound of the guns were more moan than chatter. The magic part involved the way in which one's almost certain demise was converted to the demise of the attacking enemy by the unbelievable number of rounds dispatched by the guns. Sometimes called Puff, Spook, or Spooky, their call sign was Spook; the one summoned upon occasion in Hanworth's TAOR was Spook-14. Imagine which organization flew them. (see Spook(y))

Mahgoogly - creatures that live in bushes, under, over, behind, around, near things; they make funny noises, shoot at you, hurl grenades, yet upon arrival at where you thought they may be, there is no evidence indicating anything was ever there. I'm unable to describe one; and despite hearing them often, neither do I know of anyone having seen one. Its most frightening trait was the capability, after making little noises and remaining unseen while getting closer, of suddenly becoming the enemy right before you, attempting to kill you. Let's say, for purposes of illustration, your outfit was uneventfully working along a trail when suddenly two rounds of sniper fire cracked over your heads, then silence returned. Snipers are visible you see, Mahgooglies are not; so when no one heard or saw anything further, everyone knew at least one Mahgoogly was messing around. Mahgoogly Rule #1: Never, I mean never, ever, *afgdl* never do anything sudden when in front of a person still in space-willies from a Mahgoogly. Presuming of course, one wishes to continue unassisted cardiovascular and breathing functions.

MARCAD – Marine Aviation Cadet.

Mardiv - Marine Division.

Mattel - nickname applied to the M-16 rifle, which to some resembled a plastic and metal toy. Mattel is a company that at one time produced metal and plastic toys, and used an advertising jingle "You can tell it's Mattel, it's swell." When people began dying due to inability to return fire because the first M-16s failed miserably in the combat arena, the "swell" part of the jingle took on particular meaning. Though the second model of the rifle worked rather well, the tag remained. As far as I know, the Mattel Company had nothing to do with weapons, wasn't involved in or even aware of any of this; just happened to be a well-known toy company with a catchy jingle.

MAW - Marine Aircraft Wing.

MCAS - Marine Corps Air Station.

medevac - medical evacuation; nearly always accomplished by helicopter in SEA, often at extreme risk to crew and chopper. Imagine flying your helicopter and crew into a hot firefight zone, sitting still as one of the world's largest targets for all the rifles and guns in the bushes while friendlies drag half dead people across an open area and put them in your helicopter under heavy fire. There are people breathing right now who would not be had those crews not run medevacs.

MIA - Missing In Action.

MiG - Russian design organization founded in 1939 by Artem Mikoyan (M), and (i), Mikhail Gurevich (G); the acronym is used in reference to any aircraft produced by the group, particularly Soviet military fighter aircraft (e.g., MiG-25, MiG-29, MiG-MLI). The expression normally implied MiG-21 aircraft during my combat tour.

millimeter - one one-thousandth of a meter (1/1000); abbreviated as "mm."

minimums - the lowest altitude and closest distance to an airfield an aviator may bring an aircraft without visual acquisition of the facility. A standard instrument cardholder in a single-piloted aircraft had 250 foot AGL, one-quarter mile minimums when I was flying. (see AGL, IFR)

MOD - Mate Of The Deck.

mortar - portable, muzzle-loading cannon used to fire shells at low velocities, short ranges, and high trajectories; also referred to as trench mortar.

MOS - Military Occupational Specialty; numerically designated military skill sets. (see 0300, oh-threes)

Motor T - Motor Transport; group maintaining and managing hard-surface (often goo-surface) vehicles.

NAAS - Naval Auxiliary Air Station.

nada - nothing, anything (Spanish).

NAF - Naval Air Facility.

nanometer - one billionth of a meter.

nape - napalm, from (na)pthene (palm)itate. 1. An aluminum soap of various fatty acids that when mixed with gasoline makes a firm jelly used in some bombs and in flamethrowers. 2. An incendiary mixture of polystyrene, benzene, and gasoline or jet fuel.

NAS - Naval Air Station.

NCO - noncommissioned officer; a subordinate officer appointed from among enlisted personnel.

ninguno - none, neither (Spanish).

Nomex - DuPont trademark for poly-meta-phenylene isophthalamide; an aramid (aromatic polyamide) with close-packed aromatic polymer chains that produce a strong, tough, stiff fiber with a high melting temperature; used for heat or flame resistant fabrics.

nugget - a second lieutenant or ensign; also known as gold bar, brown bar, brass bar, and in the case of an ensign, enzyme; terms normally applied in good spirit. Incidentally, the gold colored insignia worn by officers is brass, hence placement below silver insignia ranks, and the expression "brass."

nunca - never, ever (Spanish).

NVA - North Vietnamese Army; both a singular and plural expression applied to members of the regular army from North Vietnam, generally accompanied by a quantifier (e.g., an NVA, two NVA, *tacsan* NVA, an NVA regiment, a horizon full of NVA, etc.) NVA also were referred to as "Charles." (see Charles)

O&R - Overhaul and Refurbish; Naval service facilities that rebuild Naval service equipment. (see PAR)

oben alles - above everything (German).

OCS - Officer Candidate School.

oh-threes – infantry, infantry skills or tasks, such as fire team tactics, squad tactics, platoon tactics, etc. In the book, discussion of "oh-three skills" concerns how to perform and survive in an infantry combat arena.

off - voice transmission used to indicate a run on a target is complete; the reco process has been initiated (e.g., *One's off, Three's off*, etc.) The call does not imply departure from the target area but does indicate the aviator and aircraft are safe; could be used by the aviator following to gauge run commencement, presuming his eyes aren't working too hot, or things are really horrible. (see in)

OJT - On the Job Training.

okay pass - completely acceptable approach and landing on an aircraft carrier.

one - administrative section, division, department. (see one four, two, three, four, six)

one four - tactical air control section, division, department. Tactical Air Control Party (TACP). (see one, two, three, four, six)

OP, op - operation; operator; observation post. (see LP)

Opso - Operations Officer; occasionally referred to as the "Oh-oh."

OQR - Officer's Qualification Record.

ordnance - military supplies, especially weapons, ammunition, and heavy guns.

overhead - ceiling; solid structure above.

overshoot - to pass outside a quarry's radius of turn when engaged in ACM; a highly undesirable occurrence. An overshoot provides one's foe opportunities to open distance and get out of phase with one's maneuvering. If the foe is good, one may soon find the foe at his six, causing exercise of everything in one's tactical bag to force the foe's overshoot. As a rule it is singularly unhealthy to convert an attack posture to defensive by overshoot or anything else. Besides thwarting one's attack and eliciting a rather pointed embarrassment, things along this line can cost fortunes in cola at the officer's club, may terminally halt one's heart in less congenial environments.

Paddles - Landing Signal Officer.

Panama - aircraft coordination and control organization a level above Joyride; I believe that was the theory anyway.

PAR - Precision Approach Radar; paint and return, a function accomplished at an O&R facility. (see O&R)

parade - formal, rigidly maintained aircraft formation used for strict flight management; wingmen maintain close position on about a forty-five degree bearing from the lead.

passageway - hallway.

PCL - Power Control Lever; a cockpit control allowing management of engine power levels, sometimes referred to as a throttle, though it works differently than the throttle of a reciprocating engine. The net effect of increasing either is more beans from the mill.

persona non grata - an unacceptable or unwelcome person, especially to a foreign government. The government wasn't foreign when I signed up, nor was I persona non grata; and though certainly not officially decreed, that nonetheless seemed to occur upon return from combat, like it has to so many after every war of which I have heard.

pickle - we all know about food items soaked in brine or vinegar, but in this sense the word is used as a verb meaning release of ordnance from an aircraft by use of switches on the end of the stick—excuse me—control pylon. For example, one would pickle ordnance, such as Snakeyes, as the pipper covered the target.

pickle point - a location in space where ordnance is released to correctly arrive upon a target. Hitting a point in space at a specific airspeed, altitude, dive angle, heading, in balanced flight with the sight pipper on the target can be somewhat taxing in combat. (see balanced flight, pipper)

pipper - a point of light displayed on the sight panel by a lead computing sight; the idea was to have the gunsight correctly set, the pipper on the target with the aircraft in balanced flight at the ordnance release point. (see pickle point)

point - the person in front of and guiding an infantry unit in a tactical situation; depending upon viewpoint one of the warmest or coldest places a human can be positioned on this planet. As a rule points were either excellent or dead, sadly sometimes both. Also as a rule, points didn't take just a couple of rounds when hit, usually they were mashed to point-paste. If you know an actual combat version of one of these, sometime mention how cool it is they're still alive. Perhaps they'll smile. (see grunt, slack)

Pops-oh - see Big Daddy C.

port - to the left, on the left side. (see starboard)

PRC-41 - a portable (yes indeed!), UHF transceiver weighing about 7060 pounds at the end of a day in the bush. The thing started at 60 pounds, gained about 500 pounds per hour unless going uphill, in which case it gained about 500 pounds per minute. At a hint of a firefight this thing needed to be far, far away as it attracted bullets and was just too clumsy for decent bush waltzing (decent meaning one lived through it). The other side of that is while in the bush, a PRC-41 was about the only means of direct contact with tactical fixed-wing air.

pylon - fixed, usually external mount, normally but not necessarily on an undersurface of an aircraft, upon which racks of bombs, flares, rocket pods, rockets, missiles, gun pods, drop tanks, etc. can be mounted. The A4E had four wing pylons, one centerline pylon. (see rack)

rack - 1. Bed. 2. Pylon-mounted device such as a multiple ejector rack (MER) or triple-ejector rack (TER), used to carry and manage release of ordnance. (see pylon)

raison d'être - reason for being (French).

ramp - relevant to carrier landing, the part of the groove over the aft portion of the ship (the ramp), preceded by *in close*, followed by the arresting gear. (see far, far out, in close, in the middle, groove, start)

Reap, the - The Grim Reaper; death; the representative in the completely colorless cloak possibly carrying a scythe, showing only a paste-white skeletal face with dark holes for eyes unless angry about something, in which case the eyes may appear ruby-red. Look for the Reap just after Our Lady of the Luck completely turns her back, or one summons it.

recoilless - of or being a weapon designed to minimize the effect of recoil: a recoilless rifle.

Remf - Rear Echelon Muddafukkah; not all people in the rear or in safe areas were remfs.

reversal - point in an air-to-air gunnery pattern somewhere around a nautical mile, mile and a quarter or so, abeam the banner at an altitude 2500 to about 3500 feet above it depending on aircraft type; called the low reversal, where the aircraft's course is reversed. In a right-hand gunnery pattern for example, the low reverse is to the right. After the low reversal, one sets up a little old gun run, lead is calculated on the target, when in range one shoots, naturally all the rounds haul their little butts directly into the bull's-eye.

revetment - barricade against explosives.

rhodopsin - also called visual purple; pigment consisting of opsin and retinene, in the retinal rods of the eyes, that is sensitive to red light. The stuff of which night vision is made; requires about a half hour to build to a level supporting decent night vision, and instantly can be reduced to nothing by not much white light.

RIO - Radar Intercept Officer; Navy or Marine Corps flight officer in the aft seat of an F4 who plotted intercepts, ran missile shoots, handled the aircraft's radar, handled comm, was another pair of eyes, did whatever to assist the aviator in doing a better job of whatever they were doing. Aviator/RIO relationships were close; in certain situations these people could kill each other if one of them dropped his part.

RO - Radio Operator (also R/O, r/o, ro).

robot - from Czechoslovakian *robota,* meaning drudgery. 1. A mechanical device, possibly resembling a human being, capable of performing often complex human tasks on command or by being previously programmed. 2. A device that operates automatically or by remote control. 3. A person who works perfunctorily without original thought, particularly one who responds automatically to commands.

rock and roll - firefight; action. The *rock-and-roll* switch is the selector switch enabling fully automatic rifle operation.

ROK - Republic of Korea.

roll in - an act as well as a position in space; to *roll in* on a target is to commence a run upon it; normally the aircraft is rolled toward the target as the nose is lowered, there are certainly other ways to commence a run on a target. The act is normally accompanied by an "in" call.

RON - Remain Overnight.

round – single shot or volley; one projectile or bullet from a weapon that can shoot projectiles. As to definition of round for a continuous-emission energy gun, I can only speculate at something involving time, as in duration of burst at the muzzle, or duration of burn to affect an amount of damage upon a target. A standard-issue M-16 magazine in the SEA arena held 20 rounds, though most people I knew loaded 18 to preclude stressing the magazine follower return spring. It is not good at all to replace a magazine during a firefight, and then discover the return spring doesn't have the resiliency to feed rounds. That could qualify as a bad day if one lived through it, or perhaps a really bad day.

round-down - aftmost part of the flight deck on an aircraft carrier that gracefully turns down toward the spud locker; sometimes called turndown.

RPG - Rocket-Propelled Grenade; usually containing a parabolic-shaped charge for piercing.

RTB - Return to Base.

salt(y) - Navy service term for a person (or occasionally for a something) that has been in place for awhile; usually doing a job. A salt knows what to do, how to do it; as a rule is better left to whatever he is supposed to be doing. Salts generally are impatient with new people regardless of rank, particularly if the new person exhibits a know-it-all attitude, and they run the Marine Corps. Not direct it, run it. Normally a term of regard, there can be negative connotation having to do with a stagnant, narrow, resistive, uncooperative attitude. Applied context is everything.

SAM - Surface to Air Missile.

sans – without (French).

SASA - Stay Alert, Stay Alive.

SCJ - Super Cobrajet; in the early 1970s Ford constructed a few Mustangs with 429 cubic inch super Cobrajet engines, top-loader four speed transmissions, nine-inch limited-slip differentials. Everyone I know called them SCJs.

Scoot(er) - Douglas A4 Skyhawk.

SDO - Squadron Duty Officer.

SEA - Southeast Asia.

section - two aircraft.

SG - Super Guy, Super Girl, Super Gee; applies to any sex, but not a designator one could reasonably connote as even mildly desirable; a management-appointed "expert" in some area, whether qualified or not, usually not, and usually with a limitlessly narrow point of view.

ship - vessel of considerable size for deep-water navigation; a sailing vessel with three or more square-rigged masts; an aircraft; a spacecraft.

SID - Standard Instrument Departure; a published, structured IFR departure from an airfield sometimes also flown under VFR conditions. These things were designed to aggravate and confuse flight students during instrument flight training; Lord knows how they escaped into the operating universe.

Sidewinder - 1. Particularly aggressive type of rattlesnake found in the southwestern United States; 2. Type of air-to-air missile.

six - command or headquarters section, division, department. (see one, one four, two, three, four)

six o'clock - generally, not always, the most vulnerable area of a normal aircraft is directly behind it, or at its six o'clock position, and a little low. The high vulnerability of the position is due to the pilot's inability to see directly behind and below the aircraft, and there's less tracking to accomplish or lead to compute when shooting from this position. One may sit back there firing away while the target individual goes nutso trying to figure out how to crash them into a mountain or something similar. One has only to be in gun range a couple of seconds to wipe out a target. Sound easy? Locate a competent, willing cohort, and do give it a try.

Skipper - in the Marine Corps the term normally indicates a commanding officer of a line unit; where one stands in structure determines whom one calls Skipper. I've only heard the term applied generally to ship's captains, squadron commanders, and company commanders. In the Marine Corps infantry, Marine

Corps captains, the traditional rank of company commanders, are referred to as Skipper by nearly everyone, or I should say we were on Hill 10. It's a nice thing to be called, tends to focus attention to one's responsibilities toward people. (see CO)

SKS - ten-shot, 7.62 mm, semi-automatic ancestor of the AK-47. Though generally carried by VC, occasionally an NVA would be seen with one. (see AK)

slack - person directly following the point, whose job was to cut the point some slack. Normally, the slack moved to point if the point got hit; somebody, usually next in line, moved into slack. Bravo and Charley companies on Hill 10 rotated points and slacks. I've also heard this position called "slat," but not by Marines. (see grunt, point)

slats - devices that alter aircraft wing geometry by increasing chord and directing airflow, usually from the leading edge of an airfoil section. The A4's slats weren't advertised as controllable by the aviator because they operated via airflow mechanics; as wing angle of attack to the relative wind increased, slats proportionately opened. Well, as things exist on this little old spheroid, aviators are capable of comprehending aerodynamic operation; if one understood slat functioning and played into them well, people could be surprised in the air, a few colas could be won at happy hours, perhaps heartbeats could be gained in combat.

slick - 1. Relative to A4 aircraft configuration, a completely clean aircraft; no pylons, guns, nothing but basic aircraft in the air stream; the lowest drag coefficient configuration. (see clean, dirty) 2. A bomb without a retard mechanism. (see Snake-eye) 3. A helicopter without weapons.

Smoker - McDonnell F4 Phantom; so named because of the incredible amount of black gush exhausted by the engines at low altitudes when not buster.

Snake-eye - mechanical device that springs open after bomb-aircraft separation, to retard ballistic flight, enabling more accurate placement of ordnance. The actual spelling is Snakeye, which has resulted in some fairly interesting phonetics. (see slick)

snap in - to become proficient.

sortie - from French *sortir*; to go out. 1a. An armed attack initiated from a place surrounded by enemy forces. 1b. Troops involved in such an attack. 2. The flight of an aircraft on a combat mission.

speed of heat – fast; in context, say something like 200 mph on a motorcycle on a track; perhaps 600 knots or so in an A4 close to the surface; possibly 330 kph in a Ferrari F4 on the Autostrada; something over 90 mph if you're skiing; who knows what it may mean to an astronaut in a space vehicle?

Spook(y) - call sign of the Magic Dragons was Spook, which quickly became Spooky. (see Magic Dragon)

spring-loaded - an unconsciously maintained mental posture.

SRT - Standard Rate Turn; turn executed at the rate of three compass degrees per second.

standoffs - standoff weapons; designed for deli with minimal exposure of the deliverer to target defenses, thereby reducing risk; also reducing requirement to deal with the consequences of the action, as the action and effects remain unseen by the deliverer. One can RTB, get coffee, talk about his coolness, accept no responsibility for damage because it wasn't seen. Maybe that's good; it occurs to me the destruction of life, the mangling of bodies, implications of those actions ought at least to be held in full comprehension by the perpetrator. If it's easy to kill and maim people, and strategists, tacticians, and perpetrators never have to work with consequences of their actions, we're all in exceedingly deep trouble.

starboard - to the right, on the right side. (see port)

Starlight - 1. Operation conducted by the Marine Corps in the vicinity of Chu Lai. 2. Telescopic rifle sight using IR technology to provide scope-enhanced visibility in reduced-light conditions.

start - in reference to carrier landing, the beginning of the groove, followed by *far* or *far out*. (see far, far out, in close, in the middle, groove, ramp)

Steel - M60 machinegun.

stern - rear part of a ship, boat, aircraft.

Street - Thompson submachine gun; a recoil-block operated, sweeper 45-caliber, automatic weapon made infamous by gangsters of the twenties and thirties. I inherited one of these things from my predecessor, carried it a few times, saw probably six or seven of them during my tour with the infantry. The 230- grain ball rounds fired by this weapon punched through brush well, accomplished a real job on a close target, but the thing was short-ranged and heavy. Carrying the gun, a couple of fifty-round drum magazines, and a few twenty-round magazines consumed entirely too much of one's energy.

strongback - tent over a wood or aluminum frame, sometimes reinforced with plywood siding and sandbags.

synched - synchronized; in synchronization with.

T2 - North American T2A "Buckeye."

T34 - Beechcraft T34 "Mentor," the fuel-injected variety.

TACA - Tactical Air Controller Airborne; essentially the same as FACA.

Tacan - UHF (ultra high frequency) system of navigation; a *Tacan* station may be located on the ground, or in or upon a structure, aircraft, ship, vehicle. Receivers translate station transmissions into bearing and distance information, which is presented via instrumentation in radials and nautical miles (e.g., the 290 radial at 114 nautical miles). With any luck at all, radials coincide with compass points.

TACP - Tactical Air Control Party; the one four section; the small crew in a Marine infantry organizations responsible for anything concerning air support, composed of infantry organization people commanded by an aviator (ALO/FAC).

tacsan - many, much, a lot of (Japanese).

tallyho (tally) - used in traditional foxhunting to urge hounds to a fox that has been visually acquired; in aviation the expression means the subject is in sight and identified; may or may not be urging anyone anywhere. In common use the term shortened to "tally," a good response when identifying the friendly aircraft pointed out by one's wingman. An appropriate response when visually acquiring a flight of twenty hostile aircraft headed one's way might be something like, "Fucking tally, oh shit!"

tanglefoot - barbed wire strung close to the ground both at random and in various patterns, stretched tightly to trip as well as loosely to entangle.

TAOR - Tactical Area of Responsibility.

Tarawa - atoll of Kiribati, of the northern Gilbert Islands, in the western Pacific Ocean, occupied by Japanese in 1942, retaken by Marines in November 1943 after a series of particularly brutal battles.

ten-click stare - particular facial expression and out-of-focus state seen in combat, among combat veterans replaying combat, and among other people who have endured traumatic experiences.

The staring party is slack-faced, appears to be sightlessly seeking a point beyond the horizon; is actually dealing with loss, overload, etc.; attempting to order a deluge of violence and details of scenarios through which they somehow lived.

terra firma - solid ground (Latin).

the pump - a state akin to "pump," but much further along. It's a nervous, perceptive, high-energy state; as far as I know one must look right into the Reap's pasty white, black-hole-eyed face to enter it. Once there, one may experience atom vision, see protons, perhaps even electrons.

three - the operations section, division, department. (see one, one four, two, four, six)

Thumper - M79, 40 mm grenade launcher.

TOD - Time On Deck.

touch and go - brief landing where at least one of the main gear tires touches a runway or something similar before the aircraft returns to flight; not the end of a flight. On a bad day, if BAW was horrible, things just weren't going well at all, it was possible to log a few of these immediately preceding a full stop landing, although no completely astounding aviator would ever admit to that. I knew a gent whose cousin's, sister-in-law's, friend's, brother's, uncle's, employer's son heard of somebody who may have done such a thing, once.

tout au contraire - quite the contrary (French)

transceiver - transmitter-receiver.

transponder - radio or radar transceiver that responds by transmission to reception of a specific signal; in military aviation these things were called "parrots" as they "squawked" various codes for various purposes.

triple cross - weapons positioning tactic where weapons are placed such that fire along three lanes converges in a target area. The term also may refer to the fire in the target area; triple crossfire.

trops - Marine Corps tropical or summer uniform; an officer's tropical uniform could be worn with long-sleeved shirt (with or without a blouse) and field scarf, or a short-sleeved shirt with no field scarf or blouse, depending upon local directives.

turbojet - engine that takes in air that it compresses and mixes with fuel, ignites, and provides an exit path for gases from the resulting explosion; the gases rush down the provided path and turn a turbine, then exit via a tailpipe/exhaust gas tube. The functions of a turbojet engine: The intake section ducts air to the compressor section, compression causes heating of the air to, approx. 1300° F. Compressed air is routed into confined spaces often called burner cans, fuel is introduced to this superheated air generally by fine spray through jets or nozzles, then with just a small amount of electronic spark assistance, approx. four joules, or perhaps with no assistance, the mixture explodes, expands madly down the path of least resistance, leading to the turbine section. The turbine section gracefully allows the rushing gases to turn a fairly simple turbine that drives the compressor and perhaps a few mechanical and electrical devices; gases then rush out of the tailpipe/exhaust gas tube. Once in unconfined space, the rushing gases disperse and cool relatively quickly, though I wouldn't stand near the exhaust of a running turbojet, gases don't disperse and cool all that relatively quickly. One result of all this gaseous exploding and rushing about is an aircraft that, via action-reaction, zings through the atmosphere. Turbojet engines work well through a speed range from 200 to nearly 2000 knots. Problems encountered over seven or eight hundred knots have to do with getting supersonic airflow into the compressor section, and exhausting burning gases efficiently enough to produce acceptable levels of thrust. A brief view indeed; turbojet engineering is rather complex. (see turboprop)

turboprop - engines derived from turbojets; the essential difference is the exhaust gases drive a complex turbine that turns an array of shafts ultimately leading to a propeller; the turbine drive consumes all but a small amount of thrust. While this may have been wonderful to some, turboprop aircraft didn't light my fire; but they're certainly in abundant use and not nearly as noisy as their ancestors. As you can imagine, turboprop engineering also is complex. (see turbojet.)

turn around - to setup an aircraft just returned from a sortie or mission for the next sortie or mission. At Chu Lai, aircraft were refueled and reloaded; preflight inspections were accomplished by plane captains in just a few minutes. Sometimes we remained strapped in while the birds were turned around; sometimes we waited for the birds we just flew; sometimes we stacked with everyone else and took birds as they became available based on mission priority and type. Often plane captains would scramble up the ladder, lean against one's brain bucket and yell, "Sir, the (radar altimeter, ADF, radar, whatever) is out," a way of tactfully presenting a potential problem. Usually these items were nonessential to the mission, and should the mission not go, friendlies died. One had to use one's little old pumpkin head though. I mean, who benefited if one killed themselves after taking a really inadequate bird?

two - the intelligence section, division, department. (see one, one four, three, four, six)

UH34 - helicopter with a reciprocating radial engine, constructed by Sikorsky, that was just about used up by the Marine Corps in SEA. Oh my, do radial recips at or just off of idle rattle all your bones exactly right.

unq - unqualified.

VFR - Visual Flight Rules; rules for flight when the ceiling is in excess of 1000 feet and the visibility is more than three miles. (see IFR)

VMA - fixed wing Marine Attack squadron.

VMA(AW) - fixed wing Marine All Weather attack squadron.

VMFA - fixed wing Marine Fighter Attack squadron.

VMO - fixed wing Marine Observation squadron.

VMT - fixed wing Marine Training squadron.

wag - Wild-Assed Guess; when prefixed with an "s," as in "*swag*," a Scientific Wild-Assed Guess.

whup - distinct smacking sounds caused by helicopter rotor blades under certain circumstances. Specific whup sounds will garner immediate attention from any SEA combat veteran.

WIA - Wounded in Action.

WP - Willy Peter; white phosphorus.

wingy(ies) - wingman(men).

XO - Executive Officer; second in command.

yellowsheet - each time an aviator was so brash as to intrude upon squadron maintenance people to obtain a Marine Corps/Naval aircraft for whatever purpose, particularly to fly it, the aviator was obliged to first sign out the thing. When the machine was returned, the aviator signed in the craft, along with writing hopefully meaningful comments regarding any particular facet of the aircraft, such as "all ten engines failed on approach" or even worse, "E engine on board failed immediately after takeoff." Maintenance people use these little informative comments to generate repair orders, schedule maintenance and such, and may use them for poking fun at aviators. This is all done on a standard form affectionately referenced as the *yellowsheet*. Do hazard a guess as to its color.

Yo-yo - air combat maneuver employed to prevent overshoot of an opponent's radius of turn. Called *yo-yo* because one sits out there moving up and down like a yo-yo, working the plane perpendicular to that in which the target is turning while figuring how to position one's aircraft to get bullets into the target. The aviator being yo-yoed upon, if you'll pardon the manner of speech, is hardly going to sit there and allow casual sashaying into a nice saddle position at his six such that endo processing may be run. Normally, yo-yos implied at least a few minutes of joyous, extremely cool, rather precise, immensely satisfying vertical flight maneuvering activity.

zero dark thirty - long after midnight but before any hint of daylight.

zink - a unit of approx. twenty-seven nautical miles or less, used by a small group of aviators with which I flew. The expression derived from measurement of route distances on large-scale navigation and topographic charts; small mileage segments were difficult to measure using a large chart scale. When small-scale charts were unavailable, one could measure a *zink* with a pencil point, know in a normal low-altitude flight posture the distance would be covered in something less than three minutes while consuming something under 320 pounds of fuel if the aircraft was clean. Though real precision was essential, often a *zink* was a perfectly useable unit.

Zuni - 1. Five-inch diameter, pod-mounted, air-to-ground rocket; exceptionally accurate and, according to many of us, would have been rather good at certain air-to-air tasks; 2. The Zuñi: a pueblo people located in western New Mexico.

*** Note ***

This context-sensitive glossary isn't a listing of anything, nor has it been approved by anyone but a few contemporaries and me. It has been compiled specifically to clarify terms used in *Zero Dark Thirty*.

-Samuel Brantley

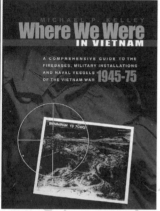

Hellgate Press
Military History & Adventure

Vietnam: From Alpha to Zebra

A Code to Keep
ISBN: 1-55571-623-7

America's Longest Held Civilian POW in Vietnam
by Ernest C. Brace

He was a former Marine hero, banished in disgrace from the Corps. Yet he maintained the military code of conduct in the torture cells of the enemy. This is the true, firsthand account of America's longest held civilian POW in Vietnam, and his courageous return to honor. Foreword by Sen. John McCain. $14.95 240 pgs. Paperback

Zero Dark Thirty
ISBN: 1-55571-624-5

by Samuel Brantley

Unlike other branches of the military, the Marine Corps required some of its combat aviators in Vietnam to spend time doing forward air control duty on the ground, with the frontline troops. For Capt. Samuel Brantley, what he would see—and do—during those seven months on the ground would change his life forever. Foreword by Conger Beasley. $15.95 288 pgs. Paperback

The Elephant and The Tiger
ISBN: 1-55571-612-1

The Full Story of the Vietnam War
by Wilbur H. Morrison

Wilbur Morrison's thorough and thought-provoking history of the Vietnam War is now available in paperback! Covers the U.S. involvement from December 13, 1954 to the fall of Saigon in 1975. Includes 14 pages of photographs. $26.95 730 pgs. Paperback

Order by phone or online today

www.hellgatepress.com   1-800-228-2275

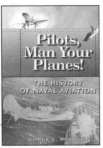